Harry C. Trexler Library
Muhlenberg College

STRENGTHENING THE POOR: WHAT HAVE WE LEARNED?

John P. Lewis and contributors:

Norman Uphoff
Samuel Paul
Uma Lele
Mohiuddin Alamgir
Sartaj Aziz
Nurul Islam
Sheldon Annis
Mayra Buvinić
Margaret A. Lycette
Richard Jolly
Thomas W. Dichter
S. Guhan
Joseph C. Wheeler

Series Editors:
Valeriana Kallab
Richard E. Feinberg

Transaction Books
New Brunswick (USA) and Oxford (UK)

Library of Congress Catalog Number: 88-24941
ISBN: 0-88738-267-3 (cloth)
ISBN: 0-88738-768-3 (paper)
Printed in the United States of America

Strengthening the Poor: What Have We Learned?

Acknowledgments

Strengthening the Poor Project Director and Guest Editor:
John P. Lewis

Series Editors:
Valeriana Kallab
Richard E. Feinberg

Associate Editor:
Melissa Vaughn

Editorial Assistant:
Valerie A. Mims

The Overseas Development Council particularly wishes to thank the International Fund for Agricultural Development (IFAD) and its President, Dr. Idriss Jazairy, for IFAD's contribution in support of this study, which enabled maximum participation by experts from the developing world. In addition, the Council gratefully acknowledges the support of The Ford Foundation, The Rockefeller Foundation, and The William and Flora Hewlett Foundation for the Council's overall program; of Lutheran World Relief, Christian Children's Fund, Church World Service, The Hunger Project, and the Rockefeller Brothers Fund for their support of ODC's work on poverty-oriented development strategies; and of The Pew Charitable Trusts for ODC's *U.S.-Third World Policy Perspectives* series.

Contents

Foreword

John W. Sewell

The alleviation of global poverty is once again beginning to capture the attention of the international community. World leaders are calling for an end to absolute poverty by the year 2000; aid agencies are redirecting staff and resources toward raising the living standards of the poorest populations; and research and academic centers are refocusing on the design of poverty-oriented development strategies.

Anti-poverty initiatives for the 1990s must, however, respond to a developing world and policy environment that in many ways differs from that of the 1970s and 1980s. Developing-country needs and capabilities are changing, as are the policies and programs of foreign aid donors.

Despite considerable social and economic progress, the problem of poverty looms larger than ever. Roughly one in five of this planet's 5 billion men, women, and children lives in absolute poverty, struggling with malnutrition, illiteracy, disease, infant mortality, and short life expectancy. Poverty trends, however, vary markedly from region to region. In East and Southeast Asia, slower population growth rates and steady advances in per capita income have contributed to a significant reduction in poverty. In South Asia, in contrast, where roughly half of the world's poor people live, more modest rates of growth have barely kept pace with the expanding population. And in Sub-Saharan Africa, where two-thirds of the people live in grinding poverty, the prospects for improvement are slight. Rapid population growth rates combined with sustained economic deterioration, falling or stagnant agricultural production, and climatic crises all contribute to widespread malnutrition across Africa. In twenty African countries, the per capita caloric intake was lower in 1985 than two decades ago.[1]

In the recent past, moreover, the repercussions of international economic decline in the 1980s have halted—and in many African and Latin American countries actually *reversed*—many of the hard-won gains of earlier decades. For sixteen African and Latin American countries, per capita income was lower in 1985 than in 1965; and in another dozen countries in these two regions it grew by less than 1 per cent during the same twenty-year period.[2]

UNICEF's major study on the impact of the recession in the 1980s, *Adjustment with a Human Face*, found evidence that child welfare—and by extension, the "physical and mental capacity of much of the future labor force"—has suffered in at least 8 countries in Latin America, 16 in Sub-Saharan Africa, 3 in North Africa and the Middle East, and 4 in South and East Asia.[3] Economists predict slow growth at best for most African and Latin American economies well into the next decade. Thus prospects for the recovery of living standards in these regions are questionable in the near future.

The problem of global poverty remains as urgent as ever. What has *changed* is the environment in which poverty will have to be addressed in the 1990s.[4] First, many men, women, and children in the developing world are generally healthier, enjoy better diets, and have greater access to education as well as health care and sanitation than at any time in the past. Just since the beginning of the 1980s, for example, an estimated two million more children are surviving annually due to the spread of low-cost vaccines and simple oral rehydration techniques.[5] Second, the poor are better organized, and they are becoming increasingly active participants in public policy decisions that affect them. Third, the relationships of the public sector to the poor have changed. In particular, many Third World governments have established administrative structures for social services. While many of these agencies may be seriously under-funded, they provide an essential framework for more and better services in the future. And fourth, aid donors are now more experienced and employ a much wider range of tools for alleviating poverty than in the past.

A number of promising initiatives in the development assistance community—aimed specifically at improving the well-being of poor men and women—are already well under way. Over the last two years, the World Bank's policy-based lending program has begun to respond to declining living standards, to identify the most vulnerable groups, and to design short-term relief programs that buffer the poor from the arduous and prolonged process of economic restructuring. Even more promising than the addition of these compensatory programs, however, is the far-reaching potential for using structural adjustment lending mechanisms to advance greater equity. The work of Sheldon Annis in this volume and elsewhere explores this new policy approach to poverty, which could involve the World Bank's dialogue with borrowing governments over such policies as tax incentives, land reform, credit schemes, commodity prices, regulations affecting cooperatives, or social security programs.

World Bank President Barber B. Conable has spoken eloquently of the need to address poverty, strengthen the role of women, and promote environmental sustainability. In the case of Asia, where more than half a billion of the world's poor live, Conable has boldly committed his agency to "support government strategies to eliminate the worst aspects of absolute poverty by the year 2000."[6] Similarly, the World Health Organization's "Health for All" campaign targets the year 2000 for bringing primary health care to deprived groups which are more vulnerable and exposed to health risks.

Important changes also may be in the offing in the aid programs of the United States. Currently the U.S. aid program is trying to do too much, in too many places, with too few resources. As a result, less than one-quarter of total U.S. overseas assistance goes to low-income countries. Growing dissatisfaction with these trends among others had led the U.S. Congress to announce plans to rewrite the foreign assistance legislation next year.

As private and official aid donors once again turn their attention to poverty-alleviation strategies, however, they face a new and difficult set of challenges. Among these are the need to restart economic growth, check environmental degradation, and lessen the impending technology gap.

Balancing trade and financial accounts, reversing the outflow of capital, and resuming economic growth in Latin America and Africa will be critical to meeting the needs of the developing world's expanding populations. Although macroeconomic reforms and economic growth are essential parts of an anti-poverty strategy, they are not by themselves sufficient. Policies and programs that are explicitly poverty-oriented are also needed.

A related crisis—that of the environment—threatens to undermine the very foundations for development progress. Between 1950 and 1983, 38 per cent of Central America's and 24 per cent of Africa's forests disappeared.[7] Shortages of fuelwood—which affect one and a half billion people in 65 countries[8]—together with the search for crop and pasture land contribute to the rampant devastation. In Brazil and Central America, for example, growing numbers of impoverished peasants are settling in fragile forest areas that cannot sustain production for more than a few years. In India, well over half of the lands suffer from degradation in one form or another; farmers there face steadily declining productivity without major new investments. As the World Commission on Environment and Development warns in its seminal report, *Our Common Future*: "The environment does not exist as a sphere separate from human actions, ambitions and needs. . . ."[9] The Commission's findings mark an historic turning point in reshaping the global community's perceptions about the relationship between the environment, poverty, and economic development. New policies are needed that can successfully integrate these three concerns.

Even as these challenges present themselves, both developed and developing countries stand on the threshold of a series of changes in industrial technologies and organization that serious observers are calling a "Third Industrial Revolution." Many developing countries, however, are poorly positioned to participate or compete in radically new developments in microelectronics, bioengineering, and materials science. While the potential of these new technologies for improvement of the human condition is great, it will not necessarily happen automatically.

Thus in the late 1980s poverty is hardly a new issue, but it needs a much more vigorous national and international response in a very different and rapidly changing setting. Direct and indirect efforts to help men and women improve their own well-being have been one of the central purposes of four decades of development cooperation. The direct address of poverty was also one of the special hallmarks of development thinking and policies throughout the 1970s. Therefore one of the first tasks of those concerned about poverty in the 1990s is to understand the lessons of the past. Those lessons are the central focus of this study, the tenth in ODC's *U.S.-Third World Policy Perspectives* series—and in substance a companion volume to *Development Strategies Reconsidered*, also directed by John Lewis and issued by ODC two years ago.

The overview essay and the chapters that follow provide an excellent synthesis of what has been learned to date about the business of "strengthening the poor"—mostly in the past 15 years, but within the longer, post-World War II perspective. This volume enjoys the distinguished leadership of John P. Lewis, who has been a prominent and active participant in the evolution of development theory, policy, and practice over the entire period analyzed in this volume. He has for years alternated between academia and government—serving on the Council of Economic Advisors under President Kennedy, as head of the USAID mission in India, as Chairman of the OECD's Development Assistance Committee, on the U.N. Committee for Development Planning, and more recently as Chairman of the three-year Task Force on Concessional Flows established by the World Bank/IMF Development Committee. While John Lewis currently spends most of his time at Princeton University's Woodrow Wilson School of Public and International Affairs, where he is professor of economics and international affairs, he is simultaneously Senior Advisor and Chairman of the Program Advisory Committee at the Overseas Development Council.

This policy study also marks the beginning of an expanded program of work at the Overseas Development Council designed to focus the attention of decisionmakers in developed and developing countries on sustainable poverty-oriented development strategies. In the next twelve months, two further sets of policy analyses will be available in the *Policy Perspectives* series. The first will explore diverging and shared interests that must be addressed in crafting environmental and anti-poverty policies for particular ecological settings—rain forests, arid lands, hillsides, cities—in the Third World. The second will focus on the politics of structural adjustment, including the special problems of nations in transition to democracy and the political risks and opportunities of pro-poor adjustment policies (see announcements at the back of this volume). We hope these studies and ODC's other work in this area contribute to a more informed and active policy dialogue on the alleviation of poverty in the decade ahead.

The Overseas Development Council particularly wishes to thank the International Fund for Agricultural Development (IFAD) and its President, Dr. Idriss Jazairy, for IFAD's contribution in support of this study, which enabled maximum participation by experts from the developing world. In addition, the Council gratefully acknowledges the support of The Ford Foundation, The Rockefeller Foundation, and The William and Flora Hewlett Foundation for the Council's overall program; of Lutheran World Relief, Christian Children's Fund, Church World Service, The Hunger Project, and the Rockefeller Brothers Fund for their support of ODC's work on poverty-oriented development strategies; and of The Pew Charitable Trusts for ODC's *U.S.-Third World Policy Perspectives* series.

Notes

[1] *Social Indicators of Development, 1987* (Washington, D.C.: The World Bank), pp. 6–7.

[2] Ibid.

[3] Giovanni Andrea Cornia, "Economic Decline and Human Welfare in the First Half of the 1980s," in Giovanni Andrea Cornia, Richard Jolly, and Frances Stewart, eds., *Adjustment with a Human Face*, Vol. 1 (New York: Oxford University Press, 1987), pp. 34–35.

[4] I am indebted to my colleague Sheldon Annis for bringing into focus four changes that are highlighted in this paragraph. For more information, see his article, "The Next World Bank? Financing Development from the Bottom Up," *Grassroots Development*, Vol. 11, No. 1 (1987), pp. 25–26.

[5] *The State of the World's Children, 1988* (New York: United Nations Children's Fund), p. 5.

[6] Barber B. Conable, "Address to the Board of Governors," (Washington, D.C.: The World Bank, September 29, 1987), pp. 20–21.

[7] Robert Repetto, *The Forest for the Trees? Government Policies and the Misuse of Forest Resources* (Washington, D.C.: World Resources Institute, May 1988), p. 3.

[8] Gus Speth, "Poverty and Environmental Degradation: Basic Concerns for U.S. Cooperation with Developing Countries" (speech before the national conference on "Cooperation for International Development: U.S. Policies and Programs for the 1990s," Michigan State University, May 17, 1988), p. 6.

[9] *Our Common Future*, Report of the World Commission on Environment and Development (Oxford: Oxford University Press, 1987), p. xi.

Overview and Summaries of Chapter Recommendations

Strengthening the Poor: Some Lessons for the International Community

John P. Lewis

The issue of poverty alleviation—more appropriately, of strengthening the poor—is being brought back toward the top of the development policy agenda.

In a sense it has always been there. If the goals of development promotion are growth, equity, and national self-reliance, then policies advancing growth diminish the average poverty of poor countries; those improving equity reduce relative poverty within those countries; and those enhancing the countries' self-reliance increase their ability to sustain gains won by and for their poor people.

Nevertheless, the focus on Third World poverty declined radically between the 1970s and the 1980s. Convinced by the start of the 1970s that "trickle-down" growth was not good enough, many developing-country governments and many of the bilateral and multilateral agencies trying to help them for most of a decade pressed programs on the equity and redistributional fronts under such rubrics as employment generation, appropriate technology, direct attacks on (absolute) poverty, redistribution with growth, integrated rural development, and basic human needs. But thereafter, starting with the impact of the second oil shock in 1979, development decisionmakers became preoccupied with the poorer countries' preemptive problems of financial and structural adjustment. Poverty issues were pushed aside, and it is only recently that emphasis has been rebuilding, not only on the need for adjustment with growth, but on an adjustment process that also affords greater equity.

The refocus on poverty, however, is not just a matter of turning back the clock. For one thing, a good deal has been accomplished during and since the last thrust of anti-poverty policy in the 1970s. In some countries the percentage (if not the numbers) of "absolute poor"[1] has diminished. In some of these countries, the poor have become more vocal; they have been organized or have organized themselves into weightier local lobbies than previously existed. Furthermore, a good deal of policy experience has accrued. There are lessons to be drawn from poverty policy's periods of high salience in the 1970s and lowered attention since.

Reflecting on this experience is the purpose of this book. In what follows, I first sketch the nature of the "reformist" anti-poverty doctrine that many official development promoters (both internal and external) adopted in the 1970s. Most of this chapter is given over to a set of lessons gleaned from efforts to implement the reformist doctrine. These are grouped under the headings of (1) productivity and subsidies, (2) center-periphery relations, (3) spatial strategies, (4) growth and equity in agriculture, (5) institutions, social sectors, and human resources, (6) women in development, (7) poverty and environment, and (8) project design, management, and assistance.

Those retrospective lessons from poverty policy's season in the sun are a mixed bag. Much of the substance of what intervenors tried to do was sound. But there were neglected priorities, and much of the doing was clumsy. The chapter winds up with some further lessons for policy that can be derived from the poverty issue's period of deemphasis in the adjustment-accentuating 1980s.

The process of writing this book began with the circulation of an early draft of this chapter to a distinguished set of development specialists who were invited to react as they pleased. Through a series of interchanges, including an authors' conference midway in the process, the other authors have chosen sectoral, regional, or other emphases and sorted their responses into the chapters that comprise the balance of the book.

In putting together the collection, we have been more concerned with timeliness than with harmony. Indeed, as editor of the volume, I expected less consensus than I got in one respect: In the early planning of the volume, we were reminded of the way differences had seemed to intensify in recent years between the two sides of the old "center-periphery" dichotomy. On the one hand, there were still plenty of establishmentarian voices who would program nationwide attacks on poverty centrally—from the top down; on the other, proponents of grassroots initiatives flowing from the bottom up (or from the periphery inward) are increasingly audible. Our cluster of authors includes representatives of both schools—although, by design, no one from the radical, "alternative development" fringe of the grassroots group, which is so skeptical of governments and all their works that its members believe local people's only hope for bettering themselves collectively is to organize into various local non-governmental groups that then may network themselves into broader populist movements.[2]

On the center-periphery issue, which is addressed in the first two chapters by Norman Uphoff and Samuel Paul, the interesting thing is that no confrontation materializes; reasoning with one another, the authors gravitate toward a synthesized middle view of the matter. But the chapters are not homogeneous; as will become clear when I refer to them individually, the authors provide a set of discrete perspectives on a common problem of continuing—and once again *recognized*—urgency.

I. The Reformist Doctrine of the 1970s

The history of development policy thought since World War II has been one of revisions. As I suggested in an earlier Policy Perspectives volume, the pattern has been roughly dialectical.[3] Much of the dominant thinking in any short period has consisted of reactions to the fashions of the preceding period—but without slipping into circularity: Over the long run, the evolution of policy thought has been linear, but it has kept zigzagging from short term to short term.

Thus, development policy strategists at the beginning of the 1970s were seized with reactions to the growth preoccupations of the 1950s and 1960s. In the aggregate, the Third World had slightly exceeded the growth target that the international community had set for the 1960s. But not only did this average cloak widening disparities among Third World countries; within many individual countries, poorer and weaker segments of the population had shared the national gains very little. Benefits had not trickled down fast enough to serve the needs of social justice or shore up the prospects for internal order.

Although it was pervasive, there is no agreed label for the new strategy that was (rather abruptly) embraced in the early 1970s by the majority of the aid establishment—notably by the World Bank under Robert McNamara, but also by most bilateral donors. We can call the strategy "reformist." Although the strategy's ideological thrust was compassionate, it was non-Marxist and not very radical. As already suggested, the new approach was concerned with unemployment and underemployment, income distribution, appropriate technology, integrated rural development, lags in the social sectors (especially affecting the weak and disadvantaged), and with basic human needs. But all of these sub-themes had a central theme: They sought to mount *direct* attacks on poverty that would not necessarily displace but augment macro development efforts. And they had certain central texts, in particular, the World Bank's *Redistribution With Growth* (1974) and the International Labour Organisation's *Employment, Growth and Basic Needs*, prepared for the 1976 World Employment Conference.[4]

Certain aspects of the new strategy followed almost inevitably from the circumstances it addressed. Thus the reformers focused more on rural than urban problems; they were not indifferent to the grinding poverty one could observe in teeming, rapidly growing Third World cities, but they recognized that poor people in poor countries were still overwhelmingly in rural areas, and reformist policy concentrated on them. Similarly, resource limitations drove the new strategy toward an emphasis on raising the productivity of the poor. Certainly aspects of the movement were concerned with enlarging consumption transfers to some of the poor, mainly "targeted" (incapacitated, very old, very young, otherwise vulnerable) groups incapable of self-support. But the strategists recognized that the volume of poverty was too great to be reversed simply by redistribution. Hence "redistribution *with* growth." The accent was placed on building the ability of the poor to produce more in their own behalf.

Granting these constraints, the driving impulse of the new approach was to do good things for the poor, and to do them *directly*—not only by macro development's indirect processes. The impulses mainly came, or were articulated from, the top, the center. But the determination was to reach down, *all the way down*, to the poorest of the poor in the villages. Such was to be the role not just of new-style indigenous developers, but also of expatriate intervenors who, working at or close to the grassroots, themselves proposed to engage in hands-on, localized development promotion.

There was a further characteristic. Nearly all of this, like the great majority of development assistance of the time, was to be conducted in a project frame. Projects were site-specific and time-bound in their design and creation. They were not only units of implementation; they were the main units of development analysis and evaluation in the transactions between aid donors and recipients.

During the 1970s, across much of the development assistance scene, there was a rush of effort to mount programs along the foregoing lines. Under McNamara, as Robert Ayres' *Banking on the Poor*[5] has detailed, this was a major thrust of the World Bank. As quickly, and partly at congressional initiative, the same kinds of "new directions" were adopted by USAID. By mid-decade most of the other OECD bilateral donors had established similar reform agendas.

II. Lessons from the 1970s

By the late 1970s, the donors were beginning to stand back to take their initial evaluative looks at their reformist handiwork. In 1979, I joined OECD's Development Assistance Committee. My first chairman's report at the end of that year noted four problematic features of the "new" anti-poverty projects that DAC members had begun to cite:

• The individual projects were confined to small geographic areas and jurisdictions, thus posing the problem of replication.

• They tended to be multifaceted and multidisciplinary, and therefore operationally difficult to coordinate.

• The projects involved heavy commitments of expatriate or national personnel from outside the area, thereby tending to increase dependence on external expertise and to complicate replication.

• Very often projects sought to escape the weaknesses of indigenous administration by establishing special project authorities that tended to weaken further the ordinary administrative system.[6]

Thus we were beginning to see the need for some revisions of reformist anti-poverty doctrine nearly a decade ago. The following (although brought down to the present) purports to be a fuller list of the lessons that could have been drawn at the end of the 1970s if the whole subject had not been shouldered aside by the prolonged adjustment crisis that intervened.

Productivity and Subsidies

The conventional reformist wisdom of the 1970s was right to emphasize enhancing the poor's productivity more than it did schemes to give them transfers and subsidies—and, indeed, to emphasize enhancing their productivity mainly by helping them find more productive work. As resource constraints tightened, the case for tilting anti-poverty policy toward productivity-building strengthened further. Redistribution is easier from a growing pie. Moreover, experience has taught a further point: A worsening distribution (as in some earlier "green revolution" instances) may be kept tolerable if there is enough aggregate growth to give some lift even to the relative losers near the bottom. Finally, productivity gains are likelier than handouts to afford escapes from dependency.

Experience has shown, however, that one way to build productivity, as will be emphasized below, is to build human capital—for example, through publicly funded education and training. Further, experience surely does not argue unexceptionally against public generosity to the poor. As also will be emphasized, the 1980s have made a broad case for cushioning the weaker sections of society against the impact of adjustment measures. Moreover, there is continuing ground for selectively targeted subsidies and transfers—to stem hunger, to aid the incapacitated, and to provide cost-effective public health benefits, especially to young children. Yet it is clearer than ever that the best way to help most of the poor is to help them raise their ability to produce.

Center-Periphery: Structuring the System

The experience of the 1970s and since has taught what we should have suspected, on the basis of general knowledge and theories of social behavior, from the beginning: Anti-poverty programs that the official political-administrative hierarchy designs and implements in a heavily, almost exclusively top-down fashion tend to be ineffective. Such efforts have a hard time reaching their grassroots clienteles through all the intervening bureaucratic layering—and a still harder time engaging local people in the conduct and management of their own poverty alleviation. The inherent limitations of centralized anti-poverty bureaucracies invite the series of structural alternatives, supplements, and follow-on considerations to which we turn next.

The Market

If those seeking to bring about changes in the villages cannot reach them effectively through the command structures of a centralized regime, one alternative is to look for self-adjusting servo-mechanisms that can accomplish some of society's purposes without, or with less, governmental intervention. Markets are a class of such devices. They are less than magical; they are flawed and imperfect; and they have to be bounded by laws and rules that are the subject of public policy. But they can indeed substitute for a lot of command decisionmaking and thus contribute generally to social efficiency.

The impact on the poor is mixed. Markets do not deal compassionately with the weak and disadvantaged. Nevertheless, freeing markets may give the poor some net gains by relieving them from discriminations that the hierarchy and the elites impose administratively. Moreover, the efficiency that market liberalization promotes is apt to create a better growth environment for poverty reduction. And letting the market settle local issues does give the poor, as market participants, some voice in local affairs—albeit only in proportion to their unequal resources.

In a revisionist program of anti-poverty policy, therefore, the market can be seen as a useful component of the appropriate policy design. Yet, plainly, it is in no sense a sufficient component.

Local Groups and Networks

If they are going to have a say in the management of affairs that affect them, the poor need to be helped to organize themselves, not only into market enterprises and groups but also into non-market organizations that can learn to influence public policies. All traditional rural societies, of course, already have well-established group structures when they commence their modernizing, development experience. But the poorer disadvantaged groups typically consist of dependent, patron-client configurations. They gain voice as they gather into newer, potentially more assertive organizational patterns. Some of these new groups (for example, cooperatives of a variety of types, including ones that are class- or caste-specific, and unions of landless agricultural workers) play mainly commercial roles, in which they seek to alter market outcomes. But others (for instance, church-related *campesino* groups in Latin America, or irrigation and education cooperatives in various regions) focus on the supply of and access to quasi-public goods. Recently various authors, including Sheldon Annis writing on Latin America and Goren Hyden on Africa, have noted the "thickening networks" of such grassroots (and predominantly indigenous) NGOs.[7] These organizations, in the view of many aid agencies as well as some developing-country governments, are taking on more important roles as instruments of poverty alleviation.

Local Government

Whether his or her own background reflects New England town meetings, Newark ward politics, or Indiana county government, an American listening to debates about how to engage the Third World poor in more effective defense of their own interests at the grassroots may sense a missing option. Non-official groups are all very well, but what about local *government*?

The fact is that the tradition of popular sovereignty at local levels in the Third World is weak and fragmented. National governments may or may not be creatures of their citizenry. But to writers like Hyden and Annis, examining governments from the perspective of African and Latin American peasants, governments are distant, semi-alien forces that staff and direct local official administrations. Local self-government is scarcely an option. The situation has not been very different in South Asia. In Pakistan and Nepal, local councils have tended to be elitist and manipulated from above. And the situation has not been much different in India; despite the *panchayati raj* reforms that began in 1959, the local self-government program has remained frail and faltering in all but two or three states at any given time.

This condition, it can be argued, is antithetical to an enduring program of strengthening the poor. Standing alone as a vehicle for popular grassroots participation, a miscellany of non-official groups and networks is not a sufficient and sustainable alternative. Except in a theocratic state, government—at the local level as elsewhere—is the one institution that has a universal, encompassing reach and a universal, or near-universal, membership. Some functions are only equitably and effectively performed within its frame. The local poor need such a frame for employing whatever political rights they have or may acquire.

But experience in a number of countries points out another clear and related lesson: At least initially, the delegation of central authority to locally selected governments is apt to aggravate inequalities between classes. This is because traditional elites are likely to be most intransigent in their traditional, local settings. Pass power to them, and the repression of the weaker and disadvantaged castes and classes is likely to worsen. Thus pro-equity reform requires a strategy for strengthening the poor politically.

Anti-Poverty Politics: Reform Regimes and Empowerment

The "bottom line" of the subject of strengthening the poor is clearly political. Although it is possible for anti-poverty reforms to be initiated without any non-local intervention, often there is a greater incidence of reformers, as well as of capacities to lever reform, in the upper reaches of the system. Thus the feasibility of reform at the local level very commonly depends on the readiness of national and provincial leaders—both official and non-official—to give greater voice to their poorer citizens. The latter can begin to build political muscle as direct anti-poverty programs provide them with employment, incomes, training, and other assets. But at the outset, the poor are likely to find local public decisionmaking stacked against them. Hence these empowering economic advances, as well as opportunities for the poor to organize, are likely to depend on the initiatives of leaders and facilitators in high places.

Such an analysis causes some people to doubt the feasibility of reform altogether on the ground that the central political and bureaucratic champions of the poor just hypothesized are apt to be members of the nation's elites. As such—if one believes either Marxist or market stereotypes—they will lack incentive to press reforms that are not driven by either class or personal-gain interests. At the end of the chapter I want to return to the proposition that this last is a remarkably brittle reading of the probabilities. Empirically—historically—there is nothing implausible about expecting some leaders to act on the basis of a *per se* interest in the welfare of the disadvantaged.

Mobilizing Local Resources

The last two items on my list of factors needed to offset the ineffectiveness of highly centralized anti-poverty structures concern the financing of programs. We have noted that much of the resources for broad-based poverty alleviation must be garnered from the poor's own accruing surpluses from improved productivity. Market processes and incentives, especially when facilitated by constructive credit programs, can be counted upon to mobilize such resources into income- and growth-enhancing private investments. But the betterment of the poor also requires the mobilization of local resources to *public* account, and this need constitutes a powerful argument for as much decentralization of public sector decisionmaking as is consistent with the country's broad national purposes. Thus the need to raise public resources locally makes a telling case for the kind of genuine local self-government already discussed. Local people are more willing to pay increased taxes or the equivalent when the revenues are being put to uses that they themselves choose and guide.

Along with the downward delegation of public sector decisions, there is a further technique—the matching grant—that outside aid donors as well as national and provincial governments can use to induce increased revenue-gathering at the local level. In a number of developing countries, local taxation has involved so much corruption—or has been so discriminatory and inequitable or otherwise unpopular—that it has been almost abandoned. A clear lesson for development promoters is the need to reconstitute the revenue function at the local level as an integral aspect of governmental rehabilitation at that level. Matching grant leverage can assist this effort.

Open Accountability

Corruption is a debilitating problem for public policy everywhere and not the least in developing countries. Delegating a greater share of consequential public sector decisions to the local level may sound like a program for proliferating corruption, but in fact the experiences of many grassroots governmental and non-governmental organizations teach the opposite. Under conditions of active local participation in public decisionmaking, the most attentive policing of implementation can be done by the clienteles and participants directly affected. Hence, the best defense against dishonest as well as unreasonably inefficient local administration can be provided by complete and open accountability of local operations to the local citizenry. For such defenses to be effective, it helps, of course, if the citizenry already includes at least a good scattering of literate and numerate members.

Spatial Strategies

Some of the lessons we have been learning are geographic. In terms of numbers of people, poverty policy's rural emphasis remains valid, but the problems as well as the sizes of cities are on the rise. What can and should *governments* do about the patterns of villages, towns, and metropolitan centers into which the populations of developing countries array themselves? How far down the structure of jurisdictions should *donor* aid programs try to penetrate? How tolerable or not are the horizontal inequities that arise among different locales in the same countries?

The Settlements Pattern

It may be, as many urban specialists argue, that trying to slow the migration of the Third World's rural poor to metropolitan centers is like tilting at windmills. The jury is still out on this issue. Despite much decentralization rhetoric, there have been few cases where significant and credible countervailing incentives in behalf of town (as opposed to metropolitan) centering have been sustained long enough to see whether it is possible to de-concentrate the upper echelons of the settlements pattern in a lasting fashion.

Whatever the prognosis for their largest cities, however, there is less doubt about the need in many countries to build more and stronger small urban settlements above the level of villages but within cycling distance from them. Such small centers have a multiplicity of administrative, trading, banking, training, educational, entertainment, and other roles to play in support of both farm and non-farm activities; and it is the role of public policy to promote their selective development. (Private locational decisions need little guidance; they tend to cluster to take advantage of and reinforce the positive externalities associated with early public sector locations. But public sector locational decision-making itself needs steering. It needs to resist the tendency to maximize political patronage by spreading public starts—schools, training centers, bank branches, supervised markets, whatever—thinly across as many villages as possible, thereby delaying the emergence of cumulative growth in a limited number of small centers.)

Despite the appalling view that Third World slums present to Western eyes (especially those of non-resident Westerners), survey research repeatedly has shown that most of the inhabitants of these slums are glad not to be back in the villages they left. Yet the needs in the cities are palpable, and our lessons to date about what policy can do to meet them are blurred and conflicted. However, Sheldon Annis, the only author contributing an explicitly urban perspective to this volume, is optimistic—less about the effectiveness of urban poverty-alleviation policy than about the growing, self-organized capacity of the urban poor (his case in point is Mexico City) to look after themselves.

Village Centering and Wholesaling vs. Retailing: Lessons for Aid Donors

Almost surely, village worship—the glorification of the smallest settlement in which one encounters the traditional society—was overdone in the 1970s. While generalizing across countries is dangerous, in many of them the individual village is the most traditional, unreconstructed jurisdiction; it is the most resistant to change, the most entrenched in customary inequalities. It is also too small to accommodate various institutions, facilities, and industries with even modest economies of scale. Hence one can argue that in many countries the traditional village should be no more than a neighborhood component of the larger unit that becomes the pivotal geographic, demographic, and administrative building block of the modernizing countryside.

In particular contexts, indigenous developers may well disagree. But what seems fairly plain as one looks back on the rural scenarios of the 1970s is that aid donors, at least, do not belong in individual villages in person—not more than fleetingly, except for learning experiences. In their major operations, the external intervenors need to *wholesale* their resources, leaving it to organizations of the internal government and/or other indigenous institutions to retail them at local (village and supra-village) levels. There are at least three reasons for the foreign agency to proceed along such arms-length lines. First, no agency could possibly deploy enough competent and knowlegeable personnel to operate very widely on a village-by-village basis. Second, if sustained for very long, such hands-on operations can generate an unhealthy dependence on expatriates. And third, even at best, foreigners are less likely to understand all of the subtleties of the local scene.

Interregional Disparities

If, as I have argued, the betterment of the poor depends importantly on the decentralization of authority and the encouragement of locally led and energized initiatives, the central authorities must expect disparities to emerge or increase between localities and between subregions. If leaders would nurture incentives they must, largely, let front-running areas run ahead.

This is a distasteful, and to some extent counter-intuitive, proposition. It does not extend to the generalized issue of rural-urban differentials, which can, indeed—depending on the country case—be the subject of moderating policies. Moreover, it is well known that horizontal disparities within the same jurisdictional levels—for example, disparities between different provinces or states or between districts within a state—can be tempered by movements in labor and capital markets, as well as by public transfers of resources from richer to poorer areas via the governments of the larger jurisdictions to which both areas belong. Nevertheless it should be a fundamental characteristic of anti-poverty policy to show more concern for inequalities among classes in given places than for inequalities between places.

Growth and Equity in Agriculture

Four of the authors of this volume—Lele, Alamgir, Islam, and Aziz—concentrate on the agricultural sector, and several of the others also focus on it in some detail. With all this collaboration, I need not here dwell long on the substantive lessons we have learned about the rural sector. But let me very briefly propose four such lessons.

First, the situation in agriculture amply illustrates the general priority for productivity and growth. In all countries where large fractions of populations depend on agriculture, there is a macro case for expanding output, whether of food or of other crops in which the country's comparative advantage is greater. Moreover, there is an equity case: It is indeed easier, on the whole, to win a better deal for the poor—both rural and urban—when agricultural production is expanding rather than static.

Second, as to equity, we now know better than ever that growth plus trickle-down in agriculture is not a sufficient anti-poverty program. As Nurul Islam demonstates in his chapter, the effects of agricultural growth on rural and urban poverty, respectively, are quite complex. Much depends on the distribution of land and other assets, on access to inputs and services, and on the nature of the farm labor force. Some of the points are surprising. For example, assistance to medium-size farmers may (via linkages and multipliers) have a greater anti-poverty effect than aid to very small cultivators. Nevertheless, as most of the authors—Uphoff, Lele, Paul, Alamgir, Aziz, Guhan, and Wheeler—in one way or another testify, experience teaches there is a predominant case for programs that deliver benefits directly to poor farming families with little or no land, provided that the programs can be operated with reasonable efficiency.

Third, there is the matter of land reform. We know that in cases where, thanks to historical accident or upheaval (Japan, Korea, China,

Taiwan) there has been a decisive transformation in the entitlements to land, this has had salutary effects on both agricultural growth and equity. By now, however, in countries where no revolutions have happened or are in prospect—especially if these are pluralistic systems given to incremental change—it is apparent (a) that elites have great capacities for delaying and/or evading thoroughgoing tenurial reforms and (b) that activists, instead of waiting for the land-redistribution millenium, should focus on building the poor's holdings of other assets, for example, "human capital."

But two cautionary footnotes need to be added to this familiar view of the land question. In the first place, care should be taken not to exaggerate the ineffectiveness of past land reforms. In some places— for example in parts of India, where land reforms are commonly said to have failed—the limited successes achieved, such as the abolition of most absentee ownership, have not been trivial. In the second place, equity seekers should not miss the opportunities for thoroughgoing reform that politics occasionally and unexpectedly creates. Such an opportunity, for example, seems recently to have been missed (with the World Bank rooting for far more radical change than was adopted) by the Aquino regime in the Philippines.

Finally, the fourth broad substantive lesson I read from donors' and indigenous governments' efforts to attack agricultural poverty in the 1970s is that in most Third World countries it is not possible to find a sufficient answer to poverty alleviation within agriculture alone. There is not enough available land to be divided into viable holdings for all hands. Maximum annual growth of farm output is unlikely to exceed 4 per cent on any sustained basis. Yet if the welfare of farmers and farm workers is to improve, output per worker will and should also grow—perhaps by 2–3 per cent annually. That leaves room for a growth of only 1–2 per cent a year in the farm labor force—at a time when the natural growth of the rural population will be considerably faster than that. This may, but it need not, mean an accelerating rush of migrants to the metropolises. But it does require the creation of more non-agricultural activities and workplaces and underscores the need for more small urban centers.

Institutions, the Social Sectors, and Human Resources

Long before the 1970s, we knew that the identities and qualities of a developing country's institutions tend to determine the character of the educational, health, population, and nutritional services supplied by the country's social sectors. We also knew that these social sector services heavily determine the present effectiveness of the country's human resources. Further, looking at cases like Japan, we knew that human resources could be the dominant factor determining economic performance. But the past couple of decades have provided some very vivid examples of these linkages.

Training Deficits and the Indirect Impact on Poverty

In Africa, the worst bottleneck on development has proved to be the shortage of trained personnel.[8] Whole cadres of professionals and para-professionals, and therefore the institutions to prepare them, need to be built, augmented, and strengthened. The inadequate supply of training can be attributed in some measure to the prevalence of very small countries and to nationalistic tensions that prevent the rationalization of training activities on a regional basis. But the short-falls cannot be put down in any simple way to the inadequacy of investment in human resource development—particularly from outside. Outlays on education claim large fractions of domestic resources, and per capita aid to Africa has been high by comparative standards. Instead, the principal problems have been allocation and organization. During the 1970s, African governments, like aid donors, got caught up in the mystique of site-specific integrated rural development projects. Little money, energy, or imagination was left for the kinds of training of whole cadres of skilled, paraprofessional, and professional personnel that could not be fitted within the bills of requirements of the discrete projects. There was little to match the broad human infrastructure development that had been done with some success in parts of South Asia a decade earlier.

The effect of these institutional and training deficits on poverty *per se* is indirect but critical. These deficits restrain African development generally and therefore the availability of material as well as human resources for attacking poverty.

Direct Links Between Poverty and the Social Sectors

There is an obvious intersection between social disadvantage and poverty. Those who are relatively deprived economically also register, in the aggregate, the highest illiteracy rates and the most serious mal-nourishment, suffer the highest infant mortality, and live the shortest lives.[9] Programs in the social sectors therefore have a high probability of benefiting the poor—provided that the poor have good access to them and find them relevant. But some of what we have learned has been less expected. Although—in developing countries generally—income per capita (the conventional macroeconomic indicator of welfare) and the various indicators of social welfare tend to move together, there are countries and regions (Sri Lanka and the Indian state of Kerala have been the most widely noted) where policy emphasis on the social sectors has caused social gains to run ahead of the economic indicators. Where this has been the case, the social advances—in themselves improvements for the poor—also have had a very clear family planning impact. Declines in infant mortality and, in particular, gains in female literacy have been associated with pronounced reductions in fertility.

There have been reverse cases as well, in which social sector advances have lagged behind those in per capita income. In Pakistan, for example, the relatively sluggish performance of education and health programs quite clearly has reflected the grip of traditional attitudes toward the status and roles of women. In such cases the difficulties of fertility reduction have been predictable, and the social sector lags may, before long, threaten the sustainability of the macroeconomic advances.

For our purposes the net of all this is that, even more than was apparent twenty years ago, strengthening the poor demands improvements in human infrastructure—both for the masses and in the training of professional and paraprofessional elites. For aid donors, as will be argued later, this translates into the need for major reforms in technical assistance design and operations.

Women in Development

During the fifteen years since the early blooming of reformist antipoverty doctrine, there has been growing recognition of the degree to which the specific roles of women in the development process have been overlooked—to the detriment of overall development goals as well as the women and their families.

Development thinking and analysis—and, to a lesser extent, development policy and action—increasingly take into account the predominance of women in the agricultural labor force in many countries, including most African countries; the dependence of much labor-intensive manufacturing for export on female workers; the heavy role of women in public works employment; the leverage female literacy exerts on family welfare; women's roles in family health; the relationship of women's status to population behavior; and the centrality of rural women's traditional work roles to energy and deforestation issues.

Appropriate poverty policy responses to these realities do not necessarily mean that indigenous governments and aid agencies must undertake special, additive programming, but that women's specific economic and household roles must receive active attention and steady follow-through across the whole panoply of poverty-alleviating efforts.

In the present volume, some of the authors have taken just this approach—building into their chapters some explicit policy lessons relating to women in development. Mayra Buvinić and Margaret

Lycette reinforce our collective emphasis in a chapter specifically devoted to some of the women-specific findings of the past decade of development research and practice.

Poverty and the Environment

We may have been into the 1980s before the environment was widely recognized as an important dimension not just of development policy, but of anti-poverty policy. Nevertheless, on the grounds that the roots of the convergence between the two subjects reach back into the preceding decade, let me interject some environment-related remarks here. (The relationship of development and environment will be explored in depth in a forthcoming volume in ODC's Policy Perspectives series.)[10]

Some environmental issues—for example, the ozone layer and the greenhouse effect—concern the poor in poor countries simply because they are members of the race. Beyond this, the junction between environment and poverty is of two kinds. First, environmental protection can compete with short-run poverty alleviation. By modifying, but also slowing down, growth into *sustainable* patterns, measures to protect the environment can retard the generation of incremental output that otherwise would be available for, among other things, reducing poverty. Moreover, budgetary and other resources may be directly reallocated from anti-poverty to pro-environment uses.[11]

The second interconnection between poverty and environment is that the problems of the poor in poor countries have intrinsic environmental aspects. Rural terrain, for example, is unequally fertile. The poor, with the weakest entitlements to resources, tend to get squeezed onto marginal lands. They have disproportionately little access to irrigation. They are the most exposed to natural misfortunes—to droughts and floods. They have to scrounge the farthest and hardest for fuel. In turn, in their marginal circumstances, they become degraders of resources and despoilers of forests—although they often are less devastating than commercial loggers or developers and official forestry departments. The marginalization point makes it clear that, *other things being equal*, whatever lessens poverty—whatever improves the real incomes of the poor—tends to reduce their pressure on marginal resources and therefore to be good for the environment.

There is a further environmental point that is significant in the centrist (top-down) versus grassroots (bottom-up) context. As already mentioned, the rural poor often are arrayed disproportionately in non-irrigated, upstream, hilly, and mountainous areas. The impulse of the grassroots poverty-alleviation school is to encourage and help them practice self-reliant development locality by locality. The trouble is that, untempered, such a policy design can neglect the downstream effects. Goat raising, for example, may seem the most rewarding calling for the hill people. But its negative externalities can extend well beyond the locality; by accelerating erosion, the goats may cause disastrous effects down below. In such cases, responsible policy must be made in a larger frame.

Another application of the same principle would concern the responsibilities for and costs of preserving natural wildlife in impoverished parts of Africa. Here the benefits that humanity derives from the preservation of the wildlife extend to people living far beyond the local area—indeed, it can be argued, they extend worldwide, and it is the responsibility of the global community to employ local people (or to subsidize them) in behalf of environmental preservation.

Project Design, Management, and Assistance

At the start of this chapter, I noted the kinds of lessons about "new style" integrated rural development and basic needs projects that DAC donors already were drawing at the end of the 1970s. The lessons have aged well. Complex, hands-on, highly localized projects are indeed hard to replicate. It is true that heavy infusions of project personnel can blight local managerial competence. In their concern to achieve scripted results, project personnel preempt initiatives, press implementation along prescribed lines, and often let their local counterparts settle into a state of ongoing dependence.

Project donors have further demonstrated—perhaps more in Sub-Saharan Africa recently than ever before—a tendency to cannibalize indigenous administrative structures. The donors have wanted "their" projects to have the best administrative vehicles that money and persuasion could buy. Under conditions where skilled local technicians and managers are scarce, this has caused the donors, for one thing, to bid against one another for the part-time services of favored local bureaucrats—a practice, common in several West African countries, that apparently is not widely regarded as unethical.

The preferred stratagem, however, has been to go the special project-authority route, seeking the creation of a new entity singly devoted to the favored project—first, to its establishment, then, often, to its operation. If the authority can get more than its share of able people and partially escape routine red tape, the formula has great appeal for the donor. But its severe cost is the weakening it can impose on the country's regular administrative system—budgetarily and in terms of personnel allocations, leaders' attention, and bureaucratic morale.

The point is not that an externally assisted project designed to strengthen the poor never again should resort to implementation by a special authority. There will continue to be instances where the function being undertaken does not fit persuasively under any portion of the existing administrative structure. Or—as has notoriously been the case with certain public works departments—the logically appropriate piece of administrative structure may be so grievously moribund as to seem beyond redemption. But in such cases, then, the new project authority should be regarded as a first step in a program of thoroughgoing and, as need be, radical administrative reform. The intention should not be simply to leave the new authority dangling in unstructured space.

Technical Assistance and Donor Coordination

As already indicated, the aid donors—by concentrating their technical assistance in Africa in the 1970s so largely on discrete local, site-specific projects—neglected the kinds of institution-building and broad expertise development that, with donor help, had been done more effectively earlier in parts of Asia. The other painful technical assistance lesson—again most visible in Africa—has been the disgraceful parochialism of such assistance. In the case of bilateral programs, supplies of expertise and training have not only, for the most part, been tied to donor-country sources; individual donors have peddled their own overlapping and competing brands of technology and doctrine in a way sure to confuse and enervate the recipient.

With literally dozens of donors weighing in on overextended country officials, there is a palpable need for improved donor coordination. This the donors have been saying among themselves with gathering vigor for at least the past eight years, and some progress has been made. But far more strenuous efforts are needed to put the recipient government in the middle of the coordination exercise and to adapt various donors' inputs to a common design on the one hand and to the donors' several comparative advantages on the other.[12]

Overambitious Design

As operating experience has piled up, the design of the prototypical anti-poverty project of the 1970s has proved too ambitious in two respects.

In the first place, often too much has been attempted along multifaceted, multidisciplinary lines. Projects that take on such complexity have been difficult to execute; it has been hard to satisfy all of their demands for staffing, sequencing, and synchronization. The fact that life is lived in the round does not mean that particular development-promoting interventions need to address a variety of its facets equally and simultaneously. Instead, something along the lines of Albert Hirschman's unbalanced growth model frequently can work: The pushes and pulls that success with one element of poverty-alleviating effort can generate can in turn induce accommodating responses in other dimensions. Local actors have most of the incentives, wit, and energy to attend to their own betterment. Interventions are needed to catalyze, not substitute for, these capacities.

The second kind of overambition concerns timing. Characteristically, anti-poverty projects, especially aid projects, have set themselves shorter than realistic timetables. Aid authorities have learned to translate their parliaments' one-year money bills into multi-year project calendars. But there are still manifold pressures to foreshorten the calendars and claim and demonstrate results sooner than the latter can mature. It is noted below that more anti-poverty effort is being channeled into non-project forms. But much of what remains in projects should be longer gaited.

NGOs: How Much of the Answer?

Just as indigenous non-governmental organizations are becoming a bigger part of the local organizational scene in many developing countries, expatriate NGOs have been playing a widening role in the development assistance community. For their part, the NGOs (the genus is highly developed in the United States and much of Europe and is beginning to gain stature in Japan) have been moving a growing fraction of their effort from relief to development. At the same time, mindful of their own operational limitations, a number of official development agencies (now including even such multilaterals as the World Bank) seem increasingly interested in shifting responsibilities as well as resources to NGOs.

Some increased reliance on NGOs certainly is in order. But as Thomas Dichter suggests in his chapter, it would be too facile to assume that NGOs can provide a principal solution to the puzzles of pro-poor aid policies. For one thing, relations between expatriate and indigenous NGOs need careful monitoring and sorting by donors. Those of the indigenous variety are of very uneven quality—but so are the expatriate ones, and some of the latter tend to be slow to interact with, and then to hand over to, their domestic counterparts.

Moreover, as between the public agency and NGO aid models, there is a problem of scale: Enlarged to the proportions of public programs, the private agencies can lose much of the flexibility that makes them attractive. Further, some of the greater cost-effectiveness that often is attributed to them reflects their use of publicly provided inputs and infrastructure. The net of the matter recalls the case of the market: NGOs are part of the answer to strengthening the poor, but by no means all of it.

III. Adjustment-Related Lessons from the 1980s

The world's Third U.N. Development Decade has turned out, more nearly, to be a Decade of Adjustment. Many of us would argue that the adjustment priority has been inescapable. If nations in a sovereign-state world are to sustain viable economic relations with one another, countries' internal and, especially, external imbalances need to be narrowed to manageable proportions. But as the adjustment process has crunched its way through the 1980s—making differing but, in many cases, arresting inroads on growth and, in particular, on the poor in many parts of the Third World—several lessons have accrued for those now seeking a revival of efforts to strengthen the poor. I would cite four:

1. The increase in non-project, including policy-based, aid probably is here to stay; those interested in using aid to strengthen the poor should learn to live with and, in part, to use this mode of transfer.

The joint efforts of the international community and developing-country governments to cope with the 1980s' prolonged adjustment crisis has shifted the balance of aid flows (as well as non-concessional transfers) away from the overwhelming dominance of project aid toward various kinds of non-project transfers. Moreover, the desire to provide quick-disbursing relief to payments deficits has not been the only motivation for the change. Program, sectoral, and other forms of non-project transfers were known to be—and again have proved to be—far more effective vehicles than project assistance for conveying advice concerning recipient countries' sectoral and broader-than-sectoral policies. Multilateral agencies such as the International Monetary Fund and the World Bank, and increasingly bilateral donors as well, have been persuaded that recipients not only need to bring their financial balances under control; to keep them healthy, they typically need to free internal markets, strengthen agricultural incentives, promote exports, rationalize their import restrictions and exchange rates, effect budgetary economies, encourage saving, and otherwise enhance efficiency. The donors have used portions of their increased non-project transfers to encourage and/or lever such reforms.

Such "policy-based lending" is not a favorite of recipients, but even if the emergency need for flexible, quick-disbursing aid diminishes, the non-project, policy-linked fraction of the aid flow is unlikely to decline much. First, the fungibility of non-project aid often is so useful to recipient governments that this softens their resistance to the policy strings. Second, the manner in which policy influence is conveyed matters greatly, and donors, including the World Bank, have been learning to engage less in rigid, detailed preconditioning and more in the kind of dialoguing that leaves the recipient to determine particulars of the policy design. Third, most recipients recognize, however reluctantly, that since aid is scarce and usually can be swamped by countervailing domestic policies, donors owe it to their own parliaments and publics to do what they can to see that the assistance is not wasted.

2. Efforts to strengthen the poor directly should not try to monopolize development assistance. This second lesson from the adjustment-stressed 1980s is a negative one that some would prefer not to see emphasized in the present context. But it belongs. The poor have a better chance of being made stronger, by themselves and with the help of others, under circumstances of economic growth; and it is a mistake to try to push all growth-promoting aid through poor-specific funnels. There are needs for infrastructure, sometimes for major industrialization, and—in this decade—for adjustment assistance. There is Nurul Islam's point, for example: Indirectly, programs benefiting middle-sized farmers may do more for the poor than ones targeted directly on the poorest farmers. As to aid, therefore, anti-poverty fighters should not strive for exclusivity; and, indeed, when some donor programs become thus constrained (as was the case with AID, for example, during the flush of the New Directions era) it behooves others to balance up total flows in other appropriate areas.

3. Adjustment 1980s-style has been harsh in its impact on the poorest sections of developing-country populations; it therefore needs cushioning and supplementing. This is the decade's central adjustment-related lesson for poverty policy. It is one with which Richard Jolly is strongly identified,[13] and that he develops in his chapter in this volume. As Jolly points out, in the absence of specific offsets, budgetary austerity and some other macro adjustments tend to hit people in the low ends of the income and asset distributions disproportionately. Measures to attenuate and soften these impacts, both by sustaining growth better and by targeting subsidies on the weakest classes, are needed to give adjustment a more "human face."

4. There is scope for putting policy leverage directly to the service of anti-poverty goals. This point overlaps substantively with the previous one, since some of the social and pro-equity reforms that policy-based lending may be increasingly used to promote may be the same ones being adopted to cushion the poor against the rigors of adjustment. But the distinction is, I think, worthwhile. First, the rationales of the two approaches differ. The one just above is defensive—a matter of damage control. Here, in contrast, I am saying: Let us use the new policy-levering aid technology positively—by putting it to the service of such good causes, for example, as land reform, health, education, family planning, urban uplift, agricultural priorities, rural centering, and constructive public works policies. Second, the array of social reforms that policy leverage can be used to promote is somewhat broader than, and does not need to be defined by, the hostile impacts that adjustment measures inflict on the poor.

The World Bank and other donors lately have started employing non-project lending to promote social reforms in just the way I am proposing. It is only fair to note that, unless used circumspectly, such leverage can generate dysfunctional tension between itself and pro-adjustment leverage; it tends to encourage increased government spending just when adjustment policy is trying to curtail it. But this only suggests the need for an enhanced tax and saving effort. The idea of having the donors tie some of their non-project grants and concessional loans explicitly to reforms favoring the poor is eminently sound.

IV. Conclusions

The lessons we can draw from anti-poverty policy's periods of prominence in the 1970s and its low salience since are numerous; nearly all of them are important; and they already have been stated in summary form. Instead of resummarizing them, I therefore single out three themes for final emphasis:

1. The alleged clash between the centrist and grassroots modes of anti-poverty policy is specious. It seems to me that Norman Uphoff and Samuel Paul are dead right in this conclusion. The two approaches can be and should be essentially complementary—and, indeed, that is what the title of this volume has been chosen to convey: One strengthens the poor partly by the provision of supplies from outside; but one does not strengthen by increasing or unnecessarily prolonging dependence. The purpose is to achieve rising welfare under conditions of growing self-reliance.

2. Development assistance still has a major role to play in strengthening the poor. Aid's part over the next decade may be somewhat diminished, but it should not become trivial. This is the view presented from the sides of both aid consumers and aid suppliers in the final two chapters of this book. Although aid to India always has been thin in per capita terms, S. Guhan argues its on-balance value, estimates that the continuing flow will remain significant, and suggests ways to improve its anti-poverty effectiveness. Guhan's views are broadly consistent with those of Joseph Wheeler, Chairman of DAC as well as a long-time USAID official, who also favors reform rather than abandonment.

The donors, it seems clear, do have to be more realistic about their operating modes. It will be scandalous if they do not very soon make substantial strides on the coordination front. This will mean centering the coordinating role in the host government itself, perhaps supported (sector by sector) by a lead donor. In particular, technical assistance must become more coherent, developmental (as in institution-building), and responsive to recipient needs and leads.

Donors (to reemphasize the point) should settle for sensible and efficient wholesaling roles. This does not mean passivity: They should require accountability and themselves monitor activities, including policy reforms, that they help support. Moreover, they can play countervailing roles against the forces of privilege and inertia in the recipient governments. But if they are wise they will leave most of the "retailing"—the direct interventions into local activities—to host-country nationals and organizations.

3. There is no reason to despair generally of the political feasibility of pro-poor reform in non-revolutionary contexts. Such reform is inherently an optimistic venture. "Political will" has to become more than a slogan. Along with initiatives at the grassroots, there must be national leadership in and/or out of the government that is determined to give the disadvantaged opportunities for political as well as economic strengthening.

It is true that such vectors of leadership typically are driven neither by class interests nor by self-interested market pressures. But this does not make them implausible. Governments seldom are monoliths. Within many of them, as well as in the leadership groups arrayed around them, there are leaders with strong, if often only intermittent, reformist purposes. It is the business of constructively intentioned donors and other outsiders to seek out these reformers and make common cause with them.

Notes

[1] The term refers to the practice, followed by a number of governments and favored by the World Bank in the 1970s, of defining a poverty line denominated in terms of income per capita or per household (the underlying logic of the line often is nutritional) and then estimating the numbers of "absolute poor" falling below that line.

[2] Recently, for example, such views are elaborated in D.L. Sheth, "Alternative Development as Political Practice," *Alternatives* XII (1987), pp. 155–171; and in Marc Nerfin, "Neither Prince nor Merchant: An Introduction to the Third System," *Development Dialogue*, 1987: 1, pp. 170–195.

[3] John P. Lewis, "Overview—Development Promotion: A Time for Regrouping," in John P. Lewis and Valeriana Kallab, eds., *Development Strategies Reconsidered* (New

Brunswick, N.J.: Transaction Books in cooperation with the Overseas Development Council, 1986), pp. 3-9.

4 Hollis Chenery et al., *Redistribution With Growth* (New York: Oxford University Press, 1974); *Employment, Growth and Basic Needs*, (New York: Praeger Publishers, 1977).

5 Robert L. Ayres, *Banking on the Poor* (Cambridge, Mass.: MIT Press, 1983).

6 *Development Cooperation, 1979 Review*, Report by the Chairman of the Development Assistance Committee (Paris: Organisation for Economic Co-operation and Development, 1979), p. 54.

7 Goren Hyden, *No Shortcuts to Progress: African Development Management in Perspective* (Berkeley, Calif.: University of California Press, 1983); Sheldon Annis, "Can Small-Scale Development be a Large-Scale Policy? The Case of Latin America," *World Development*, Vol. 15 (Autumn 1987).

8 Uma Lele almost has a copyright on the following argument. See *The Design of Rural Development: Lessons from Africa* (Baltimore, Md.: Johns Hopkins University Press, third printing with new postscript, 1979).

9 A classic statement of these interconnections (although, of course, the data need periodic updating) was provided in "Poverty and Human Development," *World Development Report, 1980* (Washington, D.C.: The World Bank, 1980), Part II.

10 H. Jeffrey Leonard and contributors, *Environmental and Anti-Poverty Strategies for the 1990s* (title tentative), U.S.-Third World Policy Perspectives No. 11, (New Brunswick, N.J.: Transaction Books in cooperation with the Overseas Development Council, forthcoming Spring 1989).

11 For the most prominent advocacy of "sustainable development," see *Our Common Future*, Report of the World Commission on Environment and Development (New York: Oxford University Press, 1987).

12 I still favor a formulation along these lines I wrote in "Coordinating aid to make it more effective—regionally and in the sphere of technical assistance," in *Development Cooperation, 1981 Review*, Report by the Chairman of the Development Assistance Committee (Paris: Organisation for Economic Co-operation and Development, 1981), Chapter III.

13 Giovanni Andrea Cornea, Richard Jolly, and Frances Stewart, *Adjustment with a Human Face*, Vols. 1 and 2 (New York: Oxford University Press, 1987).

Summaries of Chapter Recommendations

1. Assisted Self-Reliance: Working With, Rather than For, the Poor (Norman Uphoff)

However paradoxical it may appear, a strategy of "assisted self-reliance" offers important possibilities for U.S. and other donors to promote development that are lower-cost and more sustainable. Examples offered from over a dozen countries show that participatory approaches to agricultural, health, infrastructure, and other improvements can be effective and need not be small-scale. Being based on community capacity for resource mobilization and management makes these efforts more efficient and persevering.

Governments that fail to recognize and draw on the ideas, knowledge, technical capabilities, and leadership qualities of people at the grassroots take upon themselves the growing burden of not only financing but also maintaining the facilities and services being created. The alternative is to use external resources—advice, funds, training, material assistance, etc.—not so much to produce direct results as to strengthen local capacities to initiate and manage activities that produce benefits for which the poor share responsibility.

The requirements for such a strategy include:

(1) The involvement of local organizations;
(2) Working through multiple channels—not just through public sector, but also through private sector and non-governmental organizations;
(3) The use of "catalysts" to mobilize local efforts and resources;
(4) Building on indigenous traditions and technology;
(5) "Priming the pump" for sustainable resource mobilization;
(6) Use of paraprofessionals;
(7) Undertaking bureaucratic reorientation; and
(8) Taking a "learning process" approach.

Donors should recognize that "assisted self-reliance" is not a paradox, but a means to overcome past failings of development programs. These programs have been too confident that the infusion of resources—like the fueling of a machine—will produce desired results. Yet development is basically a matter of constructing structures and processes for converting scarce inputs into valued outputs. The capabilities involved are more human and social than material or mechanical—and even the latter capabilities come into being and use only through people's ideas and motivations. While material resource constraints must be taken seriously, they will remain insurmountable if decisionmakers continue to think of the poor more as "beneficiaries" than as "co-participants" in development efforts.

2. Governments and Grassroots Organizations: From Co-Existence to Cooperation (Samuel Paul)

Recent years have witnessed a growing interest on the part of donors and developing countries in grassroots organizations as an important institutional alternative for strengthening the poor. Community groups, non-governmental organizations (NGOs), cooperatives, and local governments fall within the spectrum of such grassroots agencies. These organizations generally tend to be better than central governments at adapting services to the needs of the poor. They are also more likely to enhance the political power of the poor and to nudge the bureaucracy to be more responsive to the needs of the poor. However, governments and other large-scale organizations have a comparative advantage in mobilizing resources on a large scale, developing new technologies of benefit to the poor, and promoting their nationwide diffusion. Thus *governments and grassroots organizations have differing but complementary strengths.*

Though there is a case for linkages between governments and grassroots organizations, evidence of collaboration between the two is negligible in most developing countries. National governments typically have centralized programs for poverty alleviation, whereas grassroots agencies have done much to strengthen the poor in many countries, but on a small scale and with limited national impact. There is clearly an urgent need to encourage collaboration between these two types of institutions and to design public policies that will facilitate such collaboration. Three modes of collaboration that governments might encourage can be highlighted:

1. Grassroots organizations, especially NGOs, can assist public programs for poverty alleviation by mobilizing, informing, and educating the poor. The flexibility, smallness, and highly motivated personnel

of NGOs, for example, make them well suited to perform these tasks. Collaboration for "demand mobilization" is consistent with the advocacy and "watchdog" function that many NGOs perform at the local and national levels.

2. Grassroots agencies can be invited to participate in the planning and implementation of the government's poverty-alleviation programs. The ability of grassroots agencies to listen to and adapt their services to meet the needs of the poor contributes to better planning. "Contracting out" the task of implementation to them at once reduces the burden on the bureaucracy and optimizes the use of local resources, skills, and commitment.

3. A government can draw upon the strategy and design of a grassroots initiative and build a national or regional program around it. The role of the grassroots organization in such a case is that of a "research and development laboratory" for the government program, a source of key personnel for the replication of the chosen strategies, and a model for the operating culture and systems of the new program.

International donors can play a catalytic role in stimulating these collaborative modes in several ways:

(1) The sharing of international experience in this area with developing-country governments and their leaders can yield rich dividends;

(2) Seed money for collaboration between governments and grassroots agencies can encourage governments to experiment in this important area;

(3) Lending operations, where appropriate and feasible, can include components that facilitate the participation of grassroots organizations in government projects; and

(4) Donors can assist governments in reorienting their public policies and incentive systems to stimulate collaboration with grassroots agencies.

3. Empowering Africa's Rural Poor: Problems and Prospects in Agricultural and Rural Development (Uma Lele)

In Africa, growth in agricultural production is essential for poverty alleviation; technical change in agriculture is essential for growth; appropriate balance in the availability and deployment of physical, human, and institutional capital is essential for technical change to occur; and it is the lack of such a balance in the accumulation and efficient use of different forms of capital that explains the persistence of poverty.

The poverty problem in Africa—where landlessness is relatively negligible—is mainly a problem of households in resource-poor rural areas with few obvious technological options or known solutions for increasing their production and incomes. To alleviate poverty, governments and donors have actively tried to deal with the problem of rural development for almost three decades. Despite the "gloom and doom" about Africa, much has been learned and achieved in these decades, and analysis of experience offers lessons that have important implications for policy.

The Relationship of Growth to Equity. The first set of lessons relates to the relationship of growth to equity. Experience in the 1960s (mostly in Asia) led donors and governments to believe that the "trickle-down" effect of growth does not work in addressing poverty—that a direct attack on poverty is needed instead. Experience in the 1970s (mostly in Africa) indicated, however, that "top down" approaches to allocate a large share of donor and government resources to poverty alleviation in resource-poor areas can do little for poverty alleviation when they are not accompanied by appropriate macroeconomic and sectoral policy, by an institutional framework, or by technology conducive to overall economic growth. Such efforts not only fail to create increased incomes on a sustainable basis in resource-poor areas, but also do not prepare the poor to move into employment opportunities stimulated by increased agricultural growth. Instead, they simply divert attention from a focus on broad-based growth in agriculture by postponing the growth-enabled accelerated transfer of a growing population out of resource-poor areas. They also contribute to environmental degradation.

Experience in the 1980s has told us that macroeconomic adjustment in the form of getting prices right is essential in many cases for improving overall efficiency and growth prospects. But price reforms affect incomes of the poor differently in different settings—depending on the nature of asset distribution, access to technology, credit, and markets. The many farmers living below subsistence levels may in fact be hurt by these reforms, and they may need compensatory policies to reduce their adverse impact.

The Importance of Means and Balance in Growth Strategy. A second set of lessons relate to the *means* by which growth is achieved and to its *balance*—particularly between export-crop and food-crop production. The experience of the 1960s indicated that emphasis on export crops may not ensure the employment and incomes of the primarily food-crop-producing poor. The record of the 1970s showed, however, that a well-intentioned emphasis on food security that nevertheless undermines export-crop production and ignores factors affecting improvement in food-crop productivity also may do little for poverty alleviation.

The experience of the 1980s has emphasized that while price corrections are important in shifting resources among food- and export-crop activities, they may not be sufficient for achieving growth in aggregate agricultural production. Indeed, the attempt to remove price distortions in many countries has underscored the fundamental importance of technical, institutional, and organizational complexities in alleviating poverty through growth. These complexities require a consistent, long-run strategy. Further, experience has shown that generalizations as to the effectiveness of the private, the public, or the cooperative sector are difficult, as they are complexly related to individual countries' inheritances in terms of natural resources, international markets, and politics and institutions—and consequently require country-specific solutions.

The Need for Investment in Human Capital and Institutions. Perhaps the most important lesson for poverty alleviation in Africa for both donors and governments is the fundamental need to build human and institutional capacity to address these problems. The policy implication of this clearly is to give primacy to capacity-building. Large-scale resource transfers to alleviate balance-of-payments difficulties must not be allowed to come in the way of advancing with the more basic long-run and humdrum tasks of development that enable a more genuine if less grand synthesis of the lessons learned.

Underlying Socio-Political Constraints in Recipient and Donor Countries. Finally, given the fundamental importance of foreign aid to Africa—and the role of donor advice, ideas, and skilled people until Africa builds its own human capital capacity—there is a need to address the constraints posed by perceptions and politics in both recipient and donor countries.

4. Some Lessons from IFAD's Approach to Rural Poverty Alleviation (Mohiuddin Alamgir)

This chapter summarizes the International Fund for Agricultural Development's first ten years of experience with poverty alleviation in the rural areas of developing countries—where the majority of the poor live—and draws some more widely applicable lessons from IFAD's work. The lessons cited relate specifically to the provision of credit for the rural poor, integrated rural development projects, irrigation development for the benefit of the poor, and development focused on women, ethnic populations, and cultural minorities.

The thesis of the chapter is that policymakers and aid donors should view poverty alleviation as an *economic* and not just a welfare proposition. No people are too poor, too isolated, or too marginalized to be reached and assisted cost-effectively. Whether one thinks in supply or demand terms, the rural poor represent a large untapped potential for output and demand growth. This is true even during the so-called "transition period" to structural adjustment—an effort supported by policy-based lending and now under way in a large number of countries. Measures to strengthen the *productive* base of the poor should be an integral element of adjustment efforts, ensuring the success of adjustment initiatives with minimum pain for the disadvantaged. Adjustment with this new dimension would then be synonymous with development, not just adjustment with a human face.

Planners, project designers, and aid donors should move beyond the sheer delivery of charity to formulating, in consultation with the beneficiaries themselves, development interventions that are cost-effective, sustainable, and replicable—and that build on the capacity and the creativity of poor people. Such poverty-alleviating projects and programs can be subjected to thoroughly rigorous evaluation, provided all costs and benefits are fully accounted for and correctly valued.

The starting point for an intervention on behalf of the poor should be an in-depth analysis to locate the poor, identify their characteristics, isolate the constraints under which they operate, and, above all, develop an understanding of the longer-term processes that tend to generate and perpetuate poverty.

With this backdrop, one can adapt a microeconomic approach to targeted poverty alleviation that involves the direct participation of the poor. This ensures not only that project or program benefits are not diverted away from the target groups, but also that they are sustainable beyond the life of the project. Benefit targeting is not easy without participation and structural reforms, and it cannot be effective unless supported by grassroots-based institutions and by tailored packages of basic education, training, credit, and technology—all of which are elements that enhance small and marginal farmers' ability to assume risks. NGOs can play a very useful role in promoting both participation and structural reform as well as in addressing these complementary elements.

Credit can be targeted on the rural poor by the use of ceilings on farm size, assets, or income; or by providing credit in-kind in behalf of production activities that only the target group pursues and/or with the help of mobile credit agents who can take banking services to the people. It is not necessary to insist on land or any other tangible assets as collateral. Group guarantee, assets purchased with the credit itself, and personal surety all can be good substitutes. What must be ensured is the provision of complementary support services (inputs, extension, research, etc.). While loan procedures need to be simplified, due attention has to be paid to the charging of economic interest rates so that administrative and other related costs can be recovered and so that private savings will be promoted. Care must be taken, however, that the lending institutions not unduly inflate administrative costs and that they insist on good repayment discipline. Experience shows that administrative costs can be contained and repayment performance improved by using borrower groups.

Integrated Rural Development (IRD) projects should be designed to not place an undue burden on the available management capacity of the country concerned. A simplified (fewer components) and sequential approach, building in various layers of activity as management capacity allows, can help. The unit managing the project should be given the autonomy to act flexibly in line with the complexity of the environment within which it is supposed to function; it should also have the support of relevant government agencies and strong grassroots-based institutions. Pre-design studies carefully examining all backward and forward linkages are important to ensure that production and income grow within a reasonable time horizon and in a way that generates popular enthusiasm. This should not, however, lead to limiting projects to a shorter time period. On the contrary, IRD projects should be of a longer duration (not fewer than seven years) than traditional development projects. Finally, IRD projects, which tend to concentrate on agriculture, should not ignore the needs of the landless, whose proportion is increasing in many areas.

In many parts of the developing world, it makes more sense to invest in small-scale irrigation and water-control schemes than in large-scale projects. The latter can have adverse effects on the environment and can be costly (in both capital and recurrent outlays). By contrast, small schemes—relying more directly on the recipients' knowledge of their own environment and on their contributions to investment and upkeep—frequently are more cost-effective, sustainable, and replicable.

There can be no successful development effort—no effective poverty-alleviation initiative—without direct address of the needs of women as direct beneficiaries and, where applicable, focusing on the problems of cultural minorities and ethnic populations. An integrated approach is required; gender and ethnic issues should not be brought in as afterthoughts.

5. A Turning Point in Pakistan's Rural Development Strategy (Sartaj Aziz)

Pakistan is a notable case of growth, including agricultural growth, running well ahead of social improvements and reductions of inequalities. However, intended policy changed in 1985 with the appointment of a National Commission on Agriculture. The latter has proposed a Five-Point Programme designed to achieve—by 1990—both major improvements in infrastructure (rural roads, rural electrification, primary schools, health centers, protected drinking water, and improved sanitation) and striking advances in such human dimensions of welfare and performance as literacy.

In all of its schemes for building infrastructure, sustaining growth, and promoting rural diversification (to provide increasing opportunities outside of farming for rural people as incomes and agricultural productivity grow), the National Commission on Agriculture has given particular attention to the needs of disadvantaged rural areas and of poorer and smaller farmers in all areas. It is clear that, to succeed and to be sustained, programs to benefit the rural poor directly need the active participation of the poor themselves. In Pakistan, the formal opportunity for such participation has been provided since 1979 by a structure of Union Councils and District Councils. But in practice the poor have little access to, or voice in, these bodies. There is a need for both further decentralization of development decisionmaking to individual village councils (a Union Council may encompass several villages) and to devolve more financial and planning autonomy to district and sub-district bodies.

Given these needs, early reviews (by the World Bank, for one) of the Aga Khan Foundation's Rural Support Programme (AKRSP), which is being conducted on a pilot basis in half the villages of Pakistan's Northern Areas, have been enthusiastic. But nationwide replication poses a challenge. The AKRSP operation involves a quality and density of external staffing that will be hard to match on a national scale. The pilot project's key institutional innovation—the non-official councils the project has established at the village level—will be difficult for non-governmental organizations to replicate nationwide. At the same time, local governments appear to offer a poor substitute: They tend to be driven more by patronage considerations than by developmental priorities. Moreover, they are ill-equipped and insufficiently motivated to mobilize resources to public account locally— whether by taxation or other means.

The conclusion is not that needed rural reforms are unattainable, but that they are likely to work better, and to take root, only when democratic processes and institutions have matured and there is a pool of local leadership.

6. Agricultural Growth, Technical Progress, and Rural Poverty (Nurul Islam)

The questions addressed in this chapter are: (1) how the scale and pattern of agricultural growth affect poverty, and (2) whether and how farm growth strategy can be designed to help the poor. In relation to these issues, the author assesses both the direct and indirect dimensions of the impact of growth.

Direct Effects of Growth on Poverty. First, some direct effects are inherent in the technology. Biochemical innovations, for example, tend to be more labor-intensive and more nearly scale-neutral (as between small and larger farms) than mechanical innovations. Second, there are the effects of credit arrangements and availabilities. Certain group guarantee schemes are substituting for would-be borrowers' lack of collateral. It is clear that the poor need access to an augmented supply of institutional credit more than subsidized interest rates. Third, as to markets, small farmers tend to get crowded out of *input* markets when supplies are scarce; in *product* markets, they tend not to have enough holding capacity to wait for seasonal upswings. Thus there are anti-poverty needs for abundant supplies of inputs and credit as well as strengthened national marketing systems that can stabilize prices seasonally. Finally, fragmented, traditional labor markets weaken agricultural labor's bargaining power under conditions of growth; on the other hand, the newer (green revolution) technologies tend to be labor-intensive and often are exploited most intensively by very small farmers using (cheap) family labor. Yet landless laborers tend to do better when innovations are concentrated on middle-size farmers, who do more hiring.

Indirect Effects of Growth on Poverty. These depend heavily on the openness of the developing economy in question. Protected economies can hold domestic grain prices above world levels. The impact that an expansion in domestic food production has on consumer prices depends heavily on its incidence in terms of farm size. Small farmers tend to consume the increments in their production. Conversely, middle-size farmers, by increasing marketable surpluses, make cheaper food available to urban consumers while increasing agricultural wage employment. The best policy will allow prices to fall to an extent that maintains farmers' incentives while conferring benefits on that majority of the poor who are net purchasers of food. Low food prices encourage labor-intensive industrialization.

As to the linkages associated with agricultural growth, the forward linkages are stronger than the backward ones, and the additional non-food consumption demand that agricultural expansion induces is stronger than either. Whereas the smallest farmers spend most of their income gains on food, and large farmers step up their demand for capital-intensive goods, often luxury and/or imported goods, medium-size farmers channel a large portion of their income gains toward labor-intensive—and often locally produced—consumer goods, trade, and services. This contributes to the growth of income of the poor and leads to a cumulative expansion of employment. Domestic suppliers of labor-intensive consumer goods, trade, and services must be enabled, if necessary through financial and technical assistance, to expand their outputs—preferably in the rural areas where they live.

7. What is Not the Same about the Urban Poor: The Case of Mexico City (Sheldon Annis)

Even though the Third World is rapidly becoming urban—as is the locus of Third World poverty—international donors generally have not shifted their pro-rural development bias. There are several reasons for this, but probably the most fundamental is that donors have few good, new ideas on what to do about urban poverty. Looking back, the "solutions" of the past generation range from those that now appear to make matters worse, to those that merely do not work very well, to those that work under restricted conditions but cannot realistically be replicated on a large scale. Even if donors had far greater funds, it is not clear that they would know how to keep pace with—let alone gain ground on— runaway poverty in Third World cities.

In light of the weaknesses of urban project lending, donors in the 1980s have increasingly sought to finance domestic policy changes and institutional reforms that could aid the urban poor. In recent years, the emphasis has shifted to "policy dialogue." Donors and governments are now debating: Can cheap urban food prices be sustained, and if so, at whose expense? How can tax systems be constructed to pay for urban services? How can minimum wages be set that simultaneously protect the poor and slow inflation? Who pays for and receives the benefits from physical infrastructure? Are rent control policies good for the poor? What scale of industrial investment best generates jobs for low-income workers?

For the most part, the debate over urban poverty lending has generally taken place with government officials on the one side and their technical counterparts from donor institutions on the other. In the coming decade, however, this dialogue may begin shifting into a "trialogue"; the author argues that the urban poor are becoming increasingly effective and aggressive interlocutors in their own behalf. What may change in the 1990s is not so much the questions as the discussants.

Sheldon Annis explores the popular mobilizations in Mexico City in the aftermath of the devastating earthquake of 1985. In this case, a vast "centerless" web of popular organizations emerged as an independent political force. Through street demonstrations, use of the media, manipulation of symbols, political bartering, and direct participation in reconstruction programs, the poor were able to exert considerable influence—not only on the relatively successful housing reconstruction program—but on the larger set of fundamental policy questions. Although representative organizations of the poor did not formally "negotiate" with the World Bank (the chief external donor in this instance), they nevertheless were able to transmit their ideas indirectly through the political process.

The author suggests that Mexico City may be a precursor of an increasingly strong future trend. While it is true that the urban poor always have been politically more vocal than the rural poor, the scale of mobilization and the magnitude of "social energy" that the Mexico City case captures is genuinely unprecedented. The poor are likely to challenge ever more aggressively the character of the urban policy debate. To respond, donors will have to develop new sociological understandings and new communication channels. This will not be easy. Many of the "positions" of the urban poor are directly antithetical to the doctrines of contemporary donors. Donors can expect to be pushed far harder in the future than they have been in the past.

8. Women, Poverty, and Development in the Third World
(Mayra Buvinić and Margaret A. Lycette)

Strategies to strengthen the poor need to acknowledge gender differences and be designed so that they effectively reach women both (1) because in developing countries, women bear a disproportionate share of poverty, and (2) because the welfare of poor families in these economies is increasingly dependent on the economic contributions of their women members. Among other things, the earnings of poor women help to ensure the availability of high-quality foods for infants and children, and to compensate for declines in real household income during periods of economic adversity.

To strengthen the contributions of the poor, anti-poverty interventions have to focus on increasing women's productivity and earnings and be designed or modified in response to five major constraints that they experience:

(1) Women's restricted ability (because of their dual home and market production responsibilities) to participate in projects that require substantial amounts of time from participants;

(2) Women's limited (relative to men) educational attainment, which hampers their performance in training and other projects that require reading and/or writing skills;

(3) Cultural mores that restrict women's participation in what often are more lucrative economic activities;

(4) Legal policies that constrain women's access to assets as well as modern technology and information; and

(5) Women's predominance—because of these constraints—in marginal occupations, in which it is particularly difficult to reach them through development interventions.

The experience of more than a decade of development efforts indicates that the more successful projects have targeted individual women (rather than households) and have addressed women workers in the informal sector—as the successes in micro-enterprise have revealed when compared to the record in agriculture. In addition, projects tend to be more successful when they are implemented by qualified agencies and respond to real labor market demand, as is evident from certain training interventions.

Sectoral and project efforts that seek to expand women's income-earning options need to target individual women and to complement policy reforms. Policy changes are required in legal, financial, and educational systems to address the five above-listed constraints on women's economic participation. Most important, current structural adjustment programs and similar policy reform efforts have to undergo gender-related analysis and be structured to assist poor women as well as poor men to respond to price and other incentives. This is especially important in the case of agriculture—the main income source of the majority of the poor in developing economies. Policy reforms in the agricultural sector need to acknowledge gender differences in labor allocation as well as in access to assets. Some modern technologies and programs in the sector tend to have negative implications for women. They need to be balanced, therefore, by programs specifically designed to strengthen the productivity and earnings of women farmers.

9. Poverty and Adjustment in the 1990s (Richard Jolly)

For most of Africa and Latin America, the 1980s have been a development disaster. Despite differences in their levels of economic welfare and in the sources of their problems, long-run development in Africa and Latin America has given way to the economics of survival—debt servicing, domestic cutbacks, and austerity. Per capita income since 1980 is estimated to have fallen one quarter in Africa and one tenth in Latin America. It is clear, moreover, that the poorest, weakest, most disadvantaged people in these societies have been hit hardest.

By 1986, the World Bank and the IMF, which had a quasi-monopoly on the design of the structural adjustment programs being pressed on the faltering African and Latin American economies, were recognizing the need for explicit attention to social concerns in such programming.

Meanwhile UNICEF, which had been advocating the need for such action since 1983, had initiated a set of country actions and country studies of the human dimension of adjustment that showed what was needed—and what some countries had done already. The findings were published in UNICEF's two-volume study, *Adjustment with a Human Face,* issued in 1987 and 1988. Drawing from both analysis and country experience, this study advocates:

(a) Growth- and employment-enhancing macro policies;

(b) Middle-level "meso policies" targeting fair shares of growth-promoting inputs on the poor;

(c) Restructuring of production in favor of smaller and poorer producers, women, and informal-sector workers;

(d) Restructuring of government budgets and social services toward cost-effective approaches in health, education, etc., to reach the poor; and

(e) Special nutrition and health programs to cushion vulnerable low-income groups during adjustment.

In addition to specific lines of action, this study also urged the formal adoption of national and international goals for adjusment policy that explicitly recognize the need to protect the nutritional status of vulnerable groups like children and pregnant women in the course of adjustment. It also recommended the creation of monitoring mechanisms that collect and review indicators showing if the goals are being achieved and guiding remedial action.

The World Bank and the UNICEF approaches to the protection of the poor during adjustment have been most clearly brought together by the government of Ghana in 1986 in a series of exercises, eventually involving also UNDP, WFP, IFAD, ILO, WHO, bilateral aid donors, and

NGOs. The outcome was a "Programme of Actions to Mitigate the Social Costs of Adjustment" adopted by the members of the Consultative Group for Ghana for 1988-89. This Ghanaian program can be a valuable model for other countries. Yet it is a case where the human/social dimension of adjustment came as an afterthought—and where there are still some differences between the World Bank/IMF approach and the UNICEF alternative. The first gives the right-of-way to economic adjustment, adding only such social cushioning as is not inconsistent. What is needed is an "adjustment with a human face" approach that builds adequate protection for the poor into an *integrated* program that addresses growth, equity, and adjustment objectives jointly from the beginning.

10. The Changing World of Northern NGOs: Problems, Paradoxes, and Possibilities (Thomas W. Dichter)

The focus of this chapter is on the gap between the current professional capacity of Northern NGOs and the challenge now being thrust at them for a more significant contribution and a more central role in development. Northern NGOs are being asked by multilateral and bilateral development agencies and donors to scale up and to have greater impact without compromising their grassroots orientation. At the same time, Northern NGOs are being asked by their Southern counterparts to take a less direct role in development, leaving project implementation to the indigenous NGOs.

Besides the conflict inherent in the above demands, three broad constraints stand in the way of the Northern NGOs' meeting these challenges:

1. Donor agencies are still not terribly interested in helping NGOs reflect on their work or take the necessary time to follow through on certain long-term strategies. They continue to pressure projects for success in short periods of time.

2. The culture of NGOs, while undergoing change in the direction of greater professionalism, is often still antithetical to rigorous accountability, hostile to business and government, and resistant to other themes and values that would enable them to meet a new challenge.

3. The stage of evolution of Northern NGOs as a growth "industry" is such that there is beginning to be some degree of self-justification independent of the purposes for which NGOs presumably exist. This last factor is a major obstacle to their acceptance of the Southern NGO argument for less direct, perhaps even diminished Northern

NGO involvement. Simply, almost all Northern NGOs want to stay in business.

Dichter recommends that donors be tougher on the NGOs of the North—that they demand more accountability, which in turn will strengthen them and hasten a natural sorting out and eventual division of labor. At the same time, he recommends that NGOs be encouraged to do more research and be more reflective of their own, often hidden, culture. NGOs, in their turn, must be tougher on donors (and themselves)—learning to say "no" to opportunities for which they may not be ready or in which they have no particular comparative advantage.

The author suggests that an eventual division of labor might lead to the preeminence of two broad types of Northern NGOs in the 1990s: (1) small, focused, technically skilled development "boutiques" and (2) larger "wholesalers" of development education and networks. This second type would be more in the nature of development "brokers" and would facilitate relationships between disparate parts of the systems that make up a national or regional development program.

11. Aid for the Poor: Performance and Possibilities in India (S. Guhan)

In the Indian context of limited aid availability, a very large poverty problem, and an extensive range of ongoing domestic anti-poverty programs, effective external intervention will require great *selectivity*. The chosen areas, preferably sectors with which donors have acquired familiarity, will have to be ones where aid practices and predilections—projectization, institution-building, policy reform, cost recovery—can be useful. Additionality of effort on the recipient's part will have to be induced by aiming aid at activities that, but for the stimulus and incentive of external resources, are likely to be neglected. Most important, aid will have to be made poor-specific, which will entail concentration in sectors, projects, and programs that have a high capacity to reach the poor.

S. Guhan provides specific illustrations of ways in which donors could purposively interact with India's own priorities and programs for poverty alleviation. First, aid should seek to inter-link with those *rural development programs that aim at asset transfers and wage employment for the poor*, such as the Integrated Rural Development Program (IRDP) and the National Rural Employment Program (NREP). To integrate these direct programs better with growth and redistributive processes, it is necessary to:

(1) Extend credit to the landless rural poor for the purchase of land;

(2) Fund support services such as credit, input supply, disease control, quality upgrading, design inputs, and marketing—linked, as appropriate, to projects relating to dairy, sheep farming, poultry, pisciculture, horticulture, sericulture, vegetable growing, and handicrafts—in which household-level loans and subsidies are given to the poor under the IRDP;

(3) Encourage professionally managed producer cooperatives (on the lines of the well-known AMUL model in India);

(4) Enlarge the demand for products and services generated from assets transferred to the poor; and

(5) Link employment programs to micro-level area planning designed to promote rural marketing, land consolidation, local irrigation, soil conservation, and afforestation.

Two other sectors that are prime candidates for poor-specific aid are *urban services* and *nutrition*. Urban projects—slum improvement, low-cost housing, public transport, water supply, sanitation—have a high potential for reaching the poor. External interaction in this sector can help obtain reasonable levels of cost recovery from beneficiaries, induce additionality in domestic effort, transfer international experience, and encourage inter-agency coordination. Nutrition, in the form of supplementary feeding for pregnant and nursing mothers and young children, is a critical anti-poverty intervention. It can have significant multiplier effects in reducing mortality, avoiding permanent damage to child health, and inducing a decline in fertility. Nutrition lends itself to being combined with immunization, family planning, and health education.

Participation—by beneficiaries, local communities, and non-governmental organizations (NGOs)—is of vital importance not only for effective project implementation but even more in stimulating processes that promote mobilization, replication, and self-reliance in the entire range of anti-poverty efforts. Externally aided projects can promote such participation in concrete ways:

(a) Resources and responsibilities can be channeled through local bodies and cooperatives;

(b) Elected bodies at the district level can be used for retailing sub-projects and activities to agencies at lower tiers;

(c) Similarly, associations of NGOs can be used for intermediating assistance to smaller and dispersed NGOs; and

(d) Project design can establish a variety of complementary relationships between NGOs and state-run facilities and activities.

The issue of "wholesaling" versus "retailing" of aid is related to the issue of participation. Anti-poverty projects are relatively small in loan size and more demanding in staff time when compared to projects for infrastructure, energy, or industry. It will be logical, therefore, to "wholesale" anti-poverty aid through a variety of institutions—parastatals, cooperatives, local bodies, and NGOs. Such "wholesaling" can not only reduce time and costs involved in lending but also help replication. Donors will have to be prepared to take reasonable risks in institution-building and learning through trial, error, and retrial. They will have to keep themselves closely informed of data, evaluation, research, and emerging needs and possibilities, as well as of the strengths and weakness of cooperating organizations (governmental and other) carrying out the relevant activities. Donors, too, will have to "decentralize" and "participate" if anti-poverty aid is to be something more than transactions in periodic aid-programming between the Indian bureaucracy on the one hand and money-movers on the other.

12. Sub-Sector Planning and Poverty Reduction: A Donor View (Joseph C. Wheeler)

During the past several years, aid donors and recipients have both focused heavily on issues of macroeconomic policy reform. At the same time, aid has continued to be mainly a matter of project analysis and support. But the sectoral and sub-sectoral levels of planning in between often are zones of anarchy. At these levels there is frequently a lack of coherence not only among donors, but also among the several ministries of a host government.

For illustrations of the usefulness of cogent sub-sectoral planning, the author draws on eight years of experience as head of the USAID mission in Pakistan in the 1970s. He recalls a series of plans related first to river management, subsequently to salinity control and reclamation in waterlogged areas, and later to on-farm water management. Other sub-sector strategies were pursued to bring together fertilizer supply and wheat pricing policies and to achieve a coordinated approach to agricultural research. Together, these sub-sector strategies have supported rapid growth in Pakistan's agriculture.

Pakistan in the 1970s also provided instances of sub-sectoral shortfalls, for example in the education and health fields. Reflecting on this and other country cases, as well as on recent discussions within the OECD's Development Assistance Committee—of which he is currently chairman—the author draws the following lessons:

1. Well-articulated sub-sectoral plans not only rationalize the use of resources; they galvanize political and financial support for development.

2. Highly focused and carefully researched and planned campaigns—such as those developed in the agriculture sector in Pakistan, or the more recent efforts in the child-health field focusing on immunization and oral rehydration—can capture the attention of leaders and inject enormous energy into the system.

3. Such campaigns, however, need to be designed to support, not undermine, the broader and longer-term goals of sector development.

4. A strong information base and improved measures of achievement can increase political support for primary education, public health, and small-farmer agriculture.

5. Donors and recipients should work together to avoid high-cost projects that cannot be widely replicated—by planning projects carefully, either within the framework of thoroughly researched sector and sub-sector strategies or, in the absence of such strategies, with very close attention to policy and sustainability issues.

6. Where donors have supported successful sector-level efforts, they can demonstrate to their taxpayers how aid has contributed to the gains that many of the people in poor countries have made over the past four decades.

Strengthening the Poor: What Have We Learned?

Chapter 1

Assisted Self-Reliance: Working With, Rather than For, the Poor

Norman Uphoff

The common contrast between "top-down" and "bottom-up" strategies of development, like so many oppositions, is overdrawn. There are important differences in the philosophies animating these strategies, but when it comes to implementation, donor agencies and governments confront the paradox that "top-down" efforts are usually required to initiate and even to sustain "bottom-up" capacities. One lesson donors can learn from experience in promoting more "participatory" modes of development is that neither extreme of "top-down" or "bottom-up" development is as promising as a strategy that transcends both approaches.

"Assisted self-reliance" may sound paradoxical, but it derives from assessments of what has worked—and what has not—in many countries.[1] It represents a strategy for using external resources—advice, funds, training, material assistance—not so much to produce direct results as to strengthen local capacities to initiate, manage, modify, and sustain activities that produce benefits for which the poor are responsible. There may be some continuing assistance from outside, but it is given in ways and on terms that do not displace people's own efforts to generate income, manage natural resources, enhance the quality of life, or create infrastructure.

More important than whether the *impetus* for development work among the poor comes from above or from below is the *orientation* of those who plan and support that work from above. Do they presume that they have, or can have, all the answers to the problems of the poor—that they have enough knowledge about those problems to make effective unilateral contributions? Do they assume that since they have more education and financial means, they must also possess sufficient insight and wisdom to use those resources to best effect? Do they expect to have success without learning from the poor and without giving intended beneficiaries some control over the activities being undertaken?

Conversely, do project planners and managers believe that those persons to whom development assistance is being extended have ideas, intelligence, management skills, technical capacity, and leadership qualities to contribute to the processes of development—in addition to material resources? If not, governments are taking upon themselves the whole burden of not only financing but also managing and maintaining the facilities and services being created. Such an orientation is unwise on both fiscal and psychological grounds, since it perpetuates the attitudes and relations of dependency—and dependency represents the antithesis of development at the interpersonal as well as the international level.

"Poverty alleviation" as a concept, however well-meaning it is, smacks of paternalism—as does that unfortunate term, "target group." It suggests doing things *for* the poor or *to* them, rather than *with* them. We know by now that the poor need to be actively involved in alleviating their own poverty, blending hopes and energies in concert with carefully (and jointly) designed assistance.

Two Fallacies

One reason for breaking away from thinking in terms of top-down vs. bottom-up development is to avoid two fallacies about assisting the poor. The first is the *paternalistic fallacy*: the belief that planners, technicians, and experts possess all of the knowledge, wisdom, and virtue needed to achieve development, and that the poor should be responsive and grateful beneficiaries. Similarly mistaken is the *populist fallacy* that the poor themselves possess all that is needed for their own advancement—that they can do entirely without "bureaucrats" and "technocrats." While there are some impressive self-help examples and enclaves, those regional and national programs that benefit the poor on a significant scale have been concurrent mutual endeavors from above and from below.[2]

Acceptability of Assisted Self-Reliance Approach

Before reviewing some of the experiences that support a strategy of assisted self-reliance, one should consider whether such an approach is acceptable to governments, whether they are recipients or donors of foreign aid. Three trends gaining recognition over the last five to ten years all support reorienting development efforts in this way.

First, the *volume of financial resources available* for investment in development initiatives and for maintaining them has been contracting in real terms for most developing countries. The governments of these countries have been going through multiple fiscal crises of budget deficits, burgeoning external debts, and unstable foreign exchange earnings. At the same time, governments in the richer countries face their own internal pressures limiting the resources they are able or willing to contribute to anti-poverty efforts overseas. Donor agencies cannot do "business as usual" when the volume of money available is shrinking, especially relative to needs abroad, and most developing countries cannot accept or absorb funds except on concessional terms. Such considerations require serious rethinking of the whole "aid enterprise" well beyond the scope of this discussion.

Second, *confidence in technocratic approaches has waned* as the results of the efforts of the last 30 years or so have fallen short of expectations. Technology and resource transfers have contributed to some substantial improvements. Many real gains have been registered in terms of agricultural production, mass literacy, life expectancy, and health.[3] But they are not sufficient, and they hold out little promise for similar gains in the next 30 years, as the challenges of development become more dire, dispersed, and difficult. Governments as well as most "experts" themselves are less certain now that "more of the same" will achieve what is needed. This uncertainty makes them more open to new approaches.

Third, thanks to the gains just referred to, *substantial progress in human resource development has changed the context in which development activities are undertaken.* Even among the poor, literacy and health, communication skills, and knowledge of alternative modes of technology and organization have improved. (Who knows the impact of the spreading "video revolution" in developing countries?) Rural villagers and urban slum dwellers are as intelligent as they have been all along, but now they have better-formed talents to contribute to the planning and implementation of development efforts at local levels and above.

To be more specific, a strategy of assisted self-reliance, characterized by more local initiative and control of development efforts, offers certain advantages:

• More material resources, in cash and in kind, can be mobilized locally to share the burdens of initial financing, reducing capital costs and spreading programs over a wider area;

• Limited central resources can be put to their most beneficial uses, because priority needs and preferred means can be better known;

• Beneficiaries, when they are involved in decisionmaking and implementation, are more inclined to take responsibility for managing activities as well as for contributing to their maintenance, thereby reducing recurrent costs to government;

• Local information and indigenous technical know-how can help make cost-saving and benefit-producing adaptations, avoiding the spurious "efficiency" that results from working in a uniform way everywhere.

Since locally initiated and managed development is not suitable for all services and benefits, such as major infrastructure or many research activities, assisted self-reliance is not a universal prescription or alternative. But a *broad* range of improvements can be efficiently and satisfactorily provided through locally based initiatives. A great many desirable objectives sought in the past through centrally directed efforts—employment creation, resort to appropriate technology, integrated rural development, redistribution with growth, the provision of basic human needs, direct attacks on poverty—have met with little success *and could be enhanced by much more resort to local ideas and responsibility.*

One important consideration is the sustainability of project benefits. A World Bank study of this question recently found that of twenty-five completed agricultural projects it had financed, only twelve appeared to be achieving long-term net benefits. The projects most often demonstrating sustained improvements in productivity were those that developed or strengthened institutional capabilities for beneficiary participation in management.[4]

What is surprising is not this result, but rather the persistence of thinking that development is a matter of making resource investments in a top-down way. In this there is little difference between how physical facilities are planned and built—with content and format all decided unilaterally by experts—and how training is given to local people. Questions of relevance, applicability, and sustainability are glossed over by complex processes of design, operation, and evaluation that expect nothing from intended beneficiaries except material resources and acquiescence. It should be abundantly clear by now that poverty will not be alleviated in this manner. More participatory and self-reliant means of development are needed. Fortunately there is a growing fund of experience to draw on in formulating more appropriate policies and projects.

The Poor as Participating Partners in Development

The *first* requirement for assisted self-reliance is to think in terms of not "beneficiaries" but participants in joint endeavors to improve people's productivity and well-being. A *second* requirement is making certain that the poor have organizational channels through which to make decisions, maintain communication, mobilize and manage resources, and resolve conflicts. A *third* is creating new orientations in the agencies that work with the poor. These are the common denominators of a growing number of development experiences that move away from the paternalistic and individualistic premises of most present programs. The following comments give a sense of the range and vitality of development efforts that come under the heading of assisted self-reliance.

Some of the most impressive examples are in East Asia, where agricultural and industrial development have been very dynamic:

- In Taiwan, Farmers Associations and Irrigation Associations have played key roles in that country's achieving one of the highest rates of GDP growth. Agriculture is relatively self-financing as well as self-managed, with close collaboration between farmers and technicians (whom the farmers employ).[5]

- In South Korea, the New Community Movement has changed the lives of those living in that country's 35,000 villages through a vast array of "pump-primed" local investments across all sectors of activity. At the same time, Village Forestry Associations are managing over 2 million acres of greatly needed woodland in this densely populated country.[6]

But East Asia has no monopoly on grassroots organizational capacity. Even more cases of participatory development are in evidence in South and Southeast Asia:

- In India, perhaps the best-known example is the Amul dairy cooperative system, now engaging and benefiting some 5.5 million households—mostly poor ones—in sixteen states.[7]

- Fast catching up with Amul in international attention and esteem is the Grameen Bank system in Bangladesh. Already, within two years, over 300,000 landless and near-landless persons have boosted their real incomes—by 30 per cent on average—through small loans given on a group basis; repayment rates are about 96 per cent.[8]

- In Nepal, the Small Farmer Development Programme, which started with only $30,000 of assistance from the United Nations Food and Agriculture Organization, has now spread to much of the country, making credit and technical assistance available through small groups and helping 45,000 households advance on their own.[9]

• In northern Pakistan, the Aga Khan Rural Support Project has aided self-help activities in over 500 communities—working through their own Village Organizations—improving the lives of about 400,000 persons in remote areas hardly served by the government.[10]

• In Sri Lanka, the largest irrigation system in the country— greatly deteriorated after 30 years of bureaucratic neglect and farmer misuse—was rehabilitated with USAID assistance; over 500 farmer organizations (covering 25,000 acres) now work with officials to nearly double water use efficiency. The program for participatory irrigation management is being extended to all major schemes in the country.[11]

More examples of promising self-help efforts could be given from each of these South Asian countries,[12] and the story is similar in Southeast Asia:

• In the Philippines, the National Irrigation Administration, with Ford Foundation assistance, devised what is now a national program for participatory irrigation development, operation, and maintenance.[13] More recently, the Australian-aided Northern Samar Integrated Rural Development Project, after an initial misguided concentration on infrastructure, began working with rural communities through NGOs and turned a "failed" project into one greatly valued by the people as well as the government.

• In Thailand, a provincial governor devised a system for mobilizing data from communities for joint evaluation by local people and officials, leading to what is becoming a national program of participatory development for meeting basic social needs.[14]

In Africa, the number of documented cases of "assisted self-reliance" is smaller—perhaps because the continent's more recent colonial legacy has perpetuated dependency thinking on the part of governments and populations. Yet some impressive examples do exist of what is possible with appropriate strategies:

• In Malawi, over half a million persons in 2,000 villages are now served by a gravity-flow system of piped water supply (costing about $4 per person to install) constructed and maintained by communities with appropriate assistance from the government and donors.[15]

• In Zimbabwe, a rural savings movement that started twenty-five years ago survived the difficult period of civil war and now has

200,000 members in about 6,000 savings clubs; deposits total over $2 million. In a parallel effort, the growth of a wide variety of farmer associations has helped to spur that country's "green revolution."[16]

• In Kenya, the *harambee* self-help movement, prompted and rewarded by government contributions, mobilizes funds and labor in rural areas. Such self-help groups provided about 30 per cent of all capital formation in rural areas through the mid-1970s and have contributed 8–10 per cent of total national development expenditure.[17]

• In Burkina Faso, Mali, and Senegal, a network of grassroots organizations—called the "Six S" Association—has over 2,000 peasant federations innovating to create production and employment during the dry half of the year. These federations, based on traditional work groups known as "naams," rely minimally on outside inputs. External resources are treated as a complement to local efforts.[18]

Looking elsewhere, Albert Hirschman has documented dozens of smaller-scale but nevertheless important examples of self-reliant efforts in his marvelous book, *Getting Ahead Collectively: Grassroots Experiences in Latin America.*[19] And although there may be less local initiative or support for the assisted self-reliance approach in Middle Eastern countries, Cornell University's Rural Development Committee for several years worked in North Yemen with Local Development Associations that made substantial contributions to rural development in that country.[20]

Elements of a Strategy for Assisted Self-Reliance

From the analysis of these and other experiences in various countries, certain elements of an "assisted self-reliance" strategy emerge that can be pointed out to donors as promising means. Mobilizing and utilizing local resources and talent involves no fixed design, but multiple components that can be combined in appropriate sequences and amounts. These components are briefly described here—to suggest what a strategy of assisted self-reliance is likely to involve.

1. Involvement of Local Organizations

If these essential building blocks of assisted self-reliance do not already exist, appropriate forms of participatory organization need to be introduced. Local organizations in any case deserve those types of support that strengthen them rather than lead to dependency or elite takeover. Summarizing the findings of the World Bank study cited above, Michael Cernea concludes:

> A major contribution to sustainability came from the development of grassroots organizations, whereby project beneficiaries gradually assumed increasing responsibility for project activities during implementation and particularly following completion . . . [where there was] some form of decision-making input into project activities, a high degree of autonomy and self-reliance, a measure of beneficiary control over the management of the organization, and continuing alignment of the project activities with the needs of beneficiaries.[21]

Appropriate organizations should reach beyond the grassroots level through federations of base-level organizations. These establish horizontal and vertical linkages, creating a system of local organization that has the advantages of solidarity in small groups at the base and of scale and influence operating at higher levels. It is most important that leadership at all levels remain accountable to the members of such organizations.

2. Multiple Channels for Action

The poor are best served when there are multiple levels of organization, and also parallel channels for development activity—when membership organizations operate alongside central government agencies and private businesses.[22] Any one channel helping individuals with communication, commercial activities, problem-solving, or other tasks can get "blocked" or "monopolized." It is therefore not wise to rely on just one form of institutional linkage—whether bureaucratic, local-government, cooperative, private enterprise, NGO, religious, or other. Some amount of competition as well as complementarity among these channels is advantageous for the poor majority. This means that donor programs should not concentrate narrowly on promoting just one form of local institutional development.

3. Use of Catalysts

It has been found that where local organizations and multiple channels do not exist, or where they need strengthening, the usual personnel of government are not particularly effective in mobilizing local people's energies, talents, and leadership. Accordingly, in the last fifteen years, a growing number of development programs aiming to reach and benefit the poor have resorted to specially recruited and trained catalysts—variously called promoters, organizers, facilitators, or change agents.

Most of the programs exemplifying assisted self-reliance that were cited earlier employed persons who could work closely and effectively with poor households through NGO or new kinds of government programs. Development initiatives using such change agents are often still experiments, but they are the source of a growing body of knowledge.[23]

4. Building on Indigenous Traditions and Technology

There was a time when development was seen mostly as "modernization"—when existing ways of thinking and acting were thought to need replacement, possibly coercively. In recent years, however, greater appreciation has arisen for "traditional" ways, many of which have come to be recognized as not static and usually representative of empirical adaptations to prevailing conditions. These observations point toward the use of local knowledge, materials, and skills whenever possible—to encourage better "fit" with local conditions as well as to encourage greater utilization and maintenance of investments.[24]

5. Sustainable Resource Mobilization

Some outside material and technical assistance is likely to be needed and appropriate, but it should be given as a complement to local resources, not as a gift or as something necessarily superior. All assistance should be provided in ways and on terms that are positive-sum—that neither substitute for nor discourage people's contributions. If furnished according to agreements reached with local communities, external resources can "prime the pump" to sustain and even enlarge the flows of local inputs.[25]

One of the lessons from experience is that even poor people have some financial resources they can contribute toward development efforts—if these resources are understood to be beneficial. A number of successful self-help programs—for example, the Grameen Bank in Bangladesh, the Small Farmer Development Programme in Nepal, the Rural Savings Movement in Zimbabwe—are built around group savings and credit. This strategy for grassroots development is currently being extended in a dozen countries through the U.N. Food and Agriculture Organization's People's Participation Programme.

6. Use of Paraprofessionals

To bring services closer to the people, a number of programs—for example, the Malawi self-help water supply program mentioned above—recruit (or invite) persons from the community to get training in technical subjects and skills that they can put to use for the benefit of friends and neighbors. A very impressive methodology for training "villagers as extensionists" has been worked out by the private voluntary organization, World Neighbors, on the basis of its experience with agricultural and resource conservation programs in Latin America.[26] In the health area, many parallel efforts have met with similar success under difficult conditions.[27]

7. Bureaucratic Reorientation

The staff of most government agencies are not presently prepared to work with the poor in ways that encourage and support their participation in development activities. Sometimes it will be possible and desirable to have non-governmental organizations take the lead in programs intended to engage the poor in self-reliant efforts. This is not to say that governmental agencies cannot interact constructively with disadvantaged sections of the population, but to achieve such results, a concerted effort to reorient officials' norms and behavior is usually necessary.[28]

8. Learning Process Approach

Finally, and perhaps most important, governmental and non-governmental organizations need to learn how to work in a learning process mode, in contrast to the conventional blueprinted manner.[29] This approach means working with the poor as much as possible in a flexible way, in a process of mutual learning that does not aim rigidly at pre-set targets but, instead, evolves project or program strategy on the basis of experimentation and experience. Especially if one wants to work *with* the poor rather than just *for* them, it is necessary to design and redesign efforts consistent with their own priorities and capabilities.

Working in a learning-process mode does not mean that projects are utterly open-ended. Plans must be made, and resources need to be allocated. But this mode does require that progress be continually reviewed and that plans be periodically revised in light of experience. It means that "money spent" is not equated with "development done." Building up satisfactory, widely shared knowledge about development ends and means is itself a goal. So is the formation and spread of a cadre of persons having the ideas, experience, and dedication to carry out a large-scale program that can benefit the poor majority. Learning has to be incorporated, literally, in a set of like-minded and motivated people to produce developmental results. Written instructions, no matter how detailed or imperative, cannot match the impact of a group of persons who share ideas, goals, and bonds of friendship, and who will persevere in problem-solving until valued results are achieved.

Recognizing this brings in the *normative* dimension of development work, without which "strengthening the poor" will not occur.

Such strengthening is more than a technical task. It is value-driven, and it must often confront and alter others' not-so-supportive values.[30] Part of the learning required is to understand and deal with the various values involved in poverty-oriented development. Donor agencies have a difficult time dealing with value dynamics. They claim to be functioning in an objective, value-neutral way. But anyone who has observed successful experiences in assisting the poor knows that normative factors are central in such efforts. This important lesson may be the hardest one for donors to learn and accommodate.

The overall lesson for donors is that the apparent paradox of "assisted self-reliance" is not a paradox at all. Rather, it represents a strategy for overcoming past failings of development programs. These programs have been too confident that the infusion of resources—like the fueling of a machine—will produce desired results. In fact, development is basically a matter of constructing the "machine" that converts scarce inputs into valued outputs. But the capabilities involved are more human and social than material or mechanical, and even the latter capabilities come into being and use only through people's ideas and motivations. The challenge for donor agencies is to bring their projects and other modes of assistance into line with a deeper appreciation of what is required to make a lasting contribution to the productivity and well-being of the world's poor majority.

Notes

[1] The concept has been presented more fully in Milton Esman and Norman Uphoff, *Local Organizations: Intermediaries in Rural Development* (Ithaca, N.Y.: Cornell University Press, 1984).

[2] This conclusion, as well as identification of the two fallacies, emerged from a comparative analysis of two decades of development experience in sixteen countries, ranging geographically and ideologically from China and Japan in East Asia to Turkey and Yugoslavia in the Mediterranean. See Norman Uphoff, ed., *Rural Development and Local Organization in Asia*, Vol. III (New Delhi: Macmillan, 1983), pp. 263–340.

[3] See essay by Harry Blair and Charles Mann, "Can Foreign Aid Succeed: Evidence from India," submitted to *Atlantic Monthly*, forthcoming.

[4] See Michael Cernea, "Farmer Organizations and Institution Building for Sustainable Development," *Regional Development Dialogue* (Nagoya, Japan: U.N. Centre for Regional Development), Vol. 8, No. 2 (Summer 1987), pp. 1–19. See also my assessment of World Bank integrated rural development projects in Nepal, Ghana, and Mexico: "Fitting Projects to People," in Michael Cernea, ed., *Putting People First: Sociological Variables in Rural Development* (New York: Oxford University Press, 1985), pp. 359–395.

[5] See Benedict Stavis, "Rural Local Governance and Agricultural Development in Taiwan," in Uphoff, *Rural Development and Local Organization in Asia*, Vol. II, op. cit., pp. 166–271.

[6] See S. Y. Yoon, "Women and Collective Self-Reliance: South Korea's New Community Movement," in S. Muntemba, ed., *Rural Development and Women: Lessons from the Field* (Geneva: International Labour Organisation, 1985), p. 152. On the Village Forestry Associations, see Erik Eckholm, *Planting for the Future: Forestry for Human Needs* (Washington, D.C.: Worldwatch Institute, 1979).

⁷ See S. P. Singh and Paul Kelly, *Amul: An Experiment in Rural Development* (New Delhi: Macmillan, 1981).

⁸ See Mahabub Hossain, *Credit for the Rural Poor: The Grameen Bank of Bangladesh* (Dhaka: Bangladesh Institute of Development Studies, 1984); and Andreas Fuglesang and Dale Chandler, *Participation as Process: What We Can Learn from Grameen Bank, Bangladesh* (Oslo: Norwegian Agency of International Development, 1986).

⁹ See M. Anisur Rahman, "The Small Farmer Development Programme in Nepal," in Rahman, ed., *Grass-Roots Participation and Self-Reliance: Experiences in South and South East Asia* (New Delhi: Oxford University Press, 1984), pp. 121–151. This program, like the Grameen Bank cited above, is now supported by large grants from the International Fund for Agricultural Development, which seeks to assist such activities based on local organizational capacity.

¹⁰ *The Aga Khan Rural Support Program in Pakistan: An Interim Evaluation* (Washington, D.C.: The World Bank, Operations Evaluation Department, 1987).

¹¹ See Norman Uphoff, "Activating Community Capacity for Water Management: Experience from Gal Oya, Sri Lanka," in David C. Korten, ed., *Community Management: Asian Experience and Perspectives* (West Hartford, Conn.: Kumarian Press, 1986), pp. 201–219.

¹² Reports of such efforts from India are many. One of the most innovative is discussed in Dominic Bara and Boniface Minz, *Toward Building a Self-Reliant Tribal Community: Vikas Maitri Approach to Development* (Ranchi, India: Vikas Maitri, 1981). One of the largest and most outstanding initiatives has been the Bangladesh Rural Advancement Committee, discussed in Manzoor Ahmed, "BRAC: Building Human Infrastructure to Serve the Rural Poor," in Philip Coombs, ed., *Meeting the Basic Needs of the Rural Poor* (London: Pergamon Press, 1980), pp. 362–468. A smaller but most impressive case is the Deedar cooperative, started with eight persons daily saving the cost of a cup of tea. The cooperative after twenty years includes 1,200 members with savings of 2 million *taka* and assets of 6 million *taka*. They operate agricultural, manufacturing, transport, and other enterprises for their members' and community benefit with minimal outside aid; see Jayanta Kumar Ray, *Organizing Villagers for Self-Reliance: A Study of Deedar in Bangladesh* (Comilla, Bangladesh: Bangladesh Academy for Rural Development, 1983). In Nepal, forestry management, which was taken over by the government after 1957, has been returned to rural communities with much success; one example of appropriate external aid in this is the Swiss-German Tinau project; see Rolf Suelzer and K. Sharma, *Working with the People: Some Experiences with the People-Centered Approach in Tinau Watershed Project, 1983–1986* (Katmandu, Nepal: Her Majesty's Government/Swiss Agency for Technical Assistance, 1986). One of the few self-help initiatives for improving peri-urban slums is the Orangi project outside Karachi, led by Akhter Hameed Khan, who was the moving force behind pioneering rural cooperatives in earlier East Pakistan; see Abdul Gafoor, "A Social Engineering Experiment in Pakistan: A Case Study of Orangi," *Regional Development Dialogue*, Vol. 8, No. 2 (1987), pp. 108–118. The "change agent" program in Sri Lanka, initially assisted by the Konrad Adenauer Foundation, has many features in common with these other programs; see S. Tilakaratna, "Grass-Roots Self-Reliance in Sri Lanka: Organisations of Betel and Coir Yarn Producers," in Rahman, *Grass-Roots Participation and Self-Reliance*, op. cit., pp. 152–183.

¹³ See Frances F. Korten, *Building National Capacity to Develop Water Users' Associations: Experience from the Philippines*, Staff Working Paper No. 528 (Washington, D.C.: The World Bank, 1982); and Romana de los Reyes and Sylvia Jopillo, *An Evaluation of the Philippines Participatory Communal Irrigation Program* (Manila, Philippines: Institute of Philippine Culture, Ateneo de Manila University, 1986).

¹⁴ Reported in Norman Uphoff, *Local Institutional Development: An Analytical Sourcebook, with Cases* (West Hartford, Conn.: Kumarian Press, 1986), pp. 348–350.

¹⁵ See J. Gus Liebenow, "Malawi: Clean Water for the Rural Poor," *American University Field Staff Reports*, Africa, No. 40, 1981; and Colin E. R. Glennie, *A Model for the Development of a Self-Help Water Supply Program*, Technology Advisory Group Working Paper No. 1 (Washington, D.C.: The World Bank, 1982).

¹⁶ See Ruvimbo Chimedza, "Savings Clubs: The Mobilisation of Rural Finances in Zimbabwe," in Muntemba, *Rural Development and Women*, op. cit., pp. 161–174; and Michael Bratton, "Farmer Organizations and Food Production in Zimbabwe," *World Development*, Vol. 14, No. 3 (March 1986), pp. 367–384.

¹⁷ See Barbara Thomas, *Politics, Participation and Poverty: Development through Self-Help in Kenya* (Boulder, Colo.: Westview Press, 1985).

¹⁸ Little has been published on this remarkable program. See brief accounts in Paul Harrison, *The Greening of Africa: Breaking Through in the Battle for Land and Food* (New York: Penguin Books, 1987), pp. 279–284.

[19] (New York: Pergamon Press, 1984). Hirschman's review covers activities assisted by the Inter-American Foundation. See also Sheldon Annis and Peter Hakim, eds., *Direct to the Poor: Grassroots Development in Latin America* (Boulder, Colo.: Lynne Rienner, 1988), especially studies by Judith Tendler and Kevin Healy on Bolivian cooperatives that benefit poor as well as average or better-off households.

[20] John M. Cohen, Mary Hebert, David B. Lewis, and Jon C. Swanson, "Development from Below: Local Development Associations in the Yemen Arab Republic," *World Development*, Vol. 9, Nos. 11–12 (November/December 1981), pp. 1039–1061.

[21] Michael Cernea, "Farmer Organizations and Institution Building," op. cit., p. 7. See also Esman and Uphoff, *Local Organizations*, op. cit., for evidence from 150 cases.

[22] See study cited in note 2 and cases in Uphoff, *Local Institutional Development*, op. cit., pp. 270–363.

[23] The best statement on this approach is by S. Tilakaratna, *The Animation in Participatory Rural Development*. See also the sources cited in notes 7 and 13.

[24] An excellent example of this comes from the Baglung district of Nepal, where local bridge committees working under village council auspices, with a minimum of outside help (steel cables supplied by UNICEF and a small grant from the central government), constructed sixty-two suspended bridges covering the whole district in five years. Local materials and artisans were used along with unpaid labor and management. The bridges, some as long as 300 feet, cost as little as one-quarter as much as when the government constructed them, and were built three to four times faster. See Prachanda Pradhan, *Local Institutions and People's Participation in Rural Public Works in Nepal* (Ithaca, N.Y.: Rural Development Committee, Cornell University, 1980).

[25] On this, see Uphoff, *Local Institutional Development*, op. cit., Chapter 8.

[26] See Roland Bunch, *Two Ears of Corn: A Guide to People-Centered Agricultural Improvement* (Oklahoma City, Okla.: World Neighbors, 1982); also Milton J. Esman, *Paraprofessionals in Rural Development: Issues in Field-Level Staffing for Agricultural Projects*, Staff Working Paper No. 573 (Washington, D.C.: The World Bank, 1983).

[27] A number of cases are cited in Uphoff, *Local Institutional Development*, Annex 4. One example is the Kottar Social Service Society in India, reported by John Field, "Development at the Grassroots: The Organizational Imperative," *The Fletcher Forum*, Vol. 4, No. 2 (1980), pp. 145–165.

[28] David C. Korten and Norman Uphoff, *Bureaucratic Reorientation for Participatory Rural Development*, Working Paper No. 1 (Washington, D.C.: National Association of Schools of Public Affairs and Administration, 1981).

[29] See the seminal work on this subject by David C. Korten, "Community Organization and Rural Development: A Learning Process Approach," *Public Administration Review*, Vol. 40, No. 5 (1980), pp. 480–511.

[30] When reading the best-selling book on successful American corporations by Thomas Peters and Robert Waterman, *In Search of Excellence: Lessons from America's Best-Run Companies* (New York: Warner Books, 1982), I was struck by how closely the lessons they extracted match those we drew from helping to establish farmer organization for better irrigation management in Sri Lanka (see note 11), particularly in emphasis on values, leadership, and positive-sum interpersonal relations. Donor agencies give minimal if any attention to these lessons; like many other lessons from our own American experience, they are not incorporated in our foreign assistance efforts.

Chapter 2

Governments and Grassroots Organizations: From Co-Existence to Collaboration

Samuel Paul

Developing countries vary widely in their institutional strategies for eradicating poverty. Some have depended largely on the market as the prime mover to promote growth and alleviate poverty. Others, less certain about the market's ability to foster growth with equity, have relied heavily on public sector interventions and public hierarchies. In recent years, there has been a resurgence of interest among several donors and developing countries in grassroots organizations as the preferred alternative for strengthening the poor. Community groups, non-governmental organizations (NGOs), cooperatives, and local governments fall within the spectrum of such grassroots agencies.

Community organizations often emerge from local initiatives, and in many countries such groups are a part of the social tradition. NGOs, on the other hand, generally tend to be external "intervenors" who may, among other things, create and support such community groups. Cooperatives may originate locally or come into being through governmental or NGO initiatives and support. Local governments typically are elected bodies, empowered by the state to perform specified local functions. All of these grassroots organizations are generally known for supporting collective action through the participation of local peo-

Note: The views expressed in this paper are those of the author and not of the World Bank. The author wishes to express thanks to John Lewis and Lawrence Salmen for their comments on an earlier version of this paper.

ple. Needless to say, the champions of the grassroots institutional alternative tend to distrust the capacity of the marketplace and of central governments to respond effectively to the challenge of poverty alleviation.

Institutional Alternatives: Strengths and Weaknesses

Strengthening the poor requires not only resources, but also the capacity to adapt programs to diverse and uncertain conditions together with a strong tradition of performance orientation (i.e., accountability) that is reinforced by the demand pull of the poor themselves. Neither governments nor grassroots organizations possess this set of attributes in its entirety. The limits to government action lie in the difficulties of government in responding and adapting its services to the needs of the poor, in weak public accountability for results, and in the aversion of both bureaucrats and politicians to the mobilization of demand at the local level. Even under democratically elected regimes, the poor's access to public services and programs tends to be limited by the reliance of government on standardized services that are not calibrated to the particular needs of the poor, and by the latter's inability—due to their weak political and organizational power—to demand change and hold the bureaucracy accountable. When esssential goods and services are in short supply, the chances are that the elites will have disproportionate access to them. Under such conditions, the bureaucracy will be less inclined to inform and educate the poor, or to improve the delivery of services to them.

It does not follow, however, that grassroots initiatives will provide an effective alternative to the problems just cited. Grassroots organizations are indeed likely to enhance the political power of the poor. Their interventions may also nudge the bureaucracy to be more responsive to the needs of the poor. But grassroots agencies may have limited access to funds, or may not be able to provide needed technology, research, and other infrastructure. Moreover, the benefits that flow from grassroots action may be preempted by elites—although a similar risk exists with government programs. Thus the governmental and grassroots initiatives can and should shore up one another.

Grassroots organizations are typically initiated by leaders who are committed to a cause, but not necessarily interested in replicating their endeavors nationally. The task of national replication thus falls on governments. For example, it is governments and other large-scale organizations (e.g., industry) that tend to undertake major investments to develop or adapt new technologies and promote their nationwide diffusion. Nevertheless, the grassroots agencies are generally more responsive to the needs and problems of beneficiaries. Given their greater local knowledge and commitment, they are more likely than governments to have the interests and skills to adapt development projects and programs to local conditions. The grassroots agencies' relatively small size and proximity to beneficiaries tend to make them more accountable for results. Governments and grassroots organizations, in short, have differing but complementary strengths. In the context of poverty alleviation, there is a clear case for a division of labor that exploits their comparative advantages.

Although the theoretical case for linkages between them is strong, there is not much evidence of collaborative action between these two types of institutions in the developing world. For the most part, they seem to operate on parallel tracks while they both profess to pursue the goal of poverty alleviation. In fact, it is not unusual to find an adversarial relationship between the two, with national governments defending their "top-down" approach and grassroots agencies wedded to the "bottom-up" style of operation.

Centralization: Recent Trends

The polarization between governments and grassroots organizations has been intensified by certain developments of the past three decades. First of all, many governments, including those democratically elected, moved toward greater centralization in the years after independence. Scholars have noted such a trend, interpreting it as a means for counteracting regional pressures, ethnic hostilities, and other divisive forces.[1] Mainstream economic planning approaches and systems have reinforced the belief that centralized decisions, designs, and allocations are adequate to achieve both growth and equity.[2] The argument here is not that centralization is inappropriate in all situations, but that the centralization of all aspects of planning and implementation overloads central governments while neglecting other resources and talents available in the system to get things done. Central interventions have been found to be effective, for example, in land reform, in the development of new agricultural technologies, and in preventive health. But highly centralized programs for poverty alleviation do not seem to offer many success stories. Meanwhile a few experiments in decentralization have taken place in recent decades in numerous developing countries, including Indonesia, Morocco, Thailand, and Tunisia. An evaluation of these efforts has shown that decentralization yielded perceptible improvements in resource allocation, local participation, and the extension of public services to rural areas.[3] But most developing countries seem to have moved in the opposite direction; they have failed to tap the energies of their local governments, let alone the potential of non-governmental grassroots organizations.

India's experience in center-state relations bears eloquent testimony to the conflicting pulls. A recent study argues that the country's Finance Commission and its Planning Commission have moved in oppositive directions on center-state relations.[4] The Finance Commission has endeavored to provide increased financial autonomy to the states, so that they might fulfill the functions assigned to them by the constitution. The Planning Commission, on the other hand, has brought the states into the national plan frame, leaving them very little flexibility in matters of investment. The study concludes:

> Let us remember that the country is large and diverse, but that there is also enough political, administrative and technical talent around. What is needed is greater participation of larger numbers in its affairs. Denial of such opportunity is breeding widespread frustration and resentment, causing so much waste of precious human material. That makes the country not stronger, but weaker.[5]

Grassroots Initiatives

While centralization has become a dominant feature of governments in many developing countries, grassroots organizations have emerged and flourished side by side with government in several of these countries. The relative size, local roots, and impact of these organizations vary from one region to another.[6] Many countries have had a long tradition of community groups and other local organizations playing an active role in their rural settings. In recent years, foreign NGOs have emerged as a force to reckon with in many parts of the world. In many African countries, for example, NGOs are mainly linked to foreign organizations and initiatives. In Latin American countries and in parts of Asia, on the other hand, numerous indigenous grassroots agencies are at work. As a group, these agencies are committed to the cause of strengthening the poor. Their activities range from relief works to development and empowerment. Most of them are small in size, fiercely independent, and usually critical of government programs and initiatives. There is, of course, room for government programs and non-governmental grassroots activities to co-exist and even compete in the same field; more could be done for the poor if the two sets of institutions would move from co-existence to collaboration.

There are very few definitive studies of the impact of grassroots initiatives on poverty alleviation on a national basis. Anecdotal evidence on individual NGOs and their contributions abounds. But the costs and benefits of their operations and comparisons with other institutional alternatives simply have not been assessed. That some of the grassroots organizations have had a major local impact is indisputable.[7] Whether their benefits are sustainable would depend on the extent to which they have built up local capacities and laid a foundation for increased resource mobilization for future expansion. NGOs have demonstrated innovative strategies for strengthening the poor in several countries, but on a small scale.[8] As noted above, most of them are not interested in scaling up their activities or influencing the strategies of governments for poverty alleviation. Consequently, in most countries, their activities simply co-exist with those of government and, in general, linkages between the two are sadly lacking. Under these conditions, it is not surprising that the potential for strengthening the poor has not been fully exploited in many countries.

Between these governmental and grassroots tracks, there is scope for collaboration that is only beginning to be recognized and tapped on a national basis. There are numerous ways in which governments and grassroots organizations can work together in the context of poverty alleviation; three of these will be highlighted here in view of their promise and their emerging popularity.

Collaboration for Demand Mobilization

Governments typically are weak in organizing activities to reach the poor. When the poor are illiterate and unorganized and live in inaccessible areas, the tasks of reaching, informing, educating, and mobilizing them to participate in or demand services are exceedingly difficult and call for a degree of motivation and commitment that is unlikely to be found in most public hierarchies. Grassroots organizations, especially NGOs, tend to have a comparative advantage in this regard, and may assist government programs by mobilizing and educating the poor. Their flexibility and smallness, as well as highly motivated personnel, often make them well suited to perform these tasks. The question is whether NGOs can be encouraged to play this role in ways that support and reinforce public programs for strengthening the poor. This would call for a collaborative arrangement between grassroots agencies and governments—an arrangement in which the former acts as a motivator and demand mobilizer to assure that the poor receive the services or benefits that government programs are intended to deliver to them. This role of grassroots agencies may lead them to play an advocacy and watchdog function that in turn may put them in an adversarial position vis-à-vis the local bureaucrats. Yet, even this adversarial stance may play a useful role, in that it enables the voice of the poor to be heard and helps move government services to those for whom they are intended.

This is clearly a limited form of collaboration, in which grassroots agencies are not involved in the entire range of planning and implementation activities of government programs for the poor. In some countries, NGOs and community groups do play this type of collaborative role in urban services, preventive health programs, and population activities. This role assumes special significance in countries where governments are highly centralized and the poor are inadequately organized. Some examples are given below:

• In India, a new population project sponsored by the government for the slums of Bombay and Madras has proposed that local NGOs be invited to take charge of outreach activities and motivate slum dwellers to utilize the population and health services of the municipal clinics. The role of the NGOs here is to inform, educate, and motivate the client groups. NGOs are not responsible for the implementation of all aspects of the project. They will be reimbursed for their services through a system of grants-in-aid.

• In Mexico city, FONHAPO[9]—a low-income housing authority established in 1981 by the Mexican government with World Bank support—has involved activists from the Mexican urban NGO community to augment the provision of housing credit to barrio associations, cooperatives, and community groups. This approach has in effect created a new model for relations between communities and the government and has encouraged local people to become better organized and demand greater public accountability from government (see also Sheldon Annis' chapter in this volume).

• FIDENE/UNIJUI[10] is an NGO linked to a university in the state of Rio Grande do Sul in Brazil that has played a prominent role in organizing and educating poor peasants. The methodology developed by this NGO to organize peasants has become a model emulated by others in the state. Several governmental agencies have approached UNIJUI to initiate popular education movements in other parts of the country—mainly because it has more effective outreach, and in some cases greater legitimacy, in the region.[11]

Collaborative Planning and Delivery of Services

In the second form of collaboration, grassroots organizations share actively in the planning and operations of the government's poverty-alleviation programs. The planning process takes into account grassroots views and preferences and thus blends the stereotypical top-down and bottom-up approaches. Given their comparative advantage in service delivery for the poor, grassroots organizations are given responsibility for this part of the work by governments and are compensated for same through grants-in-aid or other means. In some cases, this may take the form of "contracting out," at once reducing the burden on the bureaucracy and optimizing the use of local resources, skills, and commitment.

The following examples illustrate how collaborative planning and delivery of services to the poor have been attempted in nationwide government programs in different national contexts.

• The Zimbabwean food production program has incorporated small farmer organizations with considerable success. Despite the drought that affected Zimbabwe, like the rest of Southern Africa, in the early 1980s, smallholders managed to increase their output of maize substantially. In 1984, they produced 400,000 tons for the market instead of the 150,000 tons expected by government planners. This boost partly reflected the improved use of modern technology, but it was also the result of the contribution of the widespread system of farmer organization that had been built up to channel inputs and extension advice to smallholders. In a district with poor soils and rainfall, there was a threefold difference in output between members and non-members. Throughout the country, farmers in farmer groups were found to have higher yields and to produce and sell more maize than comparable unorganized farmers.

• In some areas of Indonesia, Kenya, and Nigeria, national population and health programs have attempted to integrate local community groups in the delivery of services. The Indonesian government provides the funds, supplies, and technical expertise needed by the program while community volunteers and village organizations mobilize demand and assist in the distribution of contraceptive supplies. In the Kenyan population program, which is aided by the World Bank, six local NGOs are actively involved as implementing agencies. In a similar project for the villages of a Nigerian state, community groups will be partners with government in building the clinics and managing the health services at the local level; government will be responsible for the procurement of drugs, the provision of technical services, and staff training.

• In Latin America and the Caribbean, the Inter-American Development Bank's program for the financing of small projects uses "intermediary" organizations such as cooperatives, producers associations, and local NGOs for channeling credit to low-income people in 21 countries. Financial assistance is limited to $500,000 per project, and no private or public guarantee is required of the borrowers.

Small urban entrepreneurs, small farmers, and women engaged in non-farm activities constitute the bulk of the beneficiaries. As of 1983, 81 projects were approved by the Bank under this scheme and implemented by a variety of intermediary organizations.

• In a World Bank-financed urban housing program for the poor in El Salvador, the government decided to entrust the planning and implementation of the key activities to an NGO (a local foundation) with considerable experience in working with the poor. The project was regarded as highly successful largely because of the dynamic role played by this NGO in planning and delivering the services in partnership with the government. The latter provided the resources, but utilized the capacity, local knowledge, and commitment of the NGO in achieving its project objectives.[12]

Collaboration for Replication

The collaborative planning and delivery-of-services mode just reviewed implies a partnership between government and grassroots agencies. The project or program design may be jointly evolved or may draw mostly upon government strategies. Since nationwide or regional coverage is required, one or more grassroots agencies may participate in this endeavor. Thus there is considerable operational collaboration.

A more subtle—and currently less common—form of linkage between the two sets of actors is possible. In this mode, a government may draw upon the strategy (design) of a successful grassroots initiative and build a national or regional program around it. Grassroots organizations thus act as innovators, testing out new strategies and performing the role of a "research and development" laboratory for the government. Furthermore, they may serve as a source of experienced personnel for the large-scale replication of the chosen strategies and as a model for the operating culture and systems of the new program. The role of the grassroots organization here is not that of a contractor or implementor, but a source of inspiration and learning, for government programs. Clearly, not all grassroots agencies qualify for this role. Governments must search for the innovators among the NGOs and decide which are yielding design and operating experiences that are worth adoption. The following examples show the potential for synergy between governments and grassroots organizations in the fight against poverty.

• The Amul Dairy of India is a widely quoted example of a successful grassroots organization. It is not as well known, however, that the government of India made a deliberate decision in the mid-1960s to draw upon the Amul experience for the design of the country's National Dairy Development Program, known as "Operation Flood." While the choice of the Amul model has been questioned by some critics, what is noteworthy is the fact that Amul in effect provided the basic building blocks for the design of the government program and acted as a source of key personnel for the new program.[13] Amul was not a contractor or partner of the national program in the conventional sense. The collaborative mode was one in which Amul was the inspirer and teacher in the replication process.

• The Grameen Bank in Bangladesh also seems to have played a similar role in the field of providing credit for the poor. It began as a modest grassroots initiative by a young professor who organized small groups of villagers to enhance their income and employment. Its success has led the government of Bangladesh to build on this strategy and to replicate its activities on a national basis. Supported by the Bangladesh Bank and seven other state-owned commercial banks, the Grameen Bank had extended its operations to 300 branches with nearly 400,000 members in five districts by 1987. The leadership of the Bank continues to be vested in the person who initiated it. Leadership is a scarce resource and is not easily replicated. The Grameen Bank and Operation Flood experiences show how this scarce resource could be harnessed to scale up important development activities nationally.

It must be emphasized, however, that such collaboration between governments and grassroots organizations has its risks and potential for abuse. First of all, many NGOs and other grassroots agencies do not have the capacity to scale up their activities on short notice. Nor do they have the skills and experience to work within the constraints of governmental administrative and accounting procedures. Most of them will require assistance and support to perform their new role effectively. Second, in large national programs, grassroots organizations may be used by governments merely as a channel for the distribution of funds. Partnership with government may encourage grassroots agencies to overextend themselves and lose sight of their primary mission for the sake of augmenting resources. Third, attracted by the availability of funds, new grassroots agencies may enter the fray without the genuine commitment and staying power that the more established agencies possess. This is likely to be one of the unintended consequences of the current international movement to goad NGOs to take on developmental tasks on a much larger scale than has been attempted before. The pace and quality of collaboration must be carefully monitored to avoid these pitfalls.

The Challenges Ahead

Like all joint endeavors, effective collaboration between governments and grassroots organizations calls for considerable investment of time and effort. It is much easier for governments and grassroots agencies simply to practice peaceful co-existence. The three types of collaboration discussed here represent a far more complex course—the third even more so than the first two. Those who plan to promote collaboration between grassroots agencies and government must have a realistic appreciation of the factors that have inhibited such approaches in the past. First, governments and grassroots agencies in many countries historically have been antagonists. Some of the best-known local NGOs started as protest movements against governments. Turning them toward collaboration will not be easy. Second, NGOs in particular prefer to concentrate on problems and target groups *selectively*, and to expand *slowly*—whereas governments are wedded to speedy replication across the land. There is thus a clash of "cultures" that may impede collaboration. Third, the financing and support services for the two sets of institutions run on parallel tracks and have hardly encouraged collaboration in the past; multilateral and bilateral donors typically finance governments, while private donors and local supporters tend to underwrite grassroots organizations. These obstacles are real and cannot be eliminated without concerted efforts for change and innovative approaches over a period of time.

In the final analysis, the poor will acquire strength only when they are aware of, and able to demand, their rights, as well as to exercise power. Public accountability can be improved only marginally by internal bureaucratic reforms—especially when the demand pull from below is lacking. Accountability tends to be biased in favor of those who wield control in the political market. Grassroots initiatives and organizations could give the poor a stronger voice. Viewed thus, demand pressures from below (from community groups, NGOs, local government, etc.) are a prerequisite for creating genuine public accountability in government. In countries where this is the missing or weak link, it makes sense to shift the balance in favor of grassroots initiatives and encourage governments to support and collaborate with them. In countries where grassroots actions are abundant, but governments are poorly organized and inefficient, greater attention needs to be given to reorienting the bureaucracy and connecting it to the potential power of grassroots action. There will be synergy only when the two tracks converge.

These shifts will occur only when the developing countries' own governments and grassroots agencies are convinced about the need for change. International donors could, however, play a useful catalytic role in promoting collaborative modes and shifts in balance such as those here discussed. First, the sharing of international experience in this regard with developing-country governments and their leaders is an important task that has yet to be addressed adequately. It is time to move beyond anecdotal evidence to more systematic documentation, analysis, and dissemination of innovative experiments and programs. Second, seed money for collaboration between governments and grassroots agencies may well nudge governments toward serious experimentation in this area. The Inter-American Development Bank's program for financing small projects and the support provided by organizations such as The Ford Foundation to NGOs in some countries are interesting examples of this approach. Third, lending operations, where appropriate, might include components that provide for the participation of grassroots agencies in government projects—as, indeed, is now the case in some of the projects of the World Bank. These are modest steps, but their cumulative impact on developing countries may well be significant over time.

Notes

[1] Glyn Cochrane, *Policies for Strengthening Local Government in Developing Countries*, Staff Working Paper No. 582 (Washington, D.C.: The World Bank, 1983), p. 46.

[2] B. F. Johnston and W. Clark, *Redesigning Rural Development* (London: Johns Hopkins University Press, 1983), Chapter 1.

[3] Dennis Rondinelli, et al., *Decentralization in Developing Countries*, Staff Working Paper No. 581 (Washington, D.C.: The World Bank, 1983), p. 4.

[4] V.M. Dandekar, "Unitary Elements in a Federal Constitution," *The Economic and Political Weekly*, October 31, 1987, p. 1865.

[5] Ibid., p. 1870.

[6] See "Development Alternatives: The Challenge for NGOs," *World Development*, Vol. 15 (Autumn 1987) for an interesting collection of articles on the role of NGOs.

[7] See Norman Uphoff, ed., *Rural Development and Local Organizations in Asia* (New Delhi: Macmillan, 1983).

[8] See Albert O. Hirschman, *Getting Ahead Collectively: Grassroots Experiences in Latin America* (New York: Pergamon Press, 1984); G. Hyden, *No Shortcuts to Progress: African Development Management in Perspective*, (Berkeley, Calif.: University of California Press, 1983).

[9] Fondo Nacional de Habitaciones Populares.

[10] Fundaçao de Integraçao, Desenvolvimento e Educaçao do Noroeste do Estado/ Universidade de Ijui. See T.R. Frantz, "The Role of NGOs in the Strengthening of Civil Society," *World Development*, op. cit., pp. 121–127.

[11] Ibid.

[12] Additional examples are given in Samuel Paul, "Community Participation in World Bank Projects," *Finance and Development* (December 1987); Also see Vittorio Masoni, "Non-Governmental Organizations and Development," *Finance and Development* (September 1985).

[13] For further details, see Samuel Paul, *Managing Development Programs: The Lessons of Success* (Boulder, Colo.: Westview Press, 1983).

Chapter 3

Empowering Africa's Rural Poor: Problems and Prospects in Agricultural Development

Uma Lele

Introduction

A dispassionate observer of the overall economic development record of aid donors and recipients over the past forty years might well ask why it is that foreign aid has achieved major successes in poverty alleviation in Latin America and Asia[1] but not yet in Africa—where, despite large expenditures of resources (especially since the early 1970s) and much experience with the results, so many items on the poverty agenda still remain incomplete, controversial, or unaddressed. In what follows, I shall explore some possible answers to this question. In order to narrow what would otherwise be an impossibly wide frame of reference, this chapter's analysis focuses largely, but not exclusively, on the development record in post-independence Sub-Saharan Africa. The discussion also has a sectoral emphasis, on agricultural and rural development, and it focuses on absolute rather than relative poverty. This is because 90 per cent of the continent's absolute poor live and work in the rural sector, compared to 60 per cent in Latin America and 80 per cent in

Note: The content of this chapter reflects research undertaken as part of a wider study on "Managing Agricultural Development in Africa" (MADIA), sponsored by the World Bank in collaboration with seven other aid donor agencies and six African governments. The views expressed in this chapter are the responsibility of the author, and do not necessarily represent the official position of the World Bank or any other entities participating in the MADIA study. In addition to registering her appreciation to the many individuals who have commented on the research, the author wishes to extend special thanks to Manmohan Agarwal for his helpful comments on previous drafts and to Peter Bocock for editing the text.

Asia. Africa's poor derive their income from a range of cropping, live-stock, and trade activities—again differing from Asia and Latin America, where employment on others' farms is an important source of income for the poor, most of whom are landless. Moreover, as in Asia, poverty has a gender dimension; female-headed households tend to be a larger proportion of poor households than in the population as a whole.

Poverty also has a regional dimension in Africa—given that income is primarily determined by crop and livestock production possibilities that are themselves influenced by regional differences in physical resource endowments. International concern about poverty in Africa has mainly focused on the plight of those who live in the poorest regions. On the other hand, population densities tend to be the greatest in areas of high land potential. From an economy-wide viewpoint, therefore, focusing on economic growth in the areas of highest population density is likely to be better for *both* growth and poverty alleviation. Specifically, the record in even the most advanced countries amply demonstrates the futility of efforts to promote long-term employment in rural areas with inadequate natural endowments (as the U.S. poverty programs of the 1960s in Appalachia testify). Rather, the solution to the problems of resource-poor regions lies in preparing for the long-term movement of people out of these areas, by investing in human capital and transportation. Low-return local employment-creation efforts not only generate a demand for perpetual subsidies, but also divert resources away from other productive areas of the country where more growth could occur.

Finally, raising agricultural productivity in areas of relatively high potential also offers the prospect of relief over the longer term for environmental problems (such as soil depletion and deforestation) created by the growth of poverty-ridden populations attempting to make a living in marginal areas from increasingly unproductive land. The faster the improvement in agricultural productivity, the faster the proportion of the population employed in agriculture will fall—and the greater will be the chances that the proportion of fallow or reafforested land will rise, as has already happened in most developed countries. The role of the non-agricultural sectors in generating productive employment—mostly through private enterprise and capital formation, as a result of the growth linkages generated by a dynamic agriculture—is thus critical for poverty reduction. In Africa in the 1970s, however, rapid growth in employment in the non-agricultural sectors occurred mainly through the public sector and through economic diversification policies pursued by governments without first ensuring the processes that will bring growth in agricultural productivity. This expansion and subsequent policy reforms that shifted relative incentives once again in favor of agriculture have critically influenced levels of poverty. I shall therefore also refer, where necessary, to trends in non-agricultural incomes and employment.

Agriculture's Role in Economic Growth and Poverty Alleviation

A large body of development theory already articulates why poverty alleviation is good for overall economic development. Broad-based growth in the productivity of smallholder agriculture results in increased employment of the rural poor, which in turn leads to strong growth linkages by influencing the pattern of overall demand; through multiplier effects, these linkages contribute to additional employment growth and help to address poverty.[2] I do not elaborate on this theory here. Instead, I intend to show that growth in agricultural production is essential for poverty alleviation in Africa; that technical change in agriculture is essential for growth; that appropriate balance in the availability and deployment of physical and human capital is essential for technical change to occur; and that it is the lack of such a balance in the accumulation and efficient use of different forms of capital that explains the persistence of poverty in Africa.

Current diagnoses of Africa's developmental crisis frequently recognize its agricultural origin. Agricultural constraints and growth potential differ greatly from one African country to another, however, and are critically affected by national development policies and political, administrative, institutional, organizational, and human capital variables, along with the availability of physical resources. By contrast, oversimplified portrayals of African agricultural problems as a continental megacrisis are one of the core explanations of the very mixed development record in Africa during the past quarter-century. They are a part of the problem in that they mask the complexity and country specificity, or indeed even micro-regional specificity, of poverty problems in Africa. Partly for this reason, the productive deployment of external assistance for poverty alleviation is also a far more complex task in Africa today than it was in much of Asia and Latin America 20–25 years ago—a difference that is manifested in the much lower success rate of donor assistance in Africa.

External Assistance and Rural Poverty Alleviation

When considering the record of poverty alleviation in Africa, it is important to note that foreign aid constitutes a large share of government expenditures and investment (35–65 per cent), and of GDP, in most small African countries. This is not simply a matter of statistical interest; it illustrates an important institutional reality: Donors by and large tend to do business with governments even when they promote private enterprise.

Large shares of aid in government expenditures are not unique to Africa. This same pattern holds for the small and poor Asian countries, e.g., Nepal and Bhutan (but not for India where aid, even at its peak, constituted less than 30 per cent of investment). This large external aid component, combined with the limited capacity of African governments to formulate and implement effective development policies, means that the strategies that donors encourage, and how they choose to spend the resources they provide, have a profound impact on poverty alleviation. This fact is frequently overlooked in discussions of African problems in donor circles, which tend to assume that fungibility of finance—including external capital—means that development failures are explained largely by the policies African governments have pursued. While granting validity to this view, I shall follow Harry Johnson in arguing that promoting growth requires achieving a balance in recipient countries of the different forms of physical, institutional, human, and organizational capital, and that because of its importance in public spending, foreign assistance can play an important role in developing such balanced capital accumulation. I shall also argue that foreign assistance achieved this objective to a greater extent in Asia and Latin America with smaller aid shares; this has not yet been the case in Africa.[3]

Another difference between aid relationships in Africa today on the one hand and those in the newly emerging nations of Asia and Latin America in the 1950s and 1960s on the other is that a single donor (the United States) was dominant in the earlier cases. In Africa, however, the picture is complicated by the presence of a large number of donors with different viewpoints and aid philosophies. Countries may receive aid from as many as 100 external sources—or an even larger number if private voluntary agencies are considered—of which 30 may be of significant size. These entities in turn may operate without any consensus among themselves as to which policies and investments should be given priority. Moreover, the priorities of individual aid agencies are liable to shift relatively quickly in line with changing international perspectives on development philosophy.

Diversity of advice and external assistance can be beneficial, provided that recipients have the capacity to evaluate such inputs competently and to deploy them effectively. Most African governments are still short of the necessary planning and implementation capacity, however, with the result that the multi-donor approach to development all too often lapses into incoherence. This has meant that poverty-alleviation efforts are far more problematic in Africa today than in Asia and Latin America in prior decades. In those years, the content of U.S. aid was largely driven by the United States' own development experience and by pragmatic (and often technocratic) solutions to problems with relatively simple (and in retrospect more easily accomplishable) objectives. For example, despite the fact that India inherited a stronger scientific and organizational base and a better endowment of trained manpower than much of Africa today, the United States deserves credit for recognizing the importance of science and technology in generating agricultural growth in India and for assisting the development of agricultural technological capacity. This was achieved through programs that helped a) to train a large body of Indian scientific and administrative personnel, b) to establish agricultural research, extension, policy planning, and implementing institutions, and c) to set up agricultural colleges on the U.S. land-grant model.[4] This capacity development was one of the most important factors underlying the launching of the "green revolution" in India, and its major contribution was holding poverty well below the levels that population growth otherwise would have caused. It should be noted, however, that the green revolution has done less to solve the poverty problem than it might have done if India had different policies—and that what empowerment of the poor *has* occurred under the existing policy regime should be credited mainly to the socially conscious educated elite who have played a key role in developing an impressive array of indigenous private voluntary organizations. This fundamental role of the elite in poverty alleviation in developing countries is seldom acknowledged in the international comunity, which more frequently views the elite only in terms of their callousness at best and rent-seeking behavior at worst.

Another factor that differentiates contemporary development planning and external assistance from the simpler days of the 1950s and 1960s is the fact that the perceptions of the development process have become more complex over time, encompassing multidimensional objectives such as poverty alleviation, protection of the environment, and promotion of private sector initiatives—with proponents of each of these (and other) specific interests playing increasingly important roles in framing donors' aid agendas. Justified as the concerns of these various lobbies are, their powerful influence on aid programming has contributed substantially to the frequent shifts of emphasis in aid rhetoric, philosophy, and practice—and to the resulting lack of continuity, stability, and predictability of many individually well-intentioned and justified activities.

Finally, the need for a balanced capital accumulation approach to poverty alleviation assumes special importance in Africa because Africa's colonial inheritance of institutional, organizational, and human capital resources was far more inadequate than Asia's and fell far short of the institutional infrastructure with which Latin America entered the second half of this century. This constraint would have inhibited the effectiveness in Africa of even the most perfectly focused foreign assistance strategies; when combined with the realities of (at best imperfectly) coordinated donor assistance, it has often in practice left African governments without the expertise to formulate their own priorities from among the kinds of aid they are offered, or to use effectively all the different types and magnitudes of assistance that they receive. This human and institutional capital constraint has been reinforced by the far lower priority assigned by donors and by African governments to the timely generation of such capital as a way of improving aid recipients' absorptive capacity.

The rest of this chapter falls into two parts. The following section briefly surveys the agricultural development performance of a group of countries and their major donors since the 1960s; and a final section presents some of the implications and lessons for future donor-recipient interactions. The material presented draws on a major ongoing World Bank study on managing agricultural development in Africa (MADIA), which has undertaken detailed analyses of a representative set of six Sub-Saharan African countries that together account for 40 per cent of the region's population and 50 per cent of its GDP.[5] The research underscores the diversity of agricultural endowments, growth opportunities, and performance in Africa—not only between but also within countries—and points to the danger of generalizing about their problems and achievements. While it documents the enormous scale of these problems, it also helps to counter some of the current "gloom and doom" about Africa by identifying cases where real and substantial progress has been made.

Some Key Features of Africa's Rural Poverty Alleviation

Perhaps the most fundamental issue in the debate about poverty alleviation is how to strike an appropriate policy balance between promoting growth on the one hand and ensuring its equitable distribution on the other. The conventional wisdom of the 1970s asserted that there are no trade-offs between achieving growth and equity. But analysis carried out under the MADIA study suggests that, if national human and institutional capacity to provide services to the bulk of smallholders is absent, significant trade-offs do in fact exist in the short and medium term, with profound implications for government expenditures, foreign exchange earnings and savings, and GDP growth.[6] Recognition of these trade-offs in practice, together with the tendency to pursue short-term objectives, has led some African countries to steer too exclusively toward one or the other goal. Differences in the nature of the political actors have been crucial in determining the substance of the chosen strategy in each case.

Country Performance

Eastern Africa provides three instructive examples of different policy approaches to the growth/equity issue in the shape of the very different priorities of Tanzania, Malawi, and Kenya during most of the post-colonial period.[7] Tanzania's rhetorical emphasis on equity objectives (over growth) was accompanied by policies that simultaneously stressed industrially led expansion (over agriculture) and social welfare in the rural sector. The government made impressive progress in the provision of primary education and (for a brief period) in improving access to rural water supply and health services (which in turn could reduce productive person-days lost to sickness). Through overvaluing the exchange rate and increasing public sector expenditures on industry, the government pursued an acute form of import substitution in industrialization, involving investments in such capital-intensive industries as fertilizers, pulp and paper, etc., at a very early stage of development. This created disincentives—especially for export agriculture—and dampened production in the traded goods sectors. By the end of the 1970s, stagnation in export earnings, accompanied by increased cost of food and fuel imports, led to a balance-of-payments crisis, rampant growth of the parallel market, and the loss of government control of the economy. This meant that official expenditures on social services could not be maintained. As a result, Tanzania has ended up losing many of the gains it made in the social sector. Ironically, attractive parallel-market prices for maize, which became a major means of barter across national boundaries for small producers living near country borders, meant that rural producers were not as badly off as their urban, public-sector-employed counterparts.[8]

Malawi's approach to development presents a sharp contrast to Tanzania's, in that Malawi did achieve rapid growth in estate-based production of export crops that was much hailed in the 1970s. But Malawi's efforts to promote the economic and social development of the majority of poor rural households (undertaken with the support of external aid agencies) have been hampered by the very policies on which its agricultural expansion was based. Specifically, land policy has favored the governmental alienation of land for the establishment of private estates and has reserved for the estate sector the right to grow certain high-value crops. Estates also have the exclusive right to sell their products (e.g., tobacco) in domestic auctions at prices substantially higher than those obtainable by smallholders (who have been required to sell their tobacco to the government's marketing corporation at prices only a third of those earned by the estates).

Malawi's extreme poverty, dependence on British grants-in-aid for the budget, and the need to earn foreign exchange and government revenues quickly resulted in an estate-based strategy of export agriculture which donors had supported initially on macroeconomic grounds. In the meantime, important foundations were laid for the provision of services to the smallholder sector through rural development programs focusing on new maize technology that were funded by donors in the 1970s. However, the rapid "alienation" of land has intensified population pressure on the remaining land; and the denial of the right of smallholders to grow high-value crops reserved for estates, together with taxation of the tobacco that they produce, has inhibited the majority of smallholders, whose incomes are well below subsistence, from undertaking the risks of adopting the new maize technology.

Given their very poor "initial" condition at independence, both Malawi and Tanzania by the end of the 1970s ran into severe economic difficulties posed by a very hostile external environment; and both have needed substantial injections of structural adjustment assistance from multilateral and bilateral donors. The extreme nature of both countries' development strategies might not have been sustainable in any case. But the substantial external shocks have meant that they have found it hard to resume a sustained broad-based growth path quickly enough through adjustment programs. A substantial long-term effort is needed to develop their economies.

Finally, employment opportunities in non-agricultural sectors have not been able to relieve rural poverty to any significant extent in either country. Tanzania suffered a decline of nearly 50 per cent in urban wages since the early 1980s as a consequence of the unsustainability of its development strategy. In Malawi, real wages in the non-agricultural sector have dropped less sharply than in Tanzania, but nevertheless are at about 80 per cent of their levels in the early 1980s.

East Africa also provides an example of a country—Kenya—that followed a smallholder-led development strategy—but with significant success in reconciling growth and equity objectives. Kenya's ability to make its smallholder tea, coffee, and other high-value crops (together with hybrid maize) major sources of domestic income and export earnings has resulted in the development of substantial linkages between the growth of agricultural output and employment opportunities in the rest of the economy. Moreover, among the six MADIA countries, Kenya has suffered the smallest decline in non-agricultural real wages since the onset of macroeconomic difficulties in the late 1970s.

Kenya's achievements stem from its more favorable initial conditions, together with its consistent support—for well over thirty years—of a smallholder-based development strategy that has been directed at broadening the economic base of formerly European-settled agriculture for the benefit of small African producers. The strategy has included several important components catering to small-scale agriculture: (1) a generally supportive macroeconomic environment (like Malawi's); (2) agricultural sector policies granting smallholders equal rights to grow export crops and earn international prices; as well as (3) the development of substantial human, institutional, and organizational resources, along with physical capital. These policies and expenditures have paid off handsomely. Moreover, export growth among small farmers has not come at the cost of technical change and progress in food-crop production. Over 60 per cent of Kenya's small farmers grow hybrid or improved maize, compared to less than 10 per cent in other MADIA countries. They also apply more fertilizer to maize than do their counterparts in other countries.[9]

The comparatively dependable near-term payoff in growth that can be obtained by concentrating resources on large-scale farmers on the Malawian model makes the temptation to take this route attractive to many African governments; their limited administrative capacity to reach the poor smallholders reinforces this tendency. In Malawi's case, using an estate-based strategy for promoting agricultural exports was made imperative by the need for a quick expansion of tobacco production in response to new world market opportunities in the mid-1960s and the need for government revenues at relatively low near-term financial and administrative costs. In practice, however, the estate sector has run into difficulties, giving new urgency to promoting growth in poor smallholder households in order to achieve sustainable long-term development.

The different approaches of Malawi, Tanzania, and Kenya to alleviating poverty on a sustained basis also reflect substantial political differences, as well as variations in the organizational mechanisms that have been deployed by each country. Malawi has operated a relatively centralized, personality-based political system since independence, while in Tanzania the ruling political party (TANU and now CCM) has overshadowed the role of the government (or indeed of any local organizations outside the party system). Neither country has been tolerant of the participatory grassroots organizations crucial for the alleviation of mass poverty. Only in Kenya has an array of voluntary self-help and cooperative organizations emerged at the grassroots to which the political system seems relatively more responsive.

MADIA countries in West Africa present an even more complex picture of technological possibilities and institutional endowments and needs than their counterparts in East Africa. Senegal poses a particularly difficult problem of fragile soils, low and declining rainfall, and a narrow production and export base centered on a single crop (groundnuts). To minimize the risks entailed by excessive crop concentration in the 1970s and the loss of protection for groundnut exports accorded by the French during the colonial regime, Senegal pursued an economic diversification strategy out of groundnuts in the "Groundnut

Basin" and into irrigated rice production in the north—and even out of agriculture into industry. The MADIA study concludes that although diversification out of a narrow productive base is essential for countries such as Senegal (especially taking into account that its rice imports now constitute nearly 40 per cent of its export earnings), speedy movement out of a long-established activity with a strong comparative advantage, especially under circumstances of limited economic alternatives, may turn out to be costly for *both* growth and equity. In much the same way as in Tanzania, Senegal's statist and elitist policies have not only caused agricultural stagnation but also effectively prevented the development of genuine cooperatives or of a competitive private sector for the benefit of a large smallholder sector.

The other two MADIA West African countries, Nigeria and Cameroon, both benefited from the oil boom in the 1970s—with Nigeria gaining earlier and to a greater extent than Cameroon. Cameroon's rural households fared better than Nigeria's during the 1970s and 1980s, partly reflecting the country's more moderate and stable macroeconomic and agricultural policies. On the other hand, Cameroon's slowness in accepting external advice has made it (like Kenya) less popular among donors than other African countries that are more receptive to suggestions.

Nigeria's experience illustrates something too often overlooked in discussions of the economic performance of African countries: the effects of political circumstances on development policy. In addition to the effects of the oil boom (which included a poor performance record in the export-crop sector), other critical factors have been: a) the failure to recognize the complex technological problems faced in increasing food-crop production; b) the instability of the policy and administrative environment (resulting from six military coups and frequent administrative changes); and c) the increasing degree of centralization of the government over time (which was needed to consolidate national integration, but was associated with the erosion of state and local governmental capacity crucial to planning and implementing development programs). These constraints to development raise questions about the long-term viability of important agriculture programs already under way.

Cameroon provides a good example of sharply different performance records within its agricultural sector, with the operation of SODECOTON (a paternalistic French-assisted cotton parastatal) on the one hand and much of the rest of the agricultural sector on the other. SODECOTON's achievements are of interest because cotton is typically grown in Africa in areas with relatively few productive employment opportunities, and because cotton development has encountered problems in much of Anglophone Africa. SODECOTON's success suggests that grassroots-oriented development approaches of the kind that have worked well in Kenya need not be the only, or even the most practical, model in countries such as Cameroon—where centralization of political power is still the norm and empowerment of the peasants has yet to occur, and where it is essential to exploit whatever opportunities poor natural resources may offer for generating smallholder incomes. Besides, in addition to an intimate knowledge of local farming systems, cotton development requires relatively complex technocratic responses, including an understanding of the international market. The program's success in achieving this is evident from the fact that smallholder cotton yields in Cameroon are ten times as high as in Nigeria, and that production has increased, although until recently Cameroon's producer prices have been lower than elsewhere in Africa. Neverthless, the slow transfer of this know-how from the French (who play a key role in running the cotton sector) to indigenous manpower does raise important questions about the need for a simultaneously more professional and more decentralized domestic power structure than currently exists in many African countries. Indeed, given the emphasis that the literature on rural development in Africa in the 1970s placed on the importance of participatory local organizations,[10] little has emerged in this respect from these efforts. African governments and their donor supporters have been unable to take on the socio-political and economic challenges involved in developing a broad human capital and organizational base. Countries at early stages of nation-building—and insecure politically—have been unwilling to decentralize power.

Cameroon's cotton development has been criticized on the grounds of its neglect of food-crop production and the adverse effect of cotton development on the environment. The MADIA study has concluded, however, that the cotton-growing areas would be more impoverished without income from cotton production. It has also found that the limited market for surplus sorghum and millet production in the cotton-growing areas has frequently been overlooked as the most binding constraint on the expansion of food-crop production by critics who attribute it to the lack of commitment to developing these crops. Finally, and contrary to populist perceptions, cotton does in fact represent an important contribution to food security at the household level (compared to the alternative of exclusive emphasis on food-crop cultivation) through the comparatively high and stable income it offers to the otherwise poor households. On the environmental issue, much clearly needs to be done to maintain and increase soil fertility in the cotton-growing areas. Environmental degradation is, however, by no means unique to export crop-producing regions—nor is the causality as straightforward as critics frequently tend to imply.

The importance of agriculture in poverty alleviation is emphasized by the fact that the non-agricultural sectors of all three MADIA West

African countries have been unable to contribute significantly to poverty alleviation in recent years. Senegal has suffered a substantial drop in real non-agricultural wages. In Nigeria, the cutback in oil revenues and the large devaluation needed to correct the inappropriate policies of the 1970s have together sharply lowered real non-agricultural wages and employment. While the effects of the oil factor have been both more recent and more modest in Cameroon than in Nigeria, a decline in non-agricultural employment and real wages has begun there as well.

Donor Performance

The MADIA study finds at best a mixed picture of donors' contributions to sustained equitable growth.

In Tanzania, the donors encouraged the overexpansion of the Tanzanian developmental effort well beyond levels that the country's human, organizational, and financial capacity could reasonably have been expected to manage. Tanzania would have been unable to expand its investment program on the scale that it did, or to pursue import-substituting industrialization (or welfare provision without policies in support of increases in production) without strong donor support.[11] Virtually the same conclusion applies to Senegal. Ironically, these two countries have both been the highest per capita aid recipients and the poorest performers in the MADIA sample. In both cases the donors heeded the governments' rhetoric and overlooked the reality—the absence of an effective development strategy or of a political environment conducive to genuine economic decentralization.

In Malawi, donors in the late 1970s provided substantial assistance to rural development projects aimed at the rural poor. While Malawi has been much praised for its good growth performance in the 1970s, it is coming under criticism for its poor equity performance in the 1980s. The experience of developing countries generally shows, however, that it is very difficult to reach marginal and below-subsistence households. Aid programs have succeeded in providing credit and extension for rural households with better-than-average land endowments, but these services now need to be spread further to reach the poor. Even in the case of the better-off households, however, until policy-based lending offered donors the opportunity, they were unable to address the adverse effects of land and pricing policies that favored the estate sector.

Malawi's experience emphasizes the fundamental need for a sound, long-term development strategy that benefits from both donor project lending and adjustment lending. The macroeconomic adjustment programs implemented to date in Malawi have been aimed at improving prices of smallholder crops, privatizing, and correcting prior biases in government expenditures in favor of "brick and mortar" investments. Without better access of small farmers to land, improved technology, and services, however, some of the measures to "get prices right" (by raising producer and consumer prices of food crops and removing fertilizer subsidies, for example) may in fact turn out to have an adverse impact on the poorest smallholders. This is because production is well below subsistence levels in nearly 60 per cent of the households in the southern and central regions, where over 80 per cent of Malawi's population lives, making them dependent on market purchases (and market prices) for their basic food needs; moreover, if these food-deficit producers are to intensify production from increasingly scarce and depleted land resources, they need to buy added fertilizer to become more able to rely on their own maize production for subsistence.[12] If structural adjustment proposals are to protect the consumption levels of the increasingly market-dependent poor in Africa while also promoting growth, donors will have to help governments to devise more imaginative, low-cost approaches to stabilizing food prices and supplies for this segment of the population. This is an area of policy in which most donors have relatively little practical experience, and the initial thrust on getting prices right and reducing the role of the government has not shown enough recognition of the complexity of this problem.

In Kenya, the country's initial endowments clearly helped to reinforce the effect of favorable subsequent policies in achieving growth with equity, but donor performance in the agricultural sector has been generally disappointing—with the exception of the sterling record of assistance for smallholder tea, coffee, and dairy development.[13] But due to export pessimism, even in Kenya (as elsewhere in Africa), donor advice and lending policies were generally against the expansion of tea and coffee production. Had Kenya followed this advice, and had the growth in its tea and coffee production been less rapid, the country's per capita income performance would have been much lower, as it suffered one of the worst terms-of-trade losses. The prices of its traditional exports vis-à-vis its imports in the mid-1980s were only a third of their level at independence. Given the immense population pressure on land as well as terms-of-trade losses, rapid advances in productivity growth will be crucial in the future for maintaining the growth record of the past.

In Nigeria, foreign aid to the smallholder sector—and especially the World Bank's assistance to the Agricultural Development Programs (ADPs)—has been important in stabilizing smallholder development efforts under the circumstances of political and administrative instability referred to earlier.[14] While the ADPs have come under criticism on a variety of grounds, the MADIA study concludes that they have played a catalytic role in getting the government of Nigeria to focus on the problems of the smallholder sector on a consistent and long-term basis. Nevertheless, both external assistance and government policy have devoted too little attention to creating the Nigerian human capital and institutional capacity needed to solve the country's complex technological, institutional, and policy problems in a country of high socio-political and resource diversity.

The Nigerian ADP experience, together with the Tanzanian and Senegalese cases cited earlier, suggests that if donors are serious about empowerment of the poor, they need to open a wider dialogue with African intellectuals and political and business leaders on a regular and consistent basis, instead of confining their contacts to governments, no matter what the degree of commitment of the latter. An important albeit modest beginning is being made in this direction by the World Bank.

In Cameroon, as in Nigeria, the World Bank was ahead of the government in making the smallholder sector the central focus of expenditures on agricultural development in the 1970s, whereas previously plantation agriculture had received priority. However, in Cameroon as elsewhere in Africa, the rural development projects financed since the mid-1970s have not achieved encouraging results. Moreover, compared to some of the Anglophone countries in the MADIA study sample, Cameroon is less advanced in clearly delineating responsibilities for policy planning in the agricultural sector—those responsibilities being splintered among various ministries and between ministries and parastatals. Thus it is not clear who will formulate and be responsible for implementing a coherent agricultural policy that focuses on the smallholder sector.

A general example of successful donor assistance has been the development of hybrid and improved maize and its widespread adoption throughout Africa, as well as the cotton development programs in some Francophone African countries referred to earlier. They both stress the fundamental importance that technological change has made to prospects of low-income households even in the face of a number of barriers. Nevertheless, only the smallholder export-crop expansion in Kenya, emanating from the government's active extension of the British colonial experience with smallholder export-crop development, can be classified as having become truly self-sustaining in a financial, institutional, and human capital sense. In this instance, the tea and coffee sectors have been managed entirely by Africans for close to two decades—without reliance on external technical assistance or institutional support and with continued success. Kenya's growing smallholder exports of these crops have earned premia in world markets for nearly fifteen years for their high quality, reflecting the sophisticated nature of the services the Kenyans have managed to provide for these producers. Given their importance, through growth linkages, the coffee and tea sectors have also generated substantial indirect employment and income in the rest of the economy.

The growth of food aid to Africa also offers examples of useful donor assistance for poverty alleviation; despite its increasing developmental orientation, however, such aid is mainly transitory and designed to alleviate specific shortages. Successes in strengthening human resources in Africa, through improvements in education, health, life expectancy, and child mortality, similarly need to be applauded—especially in view of the conditions that existed at independence in most countries. (As stated earlier, improvements in health care and access to safe water are crucial for poverty alleviation, as they enable the rural poor to reduce the number of productive days lost to sickness.) Notwithstanding these examples and the other cases noted above, however, the positive components of the donors' record amount to relatively little compared to the cumulative amount of assistance they have provided over the past decade and a half.

Finally, it is ironic but not surprising to note that most of the successes of external assistance to African agriculture noted here have come from bilateral aid grounded in former colonial history and reflect a better understanding of constraints and potentials that a long-term involvement in the countries enabled. In recent years, however, the experience available to these donors as a result of the colonial era has begun to wane, and the bilaterals have not supplemented it by developing the kind of expertise necessary for promoting the growth of tropical agriculture in the 1990s and beyond. The large traditional multilateral donors, on the other hand, have taken over the lead role in smallholder development that French and British bilateral agencies formerly provided, including functions that modest but well-conceived bilateral efforts did best in the past. It is questionable, however, whether—in a period of retrenchment and efficiency-restructuring within the donor agencies themselves—the multilaterals can in fact provide the necessary staff input to go along with their financial muscle.

Among the newer donors, U.S. experience in fostering institutional and human capital development has been stronger in Africa than that of all other donors, although weak compared to its record in Asia.[15] This is partly because of the greater instability over time of U.S. institution-building assistance in Africa, which in turn reflects changing domestic U.S. aid priorities and commitment among U.S. decisionmakers. This is an unfortunate phenomenon, since Africa needs much more assistance of this type than Asia did in earlier years, and since the success of human and institutional development often depends critically on the provision of support over a long time frame, as we have clearly shown in the MADIA study.

The broader donor record suggests that while multilateral agencies may have a comparative advantage in large-scale financial resource transfers and policy and investment analysis, their ability to promote the development of indigenous human and institutional capital (which requires fewer financial resources but a great deal more nurturing than more conventional categories of assistance) may well be limited. Indeed, the special needs of human resources development among the poor require either that larger donors clearly adopt mechanisms for decoupling the financial resource transfer function from that of developing capacity, or that the latter be handled by bilateral donors, including private foundations and voluntary agencies, which operate on a smaller resource base. These agencies should in principle be able to develop long-term partnership arrangements between African institutions and their own home-based institutions in a way that multilaterals cannot, although multilateral funding for such arrangements might be offered. However, were bilateral agencies to take on this institutional development and human-capital development function seriously, they would need to rebuild their own expertise for this purpose. Such a division of labor and specialization would of course need to take place in the context of a clear and shared long-term vision of Africa's development needs on the part of both governments and donors.

Overall, it is hard to avoid the conclusion that donors and African governments alike have lacked a long-term view of development. Despite their many good intentions, they have underrated the importance of building indigenous human and institutional capital, of diversifying the organizational and institutional base in African countries (specifically including the encouragement of grassroots organizations), of giving top priority to making efficient use of the human and institutional capital that already exists, and of tackling the many micro constraints that limit the productive potential of small farmers and defy stereotypical solutions. In these areas, of course, success depends on building up a long-term presence and the kind of comprehensive understanding of country conditions that can only be supplied by locally based personnel who are knowledgeable about local circumstances. In practice, however, all too many donor efforts have not only been strong on finances and weak on knowledge-based technological and organizational aspects, but also unduly oriented to short-term goals and directed centrally from the capital cities of donor countries. Because the development process in Africa— both in the short and medium run—depends critically on donor transfers of ideas and skills (in spite of the success achieved through indigenous efforts by some recipients), the pace of growth will be determined by improving the content and the quality of assistance programs in these knowledge-based directions.

Implications for Donors and Recipients

Swings of the pendulum between differing concerns, together with a tendency to apply stereotypical prescriptions to country-specific problems—go a long way to explain why development assistance has not achieved more in Sub-Saharan Africa over the past twenty-five years, especially given Africa's initially limited human and institutional capital stock.

Smallholder Growth versus Equity Goals

Growth versus equity has been a continuing battleground for two decades. To alleviate poverty, the donor community in the 1970s placed special emphasis on agricultural development and *within* agriculture aimed at addressing the needs of the rural poor by emphasizing food-crop projects in relatively resource-poor regions. The World Bank provided a major lead. The poverty focus of the McNamara period created a unique sense of excitement because of the genuine possibility it offered to address the problems of human suffering. However, much of this effort turned out to be "top down," mainly because Africans did not have the internal capacity to plan and implement decentralized development projects on the scale on which external financial resources became available. This in turn led to substantial external input into project planning and implementation to meet assistance targets. In responding to the aid, however, governments did, through patronage distribution, develop coalitions of socio-political support that in turn helped the process of nation-building. Efforts to promote equity constrained growth promotion. Instead of pursuing opportunities for development where clear technological solutions existed, the supporters of foreign assistance in donor countries, so crucial to aid funding, preferred deliberately targeting geographical areas with relatively poor resources on equity grounds; and this coincided with the broader socio-political objectives of African governments. Production programs in high-potential areas—especially those including export crops—were given lower priority on grounds of export pessimism and of not benefiting the poor.

Indeed, the composition of the "coalition" of interests that has opposed growth-oriented, but also smallholder-based, development of export crops in Africa has been strong but inadvertent as well as ironic. The members of this "coalition"—which includes humanitarian and environmental interests, dependency theorists, and competing crop-producing groups in the donor countries—have argued that African smallholder export-crop production threatens the achievements of poverty alleviation and food security, while spoiling the environment and international markets. The African governments themselves accepted the export pessimism theory, pursued industrialization and other forms of diversification, and in process lost shares in the world market to developed and other countries—e.g., to the United States, Malaysia, and Indonesia in edible oils; to China and the United States in cotton; and to Malaysia and Indonesia in cocoa and coffee.

With little or no growth of domestic food production in low-income, resource-poor areas—and without foreign exchange earnings from increased volumes of those export crops in which Africa has a strong comparative advantage—there was increased reliance on food imports, especially on food aid.

Economic Management Priorities: Physical versus Human Capital Investment

The record of the past twenty-five years also makes it all too clear that African governments and donors also tended to favor physical over human capital and institutional development. These priorities may be understandable: From a recipient-country government's viewpoint, investment in new roads, power lines, and water supply facilities—unlike expenditures on technical training and agricultural research—provided visible improvements in living conditions of the populations served. Donors, too, have been pleased to be able to point to tangible products of their goodwill—not to mention the usefulness of such "tangible" results to maintaining support for aid among domestic commercial interests. But the opportunity costs of this physical transfer orientation of aid have been extremely heavy.

Donor and Recipient Relationships and Their Developmental Outcomes

The historical record (including donor evaluations of their own programs) shows that donor assistance has played a very limited role in Africa's post-independence agricultural growth. Large amounts of donor assistance seem to have been allocated with the best of intentions to types of activities that have in some cases laid important foundations but had little effect on growth. Of course, country experience also furnishes outstanding examples of the catalytic role that well-conceived donor assistance has played. The effectiveness with which donors have contributed to the growth process seems to depend on the extent to which they understand the myriad micro-level constraints on growth prospects in individual areas, crops, and households. Given their greater knowledge, donors with prior colonial connections with Africa have accounted for a major share of the successes achieved, but their importance in Africa has been declining. In any case, their ability to leave behind sustainable broader indigenous systems of management has been limited.

At the same time, the inadequate external expertise and knowledge about Africa among the new, well-meaning donors is worrying, given their growing share of increasing official capital flows. Donor studies carried out for the MADIA program repeatedly note the tendency of donors to respond to Africa's problems by falling back on technological and organizational solutions arising from their own particular backgrounds and expectations—which may have little connection in practice with recipients' constraints, priorities, or organizational and human capital needs (and limitations). Time and again, these studies stress the problems associated with the lack of detailed, country-specific knowledge, including historical and situation-specific constraints. They also emphasize the pressing need for a greater institutional memory in the donor community and a better understanding of the socio-political and technological factors operating in recipient countries. Major new efforts on all these fronts are essential if the current focus of reform programs on the removal of price distortions is to be appropriately complemented by the institutional and other nonprice changes needed to give the pricing reforms a chance to work. There also needs to be far greater emphasis on the longer-term microstructural constraints relating to technologies, institutions, etc., that typically persist even while structural adjustment lending-type programs are being completed—constraints that only Africans themselves can remove with improved human and institutional capital.

Lack of a consensus among donors on means or even on specific ends—as, for instance, on the roles of the private and the public sectors, or the availability or lack of technologies—has been another fundamental constraint on the effectiveness of their assistance, in contrast to earlier experience in Asia. An objective diagnosis of a particular development problem (or definition of a particular policy goal) should be built up through data-based analysis in which Africans need to participate more actively via the mobilization of such trained manpower and institutional capacity as already has been established on the continent. This should enable development of a consensus about the steps required for solving the poverty problem. Such a consensus needs to be developed with the countries themselves, based on the greater involvement of nationals at all levels, so that there is a sustained indigenous commitment to the poverty programs and investments to be undertaken. Achieving this requires strengthening the technocracies in African governments and public sectors generally as well as promoting the development of grassroots and private institutions. Since the orientation of public policy has been centralized in many African governments, donors—forewarned of socio-political sensitivities—nevertheless need to open a wider dialogue with nationals in behalf of decentralized development. Finally, poverty alleviation requires—once again—going beyond relatively short-term structural adjustment programs to long-term developmental efforts.

Notes

[1] Uma Lele and Ijaz Nabi, eds., *Aid and Development: The Transition from Agriculture to Industrialization, and from Concessional Assistance to Commercial Capital Flows*, forthcoming, 1989.

[2] See, for example, John W. Mellor, "Agriculture on the Road to Industrialization," in John P. Lewis and Valeriana Kallab, eds., *Development Strategies Reconsidered* (New Brunswick, N.J.: Transaction Books in cooperation with the Overseas Development Council, 1986).

[3] Bruce F. Johnston and others, "An Assessment of AID Activities to Promote Agricultural and Rural Development in Sub-Saharan Africa," (MADIA report, The World Bank, Washington, D.C., February 1987). See also H.G. Johnson, "Comparative Cost and Commercial Policy Theory in a Developing World Economy," *The Pakistan Development Review* (Spring 1969), pp. 1–33.

[4] Uma Lele and Arthur A. Goldsmith, "The Development of National Agricultural Research Capability: India's Experience with the Rockefeller Foundation and its Significance for Africa," *Economic Development and Cultural Change*, forthcoming, Vol. 38, No. 2 (January 1989).

[5] The MADIA study has involved detailed analysis of six African countries (Kenya, Malawi, and Tanzania in East Africa, and Cameroon, Nigeria, and Senegal in West Africa) over the past 20–25 years. Seven other donors (USAID, UKODA, DANIDA, SIDA, the French and German Governments, and the EEC) are participating in the study, which has three main areas of focus: (i) the relationship of domestic macroeconomic and agricultural policy to agricultural performance; (ii) donors' role in the development of agriculture; and (iii) the politics of agricultural policy. Currently the results of research are being distilled into a series of book-length country-specific volumes, cross-country papers, and synthesis volumes.

[6] Uma Lele and Manmohan Agarwal, "Smallholder and Large Scale Agriculture: Are There Tradeoffs in Growth and Equity?" (MADIA report, The World Bank, forthcoming, October 1988).

[7] Uma Lele and L. Richard Meyers, "Growth and Structural Change in East Africa: Domestic Policies, Agricultural Performance and World Bank Assistance, 1963–1986, Part I and Part II," DRD Discussion Papers, No. 273 and 274 (Washington D.C.: The World Bank, Development Research Department, May 1987).

[8] Uma Lele, "The Role of Price and Nonprice Factors in Explaining Sources of Growth in East African Agriculture: Some Lessons for Governments and Donors," *World Bank Economic Review*, forthcoming; and Paul Collier, "Aid and Economic Performance in Tanzania," in Uma Lele and Ijaz Nabi, eds., *Aid and Development*, op. cit.

[9] Both Kenya and Malawi also provide examples of far higher productivity in estate-based cash-crop production than in smallholder agriculture (in sharp contrast to the established differential in favor of smallholders in South Asia). In Malawi, for example, tobacco yields in the estate sector are as much as four times as high as those in the smallholder sector, while the dualism within the smallholder sector is exemplified by the fact that larger scale smallholders typically obtain higher maize yields than their smaller counterparts, owing mainly to their ability to use hybrid seeds and fertilizers. Uma Lele, "Structural Adjustment, Agricultural Development and the Poor: Lessons from Malawi," *World Development*, forthcoming.

[10] Uma Lele, *The Design of Rural Development: Lessons from Africa* (Baltimore, Md.: Johns Hopkins University Press, rev. ed., 1979).

[11] Uma Lele, "Tanzania: Phoenix or Icarus?" in Arnold Harberger, ed., *World Economic Growth* (San Francisco, Calif.: Institute of Contemporary Studies), pp. 159–195.

[12] Uma Lele, "Structural Adjustment, Agricultural Development and the Poor: Lessons from Malawi," *World Development*, forthcoming.

[13] Uma Lele and L. Richard Meyers, "Agricultural Development and Foreign Assistance: A Review of the World Bank's Experience in Kenya, 1963–1986" (MADIA report, The World Bank, December 1986).

[14] Uma Lele, A.T. Oyejide, B. Bumb, and V. Bindlish, "Nigeria's Economic Development, Agriculture's Role and World Bank Assistance, 1961 to 1986: Lessons for the Future" (MADIA report, The World Bank, forthcoming, October 1988).

[15] Bruce F. Johnston and others, "An Assessment of AID Activities to Promote Agricultural and Rural Development in Sub-Saharan Africa," op. cit.

Chapter 4

Some Lessons from IFAD's Approach to Rural Poverty Alleviation

Mohiuddin Alamgir

The 1974 World Food Conference represented the culmination of what John Lewis in the opening chapter of this volume describes as the "reformist" revision in development policy that took place in the early 1970s. The reformers recognized that rural poverty and the hunger it spawned were inextricably linked. Consequently, the elimination of hunger required nothing less than a targeted assault on poverty itself.

The IFAD Rationale

What this recognition implied was a new development strategy whose starting point was the promotion of the productive capacity of the rural poor. This, however, was not explicitly stated in the Food Conference itself. It found its full expression later, in the mandate of the International Fund for Agricultural Development (IFAD), which was established in 1977 as a follow-up to the 1974 Conference. IFAD's mandate was to increase food production, reduce undernutrition, and alleviate rural poverty.

The new agency's conceptual foundation was the understanding that poverty alleviation is an *economic* proposition—not just a welfare one. The poor are presently operating well below their production potential, given the available technology and the possibilities of generating new technologies suited to their needs. Closing this gap requires not only quantitative and qualitative improvement of the traditional factors of production; it also—most importantly—requires education, which can make the poor aware of those social entitlements and economic opportunities to which they can gain access as they build political and social power, via mobilization and participation.

The task of rural poverty alleviation is a daunting one. First, relatively little is really known about the rural poor that can help in the design and implementation of projects and programs to be financed by an external institution. Their condition, their productive potential, even their numbers and location are too little understood. Any agency that deals with this problem, as IFAD does, must undertake in-depth poverty studies as a basis for project formulation.

Second, the fact that project and program loans have to be extended to and through governments that have themselves all too often displayed a record of neglect, of agriculture in general and of the smallholder sector and the rural poor in particular, necessitates a continuous policy dialogue with the beneficiaries.

Third, one particular dilemma of IFAD is worth noting. The Fund was intended to rely on other organizations, including the World Bank and the regional development banks, for the preparation, appraisal, implementation, and supervision of the projects it financed. The fact that these institutions are not necessarily oriented toward IFAD's mandate implied an additional responsibility for the Fund's staff, who must try to influence the policies of the counterpart institutions. This has proved to be quite a demanding task.

Fourth, as is well known, increasing awareness of the urgent need to alleviate poverty at both national and international levels has not been matched by a commensurate allocation of resources, including concessional funds. The case of IFAD is an eloquent illustration. After initial resources of $1 billion (covering the period 1978–80) and a first replenishment of another $1 billion (for the period 1981–84), the second replenishment (for 1985–87) was concluded at half that level. The Fund has tried to mitigate this by reducing its average total project costs through savings achieved by using low-cost technologies and employing local personnel and non-governmental organizations in project operations..

Understanding Rural Poverty

During its first decade, IFAD conducted in-depth poverty analyses through its Special Programming Missions and other field missions in order to learn about the poor—who they are and where they are located. This is a necessary first step in designing interventions that directly help the target group.

The next step is to develop an understanding of the complex political, social, and economic processes that generate and perpetuate poverty in different national and regional settings. A legacy of colonialism, for example, is the two-tier character of agriculture that continues to reinforce poverty in many ex-colonial societies. In some respects, the technology-based "green revolution," though it has helped production, may also have aggravated such agricultural dualism in some countries.

Another process links high population growth and the laws of inheritance with the subdivision of land and the fragmentation and marginalization of holdings. The result is a progressive deterioration in the environment. As marginalized farmers reduce fallow periods, overgraze their livestock, and bring increasingly arid, infertile, and erosion-prone land under cultivation, fragile areas are destroyed, soil and water supplies are depleted, and impoverishment is accentuated. The consequent increase in poverty in turn stimulates an increase in fertility for reasons well known—and the process perpetuates itself.

There are also cultural, ethnic, and gender-related processes that contribute to the impoverishment of tribal peoples, ethnic minorities, and rural women. What has sometimes escaped attention is that internal political fragmentation and civil strife, whether they occasion a flight of refugees or internal repressions, worsen the situation for many more people than those who are the direct victims of these developments.

National governments and international aid agencies have in general failed to take into account the fact that the rural poor are subjected to various forms of exploitative intermediation. Most important, of course, is the feudal and semi-feudal exploitation rooted in land and water relations, but the phenomenon extends also into capital, labor, and product markets. Government bureaucracies, parastatals, and even cooperatives sometimes siphon off a part of the value of the product through various fiscal, price, and non-price instruments. Such an inhospitable socio-political environment requires the mobilization of the rural poor into a countervailing productive force.

The international environment has also been detrimental to smallholder production. National policy and institutional biases against the rural poor have been further accentuated by external factors. The collapse of commodity prices and the protectionist policies of developed countries have contributed significantly to external imbalances and a heavy debt burden. The latter can be partly attributed to the high interest rates in some developed countries, over which debtors have no control. The commodity price collapse has had a particularly harsh effect on the income and welfare of smallholders producing for export and of wage laborers on large-scale commercial farms and mines.

In response to internal disequilibria and external shocks, many developing countries have undertaken adjustment measures involving stringent cutbacks in budgetary allocations. A great deal of attention has been focused on the possible harsh impact of these measures on the rural poor. IFAD is undertaking studies of the micro-level impact of structural adjustment programs on the rural poor with a view to both a) making improvements in particular projects that can shield them during transition periods and b) advancing the methods of project design.

While these welfare concerns are important, the still more important issue is the extent to which structural adjustment converts the smallholder sector into one of the economy's growth zones. One must ask how effective adjustment can take place if it does not capitalize on that part of the economy which accounts for up to 80 per cent of the country's employment and for a plurality of its output and demand.

Strategies for Rural Poverty Alleviation

The experience of many aid donors in the poverty-alleviation field persistently has presented them with a yawning gap between design and results—often due to a host of factors beyond their control. As IFAD has found out, the fundamental task for all concerned is to narrow this gap. Certain fundamentals—benefit targeting, structural reforms, support services, and people's participation—apply in each project. Careful targeting of beneficiaries has to ensure that projects work in their favor and that leakage of benefits to other groups is avoided. Anyone dealing with rural development knows that benefit targeting is nearly impossible without structural reforms in land ownership and tenure, as well as in capital and labor markets. All too often such necessary reforms either have not been undertaken or they have not been adequately implemented. In Latin America, for example, governments have failed to allocate the budgetary resources required to carry through land and tenurial reform.

Structural reforms are necessary but by themselves insufficient; they must be accompanied by the provision of basic education, training, credit, and technology packages. One critical element is enhancing the ability of small farmers to assume risks. Above all, emphasis must be placed on the building of grassroots-based institutions and on people's participation in project development from the design stage onward. This "bottom-up" approach can help ensure that projects are cost-effective, sustainable, and replicable. This is very demanding, and there must be a continuous search for effective instrumentalities to promote participation.

Regional Approaches to Poverty Alleviation

In very broad terms, IFAD's strategy in *Asia* addresses the specific needs of marginal farmers, the landless, and the tribal populations. The provision of credit, using group guarantees rather than land for collateral, has proved effective, together with other measures designed to generate off-farm employment. These include support for training, marketing, and small agro-based processing enterprises. In Asia as in other areas, small-scale irrigation and water-control schemes relying on people's participation are key measures in IFAD's strategy.

In *Latin America*, the focus has been on the needs of remote areas rarely reached by development assistance, including the Indian communities of the Andes and the mountains of Central America. The implementation of land and tenurial reforms is often an essential first step in countering the poverty processes affecting these people. IFAD has sought to assist governments in regularizing land titles and in arresting land sub-division and fragmentation. The Fund is also endeavoring to create appropriate linkages between the modern and traditional sectors, encouraging, for example, local production of farm tools and implements, local processing of agricultural raw materials, construction of feeder roads, and the development of marketing outlets.

In *Africa*, IFAD's focus is on the smallholder farming sector, women-headed households, and the nomadic pastoralists. In particular, the emphasis has been on the development of traditional crops (sorghum, millet, cassava, bananas, yams, etc.), which are low in input but highly labor-intensive and drought-resistant. Such crops are the pillars of household food security as well as the sources of employment and income, particularly for rural women. The Fund has supported research in and the development of technological packages for these "poor people's crops," including biological, environmentally safe means of pest and disease control. To bolster women's economic activities and reduce protein deficiency, the Fund is also evolving a strategy for goat and sheep production in areas where the carrying capacity of the land is sufficient to avoid environmental damage.

Regional strategies have also sought to take into account the two-way linkages between poverty and the environment. This has led to the support of conservation measures, the promotion of agro-forestry, and an attempt to develop gradually a systematic approach to the durable alleviation of the plight of the nomadic pastoralists of the Sahel and North Africa as well as the Near East. In their case, the dual purpose is to contain the expansion of deserts to marginal areas while augmenting the carrying capacity of the desert itself.

Learning from Experience

IFAD's first ten years of experience consists of over two hundred projects in ninety countries. In the day-to-day work, projects must be identified that fit IFAD's mandate; they must be thoroughly prepared as to technical, logistical, and institutional details, and must then pass the test of economic and financial viability while satisfying the social and human welfare criteria embodied in IFAD's charter. But all of that serves only to get projects started. The task of implementation, which is the responsibility of the recipient countries, is, in turn, full of pitfalls and surprises. Learning from experience and feeding the lessons back into project development—with the beneficiaries always in mind—is of the essence for an aid agency; strategy articulation is not a "one-shot" exercise.

IFAD's poverty-alleviation strategies are thus constantly evolving and being refined. For example, while IFAD's strategy as a rule tries to target the poorest 20 per cent of rural households as project beneficiaries, many a slip can occur between the definition of the target group and the ultimate distribution effects and impact of project benefits. Factors that undermine targeting range from the weak management and supervisory capability of executing agencies to indecision or shifting priorities on the part of governments. The organizational and managerial skills of the targeted beneficiaries themselves can play an adverse role, especially if training and other means of institutional support are weak. In-depth understandings of the socio-economic and cultural environment as well as of the self-help potential of beneficiaries thus are critical starting points on the road to effective project development.

Similarly, it is easy to say that a participatory approach embracing the poor themselves is fundamental to project sustainability. Yet the rhetoric of grassroots mobilization too often is not matched by action. On the contrary, local institutions have often demonstrated a bias against the poorer segments of rural populations.

Involving the poor through coercion or through requiring "voluntary" contributions of their labor is not genuine people's participation. Both public and private policies can stifle the participatory spirit. Constraints range from inadequate local leadership, limited access by the poor to decisionmaking, insufficient access to resources, and counterproductive regulations and ideologies. Most important are the isolation and alienation of the poor themselves. Non-governmental organizations have been helpful in getting around such obstacles, given the special access to the poor they have established in years of work among them. The Fund also has pressed for the decentralization of institutions dealing with rural development to bring them closer to the grassroots level.

While a participatory project may help reduce the cost of implementation and improve maintenance, sustainability, and replicability, it too can entail implementation problems similar to those of traditional economic development projects. By and large, projects that are too complicated or too ambitious break down for want of proper coordination. Rates of inflation prove higher than expected, so that physical targets go unachieved. The lack of local counterpart funds disrupts required inputs. New governments change investment priorities and administrative structures. Civil strife and natural calamities intrude. A high turnover of trained staff, especially in remote, impoverished locations, takes its toll. Assessments of the physical resource base prove overly optimistic.

Although the problems are familiar, their solutions can be innovative. For an aid agency, it is important to move quickly and responsively to ease constraints. Where counterpart funds fall short, for example, the agency should be able to work closely with borrowers to establish appropriate priorities and to reinstate the funds required to support them. In some cases, projects need to be reformulated to reflect the changing priorities or administrative structures of governments even while the focus remains fixed on the needs of the targeted beneficiaries. Active participation of beneficiaries can significantly reduce delays, which often arise from unforeseen complexities in local socioeconomic relationships, the subtleties of land relations, the attitudes of the poor toward government and local authorities, etc. The incorporation of training programs also helps to make implementation more successful.

Specific examples of IFAD's operations and the lessons derived from them can provide a closer look into the particulars of poverty-alleviation efforts.

Credit for the Poor

Lending to the poor has proven to be an economically sound proposition. From the point of view of an aid agency, a clear advantage of credit projects is the relative ease of targeting benefits to the poorest and most vulnerable groups. Ceilings on farm size, on assets, etc., can be employed. In Africa, where 40 per cent or more of food-producing households are headed by women, a distinct target group is readily at hand. In the case of landless laborers, the choice of activities covered by the project, those being trained, and the identification of the group's "target" needs can serve as a basis for eligibility. Targeting of needs is crucial to avoid a situation like the one IFAD faced in Panama, where the intended beneficiaries were the Guaymi Indians, yet credit for livestock under the project went mostly to cattle-breeding and cattle-fattening activities—in which the Guaymi people were not engaged.

Project credit can loosen the constraints that the local power structure, moneylenders, traders, and large landowners traditionally place on the rural poor. It can break down patterns of bonded labor by encouraging self-employment and micro-enterprise, which in turn can reduce the tide of rural-urban migration. To be effective, institutional credit provided to improve production, income, food security, and savings of rural households must be complemented by other types of support services, namely, appropriate technical packages, research, extension, training, and marketing.

The determination of interest rates is also critical. Low rates may not in fact benefit the rural poor, as limited supplies of cheap credit often are preempted by relatively wealthier farmers. Low rates can also discourage savings and threaten the viability of a future credit supply. As a general rule, the level of interest charged should be linked with financial norms and discipline, the relative scarcity of capital, and the viability of both credit suppliers and users. Numerous IFAD projects have established that, once given access, the poor can bear the market rate of interest and still undertake profitable economic activities.

IFAD's experience has demonstrated that credit suppliers, for their part, can also travel out to the poor countryside, providing credit by motorcycle (like the Mobile Credit Officers in Pakistan), by bicycle (like the Group Organizers in Nepal), and even on foot (like the Bank Workers in Bangladesh)—with administrative formalities kept to a minimum. The development of such cadres and simplified procedures should, in the long run, reduce the cost of credit delivery to the rural poor. However, one should not underestimate the administrative and institution-building costs in the initial phases, which have to be covered in one way or another. The interest spreads that are administratively allowed to banks may not always cover the costs of very small-scale operations. This is why, because of their inability to subsidize initial costs, some development banks have even withdrawn from smallholder credit delivery.

Administrative costs can be contained by using borrower *groups* for credit delivery. IFAD has found that loans extended for group-based activities on the basis of group eligibility can be highly effective. Group-based credit delivery promotes participation, reduces paperwork, and takes advantage of economies of scale in the investments being supported. Field evidence indicates that groups should be small and homogeneous, to ensure cohesion and efficiency. Members and leaders may, however, need appropriate training.

Group guarantee can be a more secure collateral than land or fixed assets—provided that the productive use of loans is ensured through adequate project appraisal. In most cases, for the landless poor, or for women without title to land or a claim on the physical assets possessed by their husbands, this may be the only alternative. Group credit schemes have worked well in Bangladesh, Benin, Honduras, Ethiopia, Malawi, Mali, Nepal, Pakistan, and Sierra Leone. Group formation among women has received particular attention. In Bangladesh, group membership in the Grameen Bank is 77 per cent female, and a new IFAD project in Nepal is exclusively targeted at women's groups.

Credit systems cannot be sustained, however, if governments treat credit as a transfer payment, or if loan repayment discipline is lax. Highly satisfactory repayment rates exceeding 90 per cent have been reported from IFAD projects in Bangladesh, Benin, Egypt, Ethiopia, Malawi, Mali, Nepal, Pakistan, Syria, Thailand, Tonga, Turkey, and Zambia.

This does not mean that there are no problems in credit recovery. Projects in Burkina Faso, Sierra Leone, Jordan, and Tunisia provide a few such examples. A number of reasons account for relatively low recovery: natural calamities; government policies on rural credit recovery; too rapid disbursement without adequate appraisal; poor supervision; inadequate marketing or technical packages; low output prices; lack of inputs, irrigation, and transport; loan maturities that are too long; and the failure to mobilize savings. Credit guarantee schemes that are supposed to improve viability of credit delivery to smallholders may do exactly the opposite; they may encourage loan defaults if the bank staff does not pursue recovery rigorously enough. This has been the experience in Tunisia.

Quite often it is thought that to promote effective credit use and improve repayment, credit should be extended—and repaid—in kind. This should be based on a careful assessment of loan use. In a credit project for small farmers in a remote area, in-kind delivery might need to be arranged by the credit supplier, either on its own or in collaboration with input distribution agencies. Loans in kind are also an effective means to ensure that funds are not diverted to other uses. On the other hand, reliable suppliers—or at least a diversified set of suppliers—are important to ensure the efficient delivery of loans in kind. IFAD has had difficult experiences in Benin, Mali, and Botswana because suppliers contracted for the delivery of loans in kind (work oxen, draught equipment, tractor reconditioning) fell victim to financial or other difficulties and left borrowers without recourse to other outlets. However, repayment in kind—particularly the tying of output to marketing—can be useful. In some IFAD projects, cattle loans are being repaid in offspring and short-term input loans in crops.

Finally, the importance of savings mobilization in credit schemes cannot be emphasized enough. Savings can be voluntary or compulsory, as in the IFAD Small Farmer Credit Project in Bangladesh, where group members save a small amount (one *taka*) every week and deposit it in a savings fund. In Mali, farmers are required to place their deposits in a village fund, and their access to credit is a multiple of the amount deposited. Numerous innovative means can be found to suit local customs and conditions. Policymakers should note that the propensity to save is more evident among the rural poor than among the urban poor, and that rural dwellers are more inclined to invest their savings in additional productive assets than consumer goods.

Integrated Rural Development (IRD)

IFAD's approach to integrated rural development has differed in many ways from earlier, more "traditional" concepts that often stressed integrated economic activities at the expense of social components and policy and institutional reform. A broader view is necessary, embracing the need to remove policy and institutional constraints. What is also needed is a more selective view of 1) the number of activities to be included under such projects; 2) the nature of these activities; 3) the extent and level of their proposed integration; and 4) the political and organizational preparedness of the beneficiaries to receive external assistance. This last point is critical; otherwise, even a good project concept may fall through.

A sequential approach to IRD can facilitate the design and implementation of such projects. For example, the provision of physical infrastructure, such as approach roads, irrigation channels, etc., constitutes a level of component activities that can be implemented once the development of activities providing "backward" and "forward" linkages to agriculture is under way. Such "backward" linkage activities include adaptive research, credit, and input supply, while "forward" linkages include storage, marketing, and processing. Other levels of integrated activity involving supplementary economic and social activities can be layered in as management capacity allows.

Among the conclusions that can be drawn from IFAD's initial experience with IRD is that the size of the project must be circumscribed by the demands of effective management. The larger the area covered by an IRD project, the fewer components it should have. However, while small projects are more manageable, they tend to have a high cost per beneficiary. The challenge is to formulate low-cost, small-scale IRD projects to respond to the needs of specifically targeted groups and to assure effective manageability within the manpower constraints. This is why, in a multi-sector IRD project, the Project Management Unit is an important link with the relevant government ministries and agencies on the one hand and beneficiaries on the other. However, the relative complexity of IRD projects, irrespective of their size, shows that such a link will be effective when (unlike normal bureaucracies) it can be flexible, have sufficient autonomy for change and adaptation, and have the benefit of support from strong grassroots-based participatory institutions of the beneficiaries.

Another conclusion is that the success of an IRD project depends heavily on the care taken in pre-design studies. Two areas requiring particular attention are a thorough knowledge of ongoing development activities in the project area—partly in order to avoid excessive claims on limited financial and manpower resources. The other is the potential for beneficiary involvement at the stage of project preparation.

A careful analysis of backward and forward linkages is also essential for effective design and implementation. Evaluation studies indicate that some IFAD-financed IRD projects have not paid sufficient attention to one critical forward link: marketing. Important elements of physical infrastructure (minor irrigation or soil conservation) and of social services have also sometimes been neglected.

In multi-component IRD projects, production and income increases are important to maintaining the enthusiasm of participants. Expanding preexisting production systems by increments of credit, new irrigation facilities, or the area cultivated has proven easier than effecting technical change, especially in dryland farming in Africa. Often the choice of technology package has not adequately reflected micro agro-ecological variations within the project area. To do so, such projects need to continue adaptive research with effective farmer participation.

Preliminary evaluation shows that IRD projects tend to be designed with a primary focus on agriculture. The consequence is that in areas with a large landless population and with unequal land distribution, the distribution of benefits can be skewed, unless compensatory investments are made. In many IRD projects, not enough funds have been allocated in support of either the landless or micro-enterprises.

In general, IFAD has found that a five-year implementation period for IRD projects is too short, giving rise to several kinds of inefficiencies and distortions. Most of these projects are now scheduled for a period of not less than seven years, with the first two years devoted to laying the groundwork and start-up.

Two IFAD-financed IRD projects throw additional light on the Fund's experience. The Magbosi Integrated Agricultural Development

Project in Sierra Leone, begun in 1980, was one of the first IRD projects financed by IFAD, and the Fund learned a number of useful lessons from it. Certain key assumptions on which the design project rested were either too optimistic or plainly wrong. The most intractable component proved to be swampland development—the fault being underestimation of the expertise required for such a complex undertaking. Shortfalls in the expected yield from upland rice farming pointed to the need for more intensive research on both the cultural practices of farmers and the technological packages supplied to them for increasing production. IFAD now examines each component of a technological package more closely to determine its suitability in terms of prevailing practices and conditions. Another faulty assumption was that farmers would benefit from substantially increased income from rice sales to nearby towns; in fact, however, increased production—by reducing the price of rice—had a far more modest effect on cultivator incomes than was projected. This also taught caution in terms of price projections and the need for a larger project marketing component.

Moreover, while the project provided a variety of inputs and services to farmers, it provided few formal or informal participatory/consultative mechanisms for the involvement of farmers in project management. Formation of groups was undertaken for credit delivery, but the purpose was less to have participants draw up the credit guidelines themselves than to ensure that project loans got repaid. In this respect, it was also difficult to establish whether credit facilities or other inputs were reaching and benefiting the poorest farmers.

The Magbosi project did, nevertheless, have a positive side. It demonstrated that effective extension and input delivery systems could be established in a relatively short period of time. It showed the feasibility of directly providing loans to poor women farmers and of developing a sound program of minor crops to enhance incomes. Finally, one of the distinctive features of this project was the incorporation of a monitoring and evaluation component into the project's design. While the performance of this component was not judged totally satisfactory, the experiment showed the potential usefulness of such components, which are now included in all IFAD-financed IRD projects.

Another IRD project, the Mwanza/Shinyanga Rural Development Project in Tanzania, initiated by the World Bank in 1979 and co-financed by IFAD, was unfortunately an early lesson in "don'ts" for the Fund. It combined many of the elements of poor design and implementation that have given IRD a bad name in many academic quarters. The project was unrealistic in scope and overly optimistic in its objectives. Although it was reduced in scope in 1982–83, its complexity and wide area of coverage fell victim to manpower constraints, a weak organizational structure, and communications difficulties. Farmer participation or consultation was thwarted by the low morale of field staff and lack of reliable technical packages, transport, and field equipment. Management functions were uncoordinated and poorly supervised. Staffing constraints and the failure to use resources efficiently undermined extension and training, as well as the components for seeds, livestock, road construction, and forestry. Over a three-year period, this project dominated 70 per cent of the government's development expenditure for the entire Mwanza region—with minimal results for the area's poor. Nonetheless, for IFAD there were some positive lessons. A Village Self-Help Programme was introduced as part of the project to encourage participatory development by supporting activities identified by the villagers themselves. Despite obstacles, the villagers reacted favorably, submitting more applications for small-scale activities than the program could accommodate. Similarly, the planting of village woodlots, while marred by low seedling survival rates, nonetheless impressed villagers with the potential benefits of tree cultivation for fuelwood and poles. Finally, achievements under the cassava and sweet potato research sub-component actually surpassed their appraisal targets, pointing IFAD toward increased emphasis on the improved output of such traditional crops.

Irrigation Projects

In its early years, IFAD participated in several large-scale irrigation schemes. Its experience with these led to the development of a small-scale irrigation strategy more in keeping with the Fund's micro project approach to rural poverty alleviation.

Large-scale irrigation projects have been quite successful in increasing agricultural productivity, improving farmer incomes, and creating employment opportunities. A recent review of IFAD's early investments in large-scale irrigation projects shows that six out of eight had production effects greater than, or at least equal to, appraisal estimates. In the remaining cases, it was found that production success depends equally on the provision of suitable high-production technologies (wheat and rice being the two outstanding examples), sound management of often complex projects, and the provision of complementary agricultural services. Large-scale irrigation projects can, however, have an adverse effect on the environment. They can also be costly—not only in terms of capital outlays but also in terms of recurrent expenditures. The larger the project, the longer its gestation and the slower the returns.

By contrast, small-scale irrigation and water control schemes substantially reduce total investment costs, foreign exchange requirements, and maintenance outlays. They rely more directly on the recipients' own contribution to investment and upkeep. They also fit well into a participatory, grassroots approach; are better suited to the needs of poor smallholders; and are more sustainable by them in the long run.

IFAD's Sulawesi Paddy Land Development Project, providing large-scale irrigation for trans-migrants in Indonesia, affords numerous examples of what can go wrong. First of all, land clearing, leveling, and paddy formation were subject to severe delays due to the inexperience of the lead government department in the preparation and award of tenders, the remoteness of the project areas, and other bottlenecks at the provincial level. This was further complicated by delays in the availability of farming inputs, a weak extension service, the failure of village cooperatives and farmers' groups to take hold, and a standstill on credit provision. Most critical, however, was the fact that the irrigation system itself failed to work effectively. Farmers expressed no confidence in a water delivery system that led to flooding, crop loss, and, in one instance, the loss of life stemming from quarrels over water distribution. No satisfactory means was established for controlling the distribution of water throughout the system. Water users' associations were slow in starting, and "gate men" controlling the flow of water at the head of each system were mostly under the supervision of farmers with land at the head of the system. Farmers at the system's outer reaches, facing shortages, complained of waste due to leakages in the untended supply system. Although wooden stop logs and steel plates had been provided to regulate the flow, they were soon damaged or stolen. In some cases, control structures were damaged in an effort to get additional water. A mid-term evaluation of this project, carried out in late 1986 and early 1987, recommended a number of strong remedial measures, including, in particular, steps to improve management and coordination at all levels.

Small-scale irrigation sidesteps most of these problems and shows more impressive results. For example, the IFAD On-Farm Water Management Project in Pakistan, completed in 1985, renovated 3,611 watercourses; this performance exceeded appraisal estimates by 76 per cent. This remarkable result was achieved through the establishment of 11,245 water users' associations, which also exceeded by far the project target of 2,065. These associations were highly effective in getting material and technical assistance released from the project directorate and in mobilizing labor for the renovation of watercourses. Such organization was possible because of the immediate benefits received by farmers, one of which was reduction in the inequality of water supply between "head-reach" and "tail-end"—those closest to and farthest away from the source—farmers within a watercourse command area. This has dramatically reduced litigation within the farming community. Illegal interference with water flows has virtually ceased, and the costs of maintenance have dropped sharply. The project, which relied on people's participation to achieve its main goals, has an estimated economic rate of return of 53 per cent, which is 8 per cent higher than appraisal estimates.

Women and Ethnic Populations

The most severe poverty in rural areas is often found among poor women and culturally distinct and ethnic groups, such as the indigenous Indians of Latin America and the tribal populations living in remote areas of Asia and Africa.

On behalf of women, IFAD has used a number of specially targeted approaches. In Africa, for example, the emphasis has been on women's role in food production and marketing; in Asia, the focus has been on establishing agricultural and non-farm enterprises for landless women and for women from marginal farm families. Handicrafts, livestock activities, and home economics were supported in Latin America and the Caribbean, the Near East, and North Africa.

Projects designed to reduce women's drudgery and labor in the household as well as to improve nutrition and the general quality of rural life have provided water supply, health care, labor-saving technologies, education, community development, and home economics. For example, in Mali, Burkina Faso, Senegal, and Haiti, experimental funds were established to facilitate investment by women's groups in collective and labor-saving facilities such as grain mills and community woodlots. In the Ivory Coast, IFAD has provided credit to women to acquire an improved variety of fish-smoking ovens, which have reduced the smoking time by more than 50 per cent and have contributed to the protection of the environment by substituting coconut fiber for wood as fuel.

One example from among IFAD projects that address the needs of women demonstrates both the complexities and the contradictions inherent in the issues involved—and points to some encouraging possibilities for the future. The Jahaly and Pacharr Smallholder Project in The Gambia was designed to introduce irrigated rice cultivation in two swamps traditionally cultivated by women. To free women's time for work, the project set up broad-based day care centers. Land allocation committees were formed by the project to facilitiate equitable distribution of the improved lands. Membership on these committees—nominated by the project authorities—was initially predominantly male, but IFAD succeeded in having women's participation raised to about 50 per cent. Even so, however, the land was distributed in favor of men. IFAD had to intervene again for a revision of the initial allocation so that 99 per cent of those receiving land were the women who had originally cultivated the area.

Maintaining the security of women's land tenure proved even more difficult than land distribution. Economies of scale, the physically heavy tasks of land improvement, and the more sophisticated technology introduced called for more male labor and thus more dependency on men. The coming of drought further eroded women's autonomy in decisionmaking on rice production. The overall food security of the household—traditionally under the authority of the male house head in The Gambia—became paramount.

This project presented IFAD with continuous challenges to assure that the targeted beneficiaries are in fact benefiting. The Fund's capacity to respond to complex socio-economic issues on an ongoing basis was also tested. The lessons through the implementation stage point to the need for constant vigilance.

Cultural differences pose similar problems with respect to ethnic minorities and require similar watchfulness over project design and implementation. IFAD's Alto Mayo Rural Development Project in Peru, whose major beneficiaries were the Aquaruna people, is a case in point. It was through this project that IFAD developed a clearer understanding of the overall requirements of its interventions on behalf of Indian communities. One of these is that land entitlement is the *sine qua non* for the integration of indigenous people into the national economy. Cultural viability can be safeguarded only through the continued habitation and use of traditional land. The provision of legal land titles to the Aquaruna was the IFAD's condition for this project.

A second consideration is related to education and the development of an appropriate and effective means of extension services. It became obvious that the use of Spanish in both formal schooling and informal extension and training was inhibiting communication with a people who had lived virtually isolated until the 1970s and to whom the notions of property, quantification, and monetization were alien.

Parents doubted the usefulness of school. The number of dropouts was high. Because girls attended much less than boys, a dangerous socio-cultural gap emerged between the two. "Modernized" Aquaruna young men looked for wives among the *mestizo* settlers who, in turn, responded favorably to such intermarriages since they implied access to native lands. The situation carried the seeds of ethnic extinction and was said to be responsible for the high suicide rate among the young Aquaruna women.

In July 1987, IFAD organized a seminar for project authorities, government officials, and beneficiaries on the technical, pedagogical, and administrative aspects of bilingual education in the Alto Mayo. The seminar recommended the production of an Aquaruna grammar;

the updating and expansion of the existing but largely unavailable Aquaruna/Spanish dictionary; the translation and adaptation of the current Spanish-language mathematics books into Aquaruna; the introduction of the abacus; and books on the local flora and fauna and on Aquaruna history as a means of maintaining the Aquaruna culture and identity. These recommendations are being incorporated in the project. An additional effort will be made to link school activities to community activities and parents' interests.

One noteworthy aspect of this project was the establishment, within the monitoring and evaluation unit of the project, of a division on native communities to measure the project's impact on indigenous groups. The responsible officer, an experienced sociologist/anthropologist, acts as advisor to the project's technical director.

The Fund's experiences also make it increasingly aware of the need to explore different outlets for indigenous people whose comparative advantage may not necessarily lie in farming. In the context of the Aquaruna communities, IFAD is considering activities such as hunting and gathering, afforestation, and the cultivation and export of local medicinal plants. The extensive and traditional knowledge of these forest people could make the Aquaruna the best "forest guardians" of a land increasingly subject to deforestation.

Everywhere the record of development efforts has been mixed. This should not discourage us. Neither should the recent tendency to question the value of such efforts disturb us unduly. Criticism was inevitable—and we gain from it as long as it leads to better understanding and more honest and responsible commitment. After all, the motto "learning while doing" is the most realistic and appropriate one. In IFAD's experience, the participation of the people themselves in both the learning and the doing has proved the best approach yet to the challenge of poverty alleviation.

Chapter 5

A Turning Point in Pakistan's Rural Development Strategy

Sartaj Aziz

There have been some important landmarks in the search for alternative development strategies in the past four decades. One of these occurred in the early 1970s, when it was realized that even in countries that had made reasonably good economic progress in the 1950s and 1960s, the bottom 40 per cent of the population had been virtually bypassed. As a result, the income gap between the rich and the poor and between urban and rural areas had widened, the employment problem had worsened, and the poorest people could not even meet their basic needs of food, clothing, shelter, medicine, and education.

This led to a major effort to evolve strategies and policies to reach the poor directly, promote better employment opportunities, and help meet the basic needs of the bulk of the population. Throughout the 1970s, these topics received considerable attention at many major international conferences: the World Population Conference (1974), the World Food Conference (1974), the World Employment Conference (1976), Habitat (1976), the World Water Conference (1978), and the World Conference on Agrarian Reforms and Rural Development (1979). Simultaneously, almost all multilateral agencies and donor countries began to emphasize projects and programs that could reduce poverty.

This redirection of the development effort led to many positive results, both in terms of identifying more meaningful development strategies and policies and in influencing domestic policies and programs in favor of the rural poor in many developing countries. But the cumulative impact on reducing poverty has been limited. In most

111

countries it has not been possible to operationalize the poverty-reducing strategies into specific projects or institutional arrangements. Unfortunately, this phase also coincided with a decline in the net flow of financial resources for development, particularly in the 1980s. Between 1984 and 1986, for example, total net flows of resources from DAC countries to developing countries on both non-concessional and concessional terms (measured in 1985 dollars) declined from the peak of $80.9 billion in 1984 to $53.1 billion in 1986. This decline, particularly in aid, has seriously undermined efforts and programs for the benefit of the rural poor in many recipient countries and international agencies. Even the 1985 Action Programme for the Recovery of Africa, under which the African nations undertook to carry out far-reaching reforms to strengthen the food sector and the vulnerable groups in society, has not been backed by the external resources that were promised. The international debt crisis that has dominated the development scene since the early 1980s has also shifted attention from anti-poverty programs to structural adjustment issues.

As the world prepares for the last decade of this century, there is a valuable opportunity to launch a new and more determined attack on poverty. This will require a development strategy in which agricultural and rural development is given a leading role, a serious effort to improve social and physical infrastructure in rural areas, and a genuine decentralization of administrative and political power.

A serious redirection of the development effort has been under way in Pakistan since 1985. This paper highlights some of the positive features of this effort and some of the difficulties that are emerging.

Achievements and Failures

In *economic* terms, over the past three-and-a-half decades, Pakistan has achieved an annual average growth rate of 5.5 per cent in its GDP and a reasonably satisfactory diversification of its economy. Over this period, the share of manufacturing and mining in GDP has increased from 8 per cent in 1949–50 to 20.5 per cent in 1986–87, and that of the services sector from 37 per cent to 44 per cent. Correspondingly, the share of agriculture has fallen from 53 per cent to 25.5 per cent, although agriculture continues to employ 55 per cent of the total labor force. As a result of the steady growth of GDP, per capita income in Pakistan has increased sixfold—from less than $60 in 1950 to $380 in 1985 (both in 1985 dollars).

In terms of *social* indicators, the record is not equally encouraging. By 1981–82, the overall literacy rate had hardly reached 26 per cent— 17 per cent in rural areas and 47 per cent in urban areas. The proportion of literate females in rural areas was only 7 per cent, and the female enrollment ratio was 31 per cent (of total enrollment of children between the ages of 5 and 11). Clean drinking water was available to less than 50 per cent of the population and health facilities to 45 per cent. The infant mortality rate was 121 per thousand live births, life expectancy at birth was 51 years, and the population growth rate, which itself is dependent on female literacy and social progress, was over 3 per cent. Thus a country that by economic standards was about to graduate from low-income to middle-income developing country status—by crossing the per capita income mark of $400—was almost at the bottom of the list of low-income countries in terms of social indicators.

Since about 70 per cent of Pakistan's people live in rural areas, the general neglect of social sectors has had a pronounced effect on the rural population. The manner in which the task of agricultural development has been undertaken has also widened the income and productivity gaps between large and small farmers and between farmers cultivating irrigated areas and those trying to survive on arid lands.

The Turning Point

The year 1983 marked a turning point in Pakistan's rural development strategy. With the launching of the Sixth Plan in that year, there was a major shift in investment priorities toward the social sectors. This shift was further strengthened by the new civilian government that took over in 1985. The new government announced a Four-Year Programme of socio-economic development for the period 1986–90. It also set up a National Commission on Agriculture to review the performance of the sector in the past twenty-five years and to propose strategies and policies for the remaining years of this century.

This Four-Year Programme is the first major effort to redress systematically the imbalance between economic and social progress, both between urban and rural areas and between more developed and less developed regions. The main thrust of the Programme is to undertake a massive investment program to expand the rural infrastructure by building 12,000 kilometers of farm-to-market roads; extending electricity to 90 per cent of the country's 45,000 villages; opening 40,000 primary schools, establishing 151 rural health centers and 1,180 basic health units; and providing clean drinking water to 26 million people and sanitation to 7 million people in rural areas. To implement this ambitious Programme, about 40 per cent of the country's total development outlay of $30 billion was devoted to the Programme in 1986–87 and about 45 per cent in 1987–88. This is more than twice the annual amount spent in the preceding three years. By 1990, when the Programme is completed, the total mileage of rural roads built, the number of rural schools constructed, and the villages electrified in these four years will exceed the results achieved in these sectors during the preceding ten to fifteen years.

The most ambitious target of the Programme is to double literacy—from 26 per cent to 50 per cent. This is not likely to be attained because of the inevitable time lag, but even the expected increase to 40 per cent by the end of the Seventh Plan will be a major achievement.

The setting up of the National Commission on Agriculture reflected the recognition that the success achieved so far was based on a narrow range of crops and sub-sector strategies, without a coherent analytical and social framework for the agricultural sector as a whole. Between 1960 and 1986, Pakistan attained, on average, an annual agricultural growth rate of 3.8 per cent. This could be ascribed to four major factors:

(1) An increase of 100 per cent in water availability from the canal irrigation system and from 250,000 tubewells;

(2) An increase in fertilizer consumption from 31,000 nutrient tons in 1960 to 1.78 million tons in 1987, coinciding with the introduction in Pakistan of responsive high-yielding varieties of wheat and rice;

(3) A major expansion in agricultural credit to finance tubewells, tractors, and inputs like fertilizers and seeds; and

(4) A price-support and procurement policy for crops like wheat, rice, and cotton to ensure that farmers adopting new technologies receive a stable and remunerative price.

Of these factors, the bio-chemical technologies based on new seeds and chemical fertilizer are scale neutral, but those based on tubewells and tractors are not. As a result, the yields of large and medium farmers, with better access to the package of technology requiring assured water supply and credit, are higher than the national average. Some small farmers have benefited from improved seeds and fertilizer but, without assured water and the whole range of inputs, they have not been able to participate fully in the benefits of development.

The National Commission on Agriculture, which submitted its report in April 1988, had been asked to propose agricultural policies and strategies that would not only provide a comprehensive analytical framework for the modernization of the agricultural sector as a whole, but would also include a package of technological, institutional, and policy measures for improving the productivity of small farmers. The Commission carried out a detailed study of the the obstacles encountered by farmers—particularly small farmers—and it concluded that many of these constraints can be removed through well-designed rural development programs. Farm-to-market roads, for example, open up new possibilities for growing marketable crops. The provision of electricity encourages the installation of tubewells and pumps to provide additional water. Expanded facilities for education, health, housing, drinking water, and recreation make villages more habitable and help persuade the educated youth to stay on in the rural areas rather than migrate to cities.

Continuing improvements in the rural infrastructure are also necessary to facilitate the process of rural diversification, which is an essential component of the longer term strategy recommended by the Commission. The objective of providing a decent standard of living for the country's rural population cannot be accomplished through reliance on the agricultural sector alone. Pakistan has 50 million acres of cultivated land for a rural population of 70 million. With an annual growth in population of about 3 per cent, and without a corresponding increase in cropped area, the pressure of population on the available land can only increase further. The only effective answer is massive diversification from agriculture to non-agricultural activities in the rural areas. Such a program would not only create additional employment opportunities and alternative occupations for the rural poor but also provide higher incomes to farmers selling their output to agro-industries and to those engaged in these activities.

Even if these two important tasks—the improvement of rural infrastructure and the diversification of the rural economy—are tackled successfully, the gap between developed and less-developed areas and between the rich and the poor within rural areas will not be sufficiently bridged until special attention is paid to the lowest income groups in the rural areas: small farmers, landless workers, and those living in remote and arid areas. But special poverty-reducing projects for these low-income groups will have only limited impact unless the required infrastructure is built in these areas and additional employment opportunities are generated through diversified activities.

Keeping in view the importance of the scale and sequence of these programs and interventions, the Commission has proposed that, in addition to the expanded provision of infrastructure and services in rural areas, the next step is to build village-level organizations to enable small farmers to link up with the state system, which cannot itself reach every village.

Grassroots Institutions for Rural Development

Pakistan has experimented with different models of rural development: community development in the 1950s, rural works programs in the 1960s, and integrated rural development in the 1970s. But a very important step toward an elected system of local government institutions—as distinguished from bureaucratically managed rural institutions—was taken in 1979 with the passage of local bodies legislation in each province. Under the new system a two-tier institution of elected District Councils and Union Councils was created in rural areas and elected Municipal Councils in urban areas. Elections to these bodies have been held every four years: in 1979, 1983, and 1987.

In principle, this network of local councils provides a substantial leadership resource—as a potent factor in any program of social and economic development. But experience with this type of local government has also highlighted the following inadequacies:

- The constituency of a Union Council member, based on 1,000 population, mostly defies village boundaries; there can be four villages in one ward, or four members in one village—or any combination in between. This adversely affects the natural basic unit of a village.

- The local elections over the years have led to very strong enmities, so that each village is today divided into three or four inimical groups that refuse to socialize with one another—making it impossible to have any sort of development cooperation among the population of the village.

- Since each local councilor is elected from among several contestants for the office, he usually represents the views of less than one-half of his ward and cannot effectively mobilize his constituency for development purposes.

- Grassroots organizations do not exist at present to identify the needs and problems of the rural population, mobilize the people to solve these problems themselves, and to undertake development activities with local participation.

Thus a very large number of poor people—rural smallholders, tenants, and landless workers—have no effective connection with the state system. The efforts of the government to provide inputs for agriculture, resource mobilization through cooperatives, or employment-generating programs that are intended to contribute to the betterment of life are not able to reach this large portion of the society. Nor do the poor have any organization, officially recognized and encouraged, through which they can affect decisionmaking at the local level or supply the necessary feedback to influence development decisions at the provincial or federal level.

The average villager cannot defend himself against the repression of bureaucracy at the local level, as there is no set-up through which he can mobilize his fellow villagers for his protection or assistance. There is also no organization at the village level that allows all the villagers, despite their internal differences or factions, to meet together to discuss problems facing the entire village and come up with a plan of action that they themselves can undertake, or for which they can seek help from supportive arms of the government. The constituency of the Union Council member (covering 1,000 population) or the District Council member (covering a population of about 36,000) has no meaningful grassroots *institutional* connection with the development activities of the government. The overwhelming majority of poor people living in villages therefore do not participate effectively in the development effort of the country.

To overcome these problems and carry the rural development program through to the important phase of local institution-building, reforms are needed at two different levels:

(1) To further decentralize the system of local bodies down to the village level by creating *village development councils* in all villages with a population of more than 500.

(2) To strengthen the District Councils by giving them greater financial and administrative resources and by creating a strong *district planning office* for the preparation, implementation, and supervision of development projects.

The Government has already decided in principle to move ahead with these reforms, but many political and administrative obstacles are slowing down their implementation.

Further Decentralization and the AKRSP Experience

One of the most successful examples of building grassroots institutions is that provided by the Aga Khan Rural Support Programme (AKRSP) in the Northern Areas of Pakistan. Village organizations have been established in about half of the area's 1,030 villages to undertake productive physical infrastructure projects, such as irrigation channels and link roads, and to initiate other activities to meet the needs of the people, including land improvement, livestock vaccination, and marketing of agricultural produce. The World Bank's Operations Evaluation Department has recently carried out an evaluation of the AKRSP and concluded that its performance and achievements are impressive.

The basic issue that has to be resolved in setting up village development councils in other parts of Pakistan is their status vis-à-vis the existing governmental administration and the local bodies system. The AKRSP is a non-governmental organization (NGO) that has developed good working relations with the governmental agencies operating in the Northern Areas. There is a strong body of opinion that while a non-governmental agency may, for example, be able to promote such grassroots organization, with international assistance, on a pilot basis in a selected area, it would be difficult for one or more NGOs to promote and supervise a system for rural development throughout the country. It is apprehended that neither the Provincial Governments nor the District Councils would allow such organizations to handle a large volume of resources or dispense considerable political patronage, because they need such resources and opportunities of patronage for their own political objectives.

Ideally, the village councils of the sort participating in the AKRSP should be *part* of the local government system, but so far the local government system in Pakistan has not developed to the stage where it could recruit and train competent and motivated staff necessary for establishing or promoting village-level organizations. Political rivalries and differences within the District and Union Councils would also adversely influence the implementation of the program. The chairman or other officers of the District Council, for example, would give preferential treatment to their favorite villages at the cost of others. An NGO—being non-political—could apply objective development criteria in extending various facilities to different villages and select local leadership on the basis of competence rather than political affiliation.

Both alternatives have their advantages and disadvantages. To find a workable solution, the National Commission on Agriculture has proposed transitional arrangements under which a District Support Organization would be created in each district as a non-governmental or semi-governmental unit to provide support and guidance to the village councils. After three to five years—once these units are fully established—they could be merged with the secretariat of the District Councils. The initial recruitment and training of staff for such units would be handled by a provincial Institute of Rural Development, which would also produce video tapes and other development promotion materials for the use of the District Support Organizations. Such an institute would have to be created in each province, supported by the National Centre for Rural Development. The latter already exists but would have to be strengthened for this purpose.

The AKRSP is very staff-intensive, with a professional cadre of 86 persons who are provided higher salaries and better facilities than government staff. The total population of the Northern Areas is 0.75 million, or 0.75 per cent of the country's population. It will be difficult to replicate the AKRSP staff on the same scale and quality throughout the country. The proposed program of village councils will therefore have to be implemented gradually.

Increasing Local Financial and Administrative Responsibility

A second set of issues concerns the funding of local development activities. Rural populations, generally, expect the government to provide the required infrastructure and social services through public funds. They are often unable or unwilling to raise their own resources for such purposes. One of the most positive features of AKRSP is its savings scheme, under which the village organizations have mobilized total savings of Rs.14.5 million. This is about 12 per cent of the total financial outlays under the AKRSP in the first four years. Considering the difficulties of mobilizing financial resources in rural areas on a voluntary basis, the National Commission on Agriculture has recommended an alternative system. Under this system, the power of imposing and collecting land taxes on holdings of 50 acres and more would be delegated to the District Councils, which would retain 50 per cent of the total collected for their programs and transfer 25 per cent to Union Councils and 25 per cent to the proposed village councils. If adopted, this proposal will provide a strong stimulus to the formation and functioning of village councils.

Some difficulties might arise from local rivalries and traditional feuds within villages. The Northern Areas consist mainly of remote arid lands cultivated by small farmers or livestock holders. There are very few large landowners or feudal interests. It is quite possible that, in many irrigated areas, the influential landowners would not tolerate the creation of village councils to which they or the local officials would become accountable. It would require a great deal of social engineering to develop alternative leadership for a self-sustaining development process. In practice, the setting-up of local institutions should be attempted only when such leadership has become available.

Conclusion

It is relatively easy to implement the first phase of rural development by building physical infrastructure such as roads and electricity, and by providing facilities such as schools and health centers in rural areas. The second, more difficult task is building participatory rural institutions, without which the poorest segments of the rural population cannot really overcome the obstacles that confront them. There are some successful examples of grassroots institutions on a pilot scale, but these often depend for their success on the high-quality expertise and motivation of outside experts. It is hard to multiply such expertise on a sufficient scale for other project areas. The difficulties of extending the models attempted in pilot projects to the rest of the country are further compounded in countries with a multi-party political system. When democratic processes and institutions have matured and there is a pool of local leadership, it will become more feasible to build grassroots development institutions as a part of the political and administrative decentralization of the country.

In Pakistan, despite these difficulties, a viable approach has been identified and the process of setting up village-level councils is about to begin. It would be unrealistic to expect that the system will spring up throughout the country in a short time, but in the next five to seven years it should be possible to set up effective and functioning councils in at least half of the 30,000 villages that have a population of more than 500 people. At the same time, with the completion of infrastructure in most rural areas by 1990, it should be possible to accelerate the pace of agricultural diversification toward high-value-added sub-sectors like livestock and horticulture, which have greater backward and forward linkages as well as greater employment potential.

Thus the next phase of rural development in Pakistan will have two interrelated dimensions: 1) a sustained process of agricultural diversification to provide higher incomes and more job opportunities in rural areas; 2) the building of grassroots institutions to enable the rural poor to take advantage of these development opportunities. If this phase is successfully completed, the incidence of rural poverty in Pakistan should be much lower by the year 2000 than it is today.

Chapter 6

Agricultural Growth, Technological Progress, and Rural Poverty

Nurul Islam

How do the pace and the pattern of agricultural growth affect poverty? Are there ways in which an agricultural growth strategy can be designed to have a positive impact on poverty?

Theoretical and empirical analysis has led to divergent answers to these questions. Much depends on the nature of technological progress and its diffusion among different groups of farmers, on its impact on the growth of income and productivity, as well as on the initial conditions under which the growth process is initiated—particularly the distribution of assets, especially land. Frequently, access to land as well as to fixed and working capital for financing modern inputs is unequal, as is access to education, training, and research. For growth to reduce poverty and promote equity, the access to all of these factors must be widely diffused. In many countries, experience with the direct redistribution of assets, particularly land, and with public measures directing inputs or resources to poor farmers, has not been very promising. The political and administrative obstacles in the way of direct assaults on poverty are very substantial. This enhances the importance of the poverty-alleviating effects of the growth process itself. To the extent that the latter are positive, the need for a more direct redistribution of assets for poverty-alleviating measures may be less urgent.

In fact, it is advisable to pursue efforts on both fronts—that is, to a) maximize the so-called "trickle-down" effect of growth on poverty while b) undertaking direct poverty-alleviating measures. An appropriate balance between the two is needed so that, in the long run, direct

121

poverty-alleviating measures do not adversely affect the savings, investment, and technological progress that contribute to growth.

Direct Effects of Growth on Poverty

Technology

The biological and chemical innovations that have generated most of the rapid growth in Third World agriculture have been scale-neutral in terms of cost per unit. Technologically speaking, therefore, big farmers do not enjoy a differential advantage because of economies of scale. Mechanical innovations, however, have tended to be capital-using and labor-displacing, especially when incentive structures and macroeconomic policies lower the relative cost of capital below its opportunity costs—either because of a subsidized interest rate policy, or because of overvalued exchange rates (where capital equipment comes from abroad). This affects the poor adversely, since most of the poor are either wage-labor or sharecroppers.

Yet not *all* mechanization has a net adverse effect on employment. In some instances, mechanization reduces the time required for land preparation and harvesting, and it increases cropping intensity and hence labor requirements and employment. Even if labor input per unit of output declines, larger output increases the net volume of employment. This is apart from the indirect employment generation in the manufacture, maintenance, and repair of equipment.

The direct poverty-alleviating impact of technological progress depends on a) how far it spreads to the small farmers, sharecroppers, or tenants and b) how much it increases the employment of the rural poor. Empirical evidence to date confirms that technology *has* spread, though with a time lag, to the small farmers and sharecroppers, who are usually more risk-averse and hence wait until after the income-augmenting effects of new technology are well demonstrated. However, for the spread to occur, two obvious requirements are that high-yielding modern inputs be plentifully available and that infrastructure (i.e., a road and transportation system for the marketing and distribution of improved inputs as well as training, education, and extension facilities) likewise be widely available. Another matter of high priority is the development—through adaptive and region-specific research—of new technologies suitable for diverse agro-ecological conditions, (e.g., differing water, soil, and climatic conditions). In the past, technological progress has often been confined to principal cereals—for example, wheat, rice, maize—and to regions well endowed with irrigation potential and good quality soil, bypassing poor or rain-fed soils and so-called "inferior" crops such as sorghum, millet, and roots and tubers, etc. Yet the agro-ecologically disadvantaged regions are often very poor; poor farmers are also often found to be producing traditional crops that have scarcely benefited from yield-increasing technological innovations. In addition, in contrast to the high-yielding varieties of wheat and rice, those improved crop varieties that reduce dependence on purchased inputs generally facilitate easier access to new technology, and its faster adoption, by resource-poor small farmers with limited access to credit. Examples are drought-tolerant or pest- and disease-resistant crop varieties, short-maturing varieties that increase cropping intensity, and the biological fixation of nitrogen. These and similar technological innovations enable a rapid increase in the productivity and income of small farmers and thus tend to reduce the conflict between growth and equity and poverty alleviation.

Credit

How effectively do the poor participate in the market mechanism so that they can gain fully from the benefits of technological progress? Especially relevant in this context is the access of the poor farmers to the markets for credit, labor, inputs, and outputs.

Rural credit markets are inadequately developed, fragmented, and fraught with imperfections. Nor are there adequate institutions for the mobilization of rural savings, or profitable investment opportunities for such savings—due partly to lack of information or knowledge as well as of transport and communications infrastructure, and partly to the discriminatory pricing and exchange rate policies that depress returns to agricultural investment.

The risks and uncertainties of providing small farmers access to the credit market are frequently overestimated by private lenders; tenants, sharecroppers, and small farmers either lack secure title to land or do not own sufficient land to serve as collateral for loans. Furthermore, the transaction costs of dispensing and supervising small loans are very high, thus limiting the access of small cultivators to institutional sources of credit.

Delinking credit from the ownership of land as collateral has been tried in a very limited way; the uncertainties of crop failure on the one hand, and of price fluctuations on the other, increase the risk of default and constrain the supply of crop-based loans. Public measures designed to reduce, insure against, or compensate for the price fluctuations can lower the risks for credit institutions—but they involve budgetary costs. Similarly, public subsidy of credit agencies can offset the high costs of small loans—but likewise cost budget money. On the other hand, innovative credit schemes based on group lending or group guarantee by borrowers have contributed to the reduction of both the risks and administrative costs.

Experience to date indicates, however, that what is important is not a low or a subsidized rate of interest but access to an elastic supply of loanable funds. Small farmers have demonstrated their ability not only to pay high rates of interest but also to repay on time. What is needed is vigorous competition in the provision of credit through a multiplicity of lenders, both public and private. The credit market is often interlinked with the markets for land and for output; landowners and traders are frequently moneylenders. Different credit institutions developed through public initiative, growth of marketing intermediaries, and possible institutional change in the land structure—all of these will help increase competition in the credit market, delink the different factor markets, and widen opportunities for small farmers. No less important are legal procedures and institutions for the enforcement of contracts; their weaknesses have adversely affected the viability of credit institutions.

Markets for Outputs and Inputs

In the markets in which they sell and buy commodities, small farmers suffer from a relative disadvantage vis-à-vis big farmers. Often, small farmers with limited resources to hold stocks must sell immediately after harvest at a price lower than the annual average price or the price that prevails later in the year; they buy later in the year, when prices are higher, to meet their own consumption needs. In remote or distant regions, they either receive lower output prices, or pay higher prices for inputs because of high costs of transportation, marketing, and distribution. Furthermore, when inputs are in short supply and there are few suppliers—often public distribution agencies—small farmers are likely to lose out, since big farmers with higher status in the power structure have greater access to the public distribution system.[1] Hence what is necessary in a crucial sense is an abundant supply of inputs and credit, as well as a strengthened marketing system to expand and stabilize supplies over time, especially to meet the seasonal variations in requirements of inputs and credit.

Innovation, Employment, and Poverty

The impact of accelerated agricultural growth on rural labor through increased employment and/or an upward pressure on real wages depends on the pattern of growth, including the composition of output and the choice of techniques, as briefly mentioned earlier. In many developing countries, a high rate of growth in population, and therefore in the rural labor force, tends to exceed growth in employment opportunities. The labor market is frequently fragmented or imperfect, with the result that few employers, sometimes acting as both traders and/or creditors, can choose from among a large number of workers seeking employment. Frequently, wages are determined by convention, old habits, or family links. Big landowners often prefer to employ workers known personally to them, and about whose availability, especially at times of peak seasonal demand, they feel sure. Personal contacts and family links influence employment and wages, promote preferential treatment for those within rather than outside a village, and constrain inter-village mobility and employment opportunities, both short and long run. Two factors can help strengthen workers' participation in the market. First, education can improve the perception of alternative opportunities and encourage mobility of labor; it can also enhance awareness of workers' rights and help farmers to organize and build bargaining strength. Second, employment opportunities in the non-farm sector, including urban employment, improve the relative wages of rural labor.

Technological progress requires a careful husbanding and applica-tion of modern inputs and increases the use of labor in such operations as land preparation, transplanting, weeding and harvesting, etc. In many instances, small farmers, sharecroppers, or tenants make more intensive use of modern inputs, i.e., higher inputs of fertilizer, modern seeds, and water per acre than do large farmers, at least in the long run, and produce a greater output per acre—even though they fre-quently pay higher prices for inputs and high interest rates for credit. They maximize net returns (net of purchased inputs) per unit of land by driving down the marginal product of labor to a level at which the average income of the family (total product divided by numbers of family members) is adequate to provide an acceptable subsistence wage. Moreover, with tenants or sharecroppers competing for very scarce land, tenancy arrangements with landlords are likely to involve very intensive use of inputs, especially when the owners share a part of costs and sometimes also provide credit. Higher output per acre can compensate for higher per acre application of purchased inputs and still leave net income per acre at a level higher than that obtained on large farms.[2]

Technological progress in agriculture can have different employ-ment effects, depending on the size of the farms involved. From the point of view of very poor or landless laborers, employment oppor-tunities tend to be positively related to the share of middle or large farmers in the expansion of output; with increased income, these bet-ter-off farmers tend to reduce their own rate of participation in the labor force and to hire additional labor. Conversely, small farmers meet increased requirements for labor by working more hours themselves. Therefore the interests of small farmers and those of landless laborers without access to non-farm employment opportunities do not coincide.

The concentration of technological progress on small farms alone may not expand the wage-employment opportunities of the landless as much as if landowners, especially the middle farmers, also participate in technological progress. This may imply, however, that income distribution in fact worsens as the rich gain proportionally more than the poor, while the absolute còndition of the poor improves.

Indirect Effects of Growth on Poverty

Technological change in agriculture has indirect effects of two kinds on the alleviation of poverty. The first is the impact of technological change on the supply of food and on its relative price and, consequently, on real wages and employment in both the agricultural and non-agricultural sectors. The second is the multiplier effect on income and employment in the non-agricultural sectors set in motion by the increase in agricultural production and income. Both of these indirect effects are greater if the gainers in the first instance include many not-so-poor middle farmers. But the direct effect on poverty is greater if the beneficiaries in the first instance are exclusively the poor, especially the smallest farmers and landless laborers.

Growth Patterns, Food Supplies, and Prices

The effect of increased agricultural production on domestic food prices depends on how closed or open the economy is to international trade. In an open economy, domestic prices will be equal to world prices, whereas in a closed economy, variations in domestic production will affect the domestic price. In reality, the economies in developing countries are in an intermediate position; they are neither completely closed nor totally open to international trade. Domestic prices diverge from world prices due to tariffs and quantitative restrictions on exports and imports. For a commodity that is domestically produced and partly imported under tariffs, the domestic price is higher than the world price by the amount of the tariff. The domestic price falls when the shift in supply function or increase in productivity is large enough to cause domestic supply at the prevailing price to exceed domestic demand. The new domestic price, however, may remain at a level higher than the world price. There will still be no imports at that price; tariffs remain prohibitive. But with a further increase in productivity and a shift in the supply function, the domestic price may fall to the level of the world price, and the country may change from importer to exporter status.

The domestic price can be lower than the world price either because there is an export tax, the incidence of which falls fully or partially on the exporter, or because consumers pay subsidized prices that are implemented either through public procurement of domestic output at less than world prices or through subsidies on imports. With an export tax, an increase in productivity and a shift in the supply function would not affect the domestic price. In the second case, what happens to the domestic price depends on the government price policy: It can let prices fall below the previously fixed prices to match the reduction in cost while subsidies are maintained, or it can abolish subsidies, keeping prices unchanged. If the cost reduction is large enough, it can reduce both price and subsidies.

The higher the rate of growth in marketable surplus in relation to demand, the greater the decline in the relative price of food—insulated partially or fully from the world market. The magnitude of the marketable surplus depends not only on the rate of growth in food production, but also on how the increase in production is distributed among different categories of farmers. Medium and large farms have a higher ratio of marketable surplus to output than do small farms. If the increase in food output is generated largely by small farms, this will result in a small marketable surplus. Small farmers have high income elasticity of food demand; they may frequently have a larger family size and a greater dependency ratio. Accordingly, an increase in output on the small farms tends to be consumed by the farmers themselves. If, on the other hand, a substantial increase in food production is provided by a very few large producers, then the fall in price is likely to be so large as to discourage production and detract from the favorable effects on employment and income flowing from increased production by large farmers. This is because the market demand for food will be constrained in the absence of an adequate increase in income of the small farmers, who are far more numerous. There has, therefore, to be an appropriate balance in the distribution of increased output among the different categories of farmers so that a fall in price resulting from an increase in output is not so severe as to discourage production.

The indirect favorable impact on food prices is most likely to be realized if the increase in production takes place mainly among the middle and small farmers, but not *only* among small farmers. In many countries, governments intervene to stabilize farmers' prices or to support minimum prices through buffer stock operations. The politically vocal or organized large and middle farmers may exercise pressure to support prices at levels that allow farmers—especially big farmers—to reap excess profits from cost-reducing innovations rather than pass them on to the consumers. The optimum policy therefore calls for allowing prices to fall to an extent that maintains producers' incentives while conferring benefits on the net purchasers of food. Given the differential impact of technological progress on different categories of farmers, or different farm sizes, a steep decline in price may reduce the net income of the small farmers who, at least in the early stages of the diffusion of new technology, do not benefit, or do not benefit adequately, from cost-reducing innovations. Thus the price of progress may be that, initially, the pioneers or the early innovators earn excess profits.

Low food prices resulting from cost-reducing innovations directly improve the real income of the poor, who are the net purchasers of food.[3] By making available a large supply of the principal wage good—food—at a stable and low price, technological progress in food production facilitates the adoption of an employment-based development strategy, especially in the non-farm sector. Otherwise, as employment and income of the poor expand, given their high income elasticity of demand for food, a rapid increase in food demand is likely to put an upward pressure on food prices.

Furthermore, a fall in food prices improves the terms of trade of the non-farm, industrial sector and tends to lower wages in the non-farm sector and to encourage labor-intensive industrialization and the substitution of labor for capital in various processes and products. Thus food price declines also enhance the competitiveness of labor-intensive products in the world market and thus promote exports, which in turn adds further stimulus to the expansion of output and employment in the non-farm sector.

The role of marketing, distribution, and transaction costs in the movement of food from rural producers to urban consumers is crucial. An increase in such costs would offset the cheapening effects of technological progress on the relative price of food.

Intersectoral Linkages

Increased agricultural output and income have a multiplier effect on income and employment. There are certain linkages within the agricultural sector itself: For example, an expansion of income in staple food or cereal production leads to a higher percentage being spent on horticulture and livestock products. When carried out on small farms—as they are in many developing countries—these activities are labor-intensive and help expand employment and income of the poor.

An increase in agricultural production affects the rest of the economy via intersectoral linkages. On the one hand, it leads to increased demand for inputs such as fertilizers, pesticides, irrigation equipment, and other tools and implements; on the other hand, it stimulates demand for processing, marketing, and distribution of agricultural output. Empirical evidence suggests that the forward linkages (i.e., marketing, distribution, and processing, etc.) of agricultural products provide a much stronger linkage than the backward linkages (i.e., expanded use of production inputs). More important than the production linkages are the consumption linkages—stemming from the expenditure of incremental agricultural income on non-agricultural goods and services—produced in both rural and urban/semi-urban areas.[4] These linkages include the stimulation of not only a wide variety of manufactured consumer goods, but also trade and other services; they are frequently highly labor-intensive. The employment-creating role of small and cottage industries has received much attention. But the role of rural trade and services (which include housing, education, health, transportation, and personal services, etc.) as a source of employment and income for the poor has not been sufficiently recognized.

The growing demand for non-agricultural goods and services (upon which, of course, employment expansion depends) must originate primarily from agricultural growth, especially the expenditures of middle and large farmers who devote larger shares of their income gains to non-farm, labor-intensive goods and services. The expenditure patterns of very small farmers, who spend a higher proportion of incremental income on food than on non-food items, provide a weak intersectoral linkage. Wherever the middle farmers are numerous, their absolute aggregate expenditure on non-food items is often as great, if not greater than, the aggregate expenditures of a larger number of small farmers. Starting from this large base, the fact that middle farmers channel higher percentages of whatever increments on income they get into expenditures on non-food items provides a strong stimulus for the non-farm sector's output and employment. In Malaysia, a study in which the largest farm size covered was 15–20 hectares showed that middle farmers (defined as those from the fourth through the seventh deciles in terms of farm size) spent 63–66 per cent of their incremental income on non-farm goods and services in 1972–73. Of the non-farm goods, about three-fifths were produced locally and two-fifths came from outside the region. In Africa, the shares of incremental income that medium-size farmers spent on non-farm goods and services were lower, i.e., 24 per cent in 1976–77; those on locally produced goods and services were about 11 per cent. But the incremental income shares spent on livestock and horticultural products, which were also highly labor-intensive and locally produced, were higher—as high as 30 per cent. In Bangladesh, the shares spent by middle farmers on non-farm goods and services were about 25–30 per cent.

The expansion of the non-farm sector in the rural areas provides employment and income for the rural poor; this, in turn, creates additional demand for food as well as non-food commodities, thus setting in train successive rounds of income and employment expansion. In Malaysia, an increase of $10 in agricultural income was associated with an increase of $8 in rural non-farm income; in India, a 10-per-cent increase in agricultural employment was estimated to lead to a 10 to 13-per-cent increase in non-farm employment.[5]

However, the consumption expenditure patterns of the richest or largest farmers do not have strong positive interlinkages for income and employment expansion in the non-farm sector. First, the propensity of these farmers to spend on *imported* goods is high—constituting a leakage from the domestic multiplier effect. Second, the saving propensity of these farmers is also high and constitutes a leakage from the consumption expenditure stream. It is true, of course, that if these savings are invested in labor-intensive activities, whether rural or urban, they have positive employment effects. Nevertheless, the net leakages tend to be greater than in the case of the medium farmers, whose consumption patterns are more domestically oriented.

The demand pull provided by agricultural growth needs to be matched by an elastic supply response from the non-farm sector. A few preconditions need to be met if the rural non-farm sector is to respond strongly and positively to the stimulus provided by increased expenditures by the farm sector. Most important among these is the availability of physical infrastructure—a road and transport system, a communications system, rural credit to finance both current and investment costs of non-farm activities, as well as education, extension, and training relating to non-farm activities. The role of government policy in either directly providing—or stimulating the private sector to provide—these prerequisites is crucial.

Conclusion

Targeting rural technologies and public investments on small farms leads to immediate gains in equity and production—although not necessarily to gains for the landless or for marginal farmers, who cannot respond by expanding output. If the focus is exclusively on *small* farms, the indirect impact on growth in income and employment through the expenditure multiplier is not likely to be as high as it would be if the increase in production largely took place in the first instance on middle-size farms. Focus on *middle-size* farms, on the other hand, may have a high multiplier effect on growth, with a favorable impact on absolute poverty—but at the cost of worsening the relative distribution of rural incomes.

Therefore, there is a trade-off between growth and equity or poverty alleviation; a balance needs to be struck by targeting technology and investment on a broader range of farm-size groups, including *both* small and medium farms. The degree of absolute poverty initially, the relative distribution of farm sizes, and the urgency of immediate action to relieve poverty will all affect the appropriate policy choices.

Notes

[1] Mahabub Hossain, "Fertilizer Consumption, Pricing, and Foodgrain Production in Bangladesh," in Bruce Stone, ed., *Fertilizer Pricing Policy in Bangladesh* (Washington, D.C.: International Food Policy Research Institute and Bangladesh Institute of Development Studies, 1987).

[2] Michael Lipton and Richard Longhurst, "Labor and the MVs," and "Putting Together the MV-Poverty Mystery," in *Modern Varieties, International Agricultural Research, and the Poor,*" Consultative Group on International Agricultural Research, Study Paper No. 2 (Washington, D.C.: The World Bank, 1985), pp. 49–64 and 87–100.

[3] John W. Mellor and Gunvant M. Desai, "Agricultural Change and Rural Poverty: A Synthesis," in *Agricultural Change and Rural Poverty: Variations on a Theme by Dharm Narain* (Baltimore, Md.: The Johns Hopkins University Press, 1985), pp. 192–199; and John W. Mellor, "Food Price Policy and Income Distribution in Low-Income Countries," *Economic Development and Cultural Change*, Vol. 27, No. 1, October 1978, pp. 25–26.

[4] Steve Haggblade, Peter Hazell, and James Brown, "Farm/Non-Farm Linkages in Rural Sub-Saharan Africa: Empirical Evidence and Policy Implications" (unpublished discussion paper, Agricultural and Rural Development Department, The World Bank, May 1987), pp. 113–125; and Peter Hazell and Ailsa Roell, *Rural Growth Linkages: Household Expenditure and Patterns in Malaysia and Nigeria*, Research Report No. 41 (Washington, D.C.: International Food Policy Research Institute, September 1983), p. 12.

[5] Hazell and Roell, ibid., p. 12; Steve Haggblade et al., ibid., pp. 113–125.

Chapter 7

What is Not the Same About the Urban Poor: The Case of Mexico City

Sheldon Annis

How Aid Donors Think About Urban Poverty

Few changes on the global landscape have been as dramatic or socially far-reaching as Third World urbanization. In 1950, when the largest city in the world was New York, six of the world's ten largest cities were located in Europe and the United States. But since then, Third World cities have been growing approximately three times faster than those in the industrial world.[1] By the turn of the century (when for the first time in human history half the world's population will be urban), 18 of the world's 21 largest cities will be located in the Third World.[2] At this rate, the Third World will absorb nine-tenths of all global urban growth over the next 30 years.[3]

As the world's population becomes proportionately more urban— and as the urban population becomes proportionately more Third World—poverty, too, is urbanizing. Third World cities themselves are growing very fast, but squatter settlements, shanty towns, and low-income neighborhoods *within cities* are growing about twice as fast.[4] In the very poorest countries, such as Haiti and Burundi, as many as half of all city dwellers live in absolute poverty; in India, about 40 per cent; and in less poor countries such as Morocco or the Philippines, about 30 per cent.[5]

Note: The author wishes to express special thanks to the Inter-American Foundation, the World Bank, and The Ford Foundation for their support of the research on which this essay draws.

Curiously, despite the accelerating growth of Third World cities—and the poverty that grows with them—the trends of aid donors have not followed the demographics. As John Lewis points out in the overview essay of this volume, the "populist aid doctrine" of the 1970s has steadfastly held to a "pro-rural tilt." Overall, only about 8 per cent of all multilateral and bilateral development assistance is explicitly directed to urban problems.[6] The urban and housing program of the U.S. Agency for International Development (USAID) spends $200–300 million per year worldwide out of its $2–3 billion budget.[7] The World Bank—whose urban poverty lending has averaged about 3.5 per cent of total lending in recent years—has recently re-merged its infrastructure, water, and urban departments, signaling reluctance to treat "urban" as a stand-alone poverty problem.[8] The Inter-American Development Bank only recently *formed* an urban planning unit—in a sense, just catching up to where AID and the World Bank were 15 years ago. Indeed, if dollars from donors define "strengthening the poor," then it is hardly accidental or a matter of editorial bias that most of the chapters of this volume focus on rural themes.

There are four nominal reasons—and one much more fundamental reason—why development donors are likely to hold to their pro-rural course in the 1990s.

First, although an increasing proportion of the poor are urban or urbanizing, a majority of the very poorest people remain rural.[9] Poor though they are, in most countries the urban poor still are relatively privileged compared to their rural counterparts.

Second, even if donors are rural-biased, national development policies are generally urban-biased. It is not uncommon for Third World countries that are 60–70 per cent rural to allocate about 70–80 per cent of their budgets to urban sectors.[10] So donor bias is, at best, only a corrective.

Third, the concept of urban poverty alleviation carries with it a built-in paradox: "Solving" the problem makes it worse. Migrants are attracted to opportunity, and making life better in the city attracts more migrants; therefore, most donors would argue, the best way to help both countryside and city is to make life better for the rural poor.[11]

Fourth, in the 1980s donors have come to view most of the common prescriptions of the 1970s—particularly prescriptions that the poor themselves generally favor—as problems in their own right. Yesterday's solutions are today cast pejoratively as "subsidies" for food, housing, education, fuel, and transportation. Such subsidies are almost invariably seen as fiscal "black holes" that are politically manipulated and disproportionately appropriated by the non-poor.

This fourth reason suggests a fifth, even more basic reason: Namely, the best urban ideas from the populist era have not worked very well. Quite honestly, no one who knows the turf well knows what to do, leading to a kind of intellectual agnosticism that weighs heavily against boldness. Today's urban technicians are generally to be found pondering a set of project options that—they believe—range from those that flatly make matters worse, to those that merely do not work very well, to those that work under restricted conditions but cannot realistically be financed or implemented on a wide scale.[12]

Take, for example, the case of housing. Since the most buoyant days of the Alliance for Progress, when John Kennedy encountered tens of thousands of people in the streets of Latin American cities, and later, when Robert McNamara was met by hundreds of thousands of street dwellers in Calcutta, development donors have wanted to help build decent, affordable houses for the poor. Yet in the end, every round of publicly supported house-building has proved to be "too expensive"— even with genuine innovation in technology, materials, financing, and institutional support.[13] Even with self-help, mutual help, sites and services, progressive slum upgrading, institution-building, and wholesaling rather than retailing, the simple truth seems inescapable: Even *if* we could assume honesty, bureaucratic efficiency, good use of technology, and community participation, no system of state-sponsored housing can keep pace with—let alone gain ground upon—cities that grow 3–5 per cent in size year after year.[14] The problem is that in housing in particular, but in urban projects generally, donor resources and existing project instruments so thoroughly "underwhelm" the needs of cities as to be trivial by all but the kindest or most self-serving of standards.

Given this ambiguous state of the art, what are donors left to think about urban poverty alleviation? Where next? For that matter, what now?

The Policy Content of Urban Poverty Projects: Who Is Asking?

For most of the past two decades, urban poverty lending has been a two-sided debate between governments and donors. In staging this debate, donors have always believed that the policy content of their lending was more important than the actual amounts of dollars transferred. No one disagrees that good projects nested within bad policies are exercises in futility; so, in large measure, the contemporary debate focuses on what precisely constitutes "good policies." How are the needs of the urban poor balanced against the needs of the rural poor, the requirements of growth, the constraints of austerity? If one could listen in on this "policy dialogue," the kinds of urban poverty questions that one would surely hear being debated between donors and governments are: Can cheap urban food be sustained, and if so, at whose expense? How can tax systems be constructed to pay for urban services? How can minimum wages be set that simultaneously protect the poor and slow inflation? Who receives the benefits of physical infrastructure? Who pays for it? Where in metropolitan areas should the poor be housed? To what extent can open admissions and free tuition be maintained in public universities that serve the poor? Are rent control policies good or bad for the poor? What scale of industrial investment best generates jobs for low-income workers?[15]

In most respects, these "new" policy questions are, I believe, the right ones. But even so, the coming decade may hold some major shifts in thinking about urban poverty. For what may change is not so much the questions as the discussants.

The key assertion of this essay is that the urban poor are becoming increasingly effective and aggressive interlocutors in their own behalf. An indirect "trialogue"—involving not only donors and governments, but also the organized poor—may increasingly challenge the assumption of "dialogue." In the 1990s, we may find ourselves spending considerably less time asking whether we know the right questions and shift our attention to a more profound issue: Who is asking, and even more important, who is deciding?

To illustrate how and why this is so, I here describe the milieu of Mexico City—which may offer a glimpse into Latin America's (if not necessarily the Third World's) urban future.

Urban Growth and Popular Organizations in Mexico City

By the turn of the century—only a decade from now—roughly three-fourths of more than half a billion Latin Americans will live in cities.[16] Latin America will be as urbanized as North America, Europe, East Asia, or the Soviet Union.[17] The world's two largest megacities—by a considerable margin—will be Mexico City, with a projected 26.3-million population by the year 2000, and São Paulo, with a projected 24.0 million.[18]

In Mexico City, which has been incorporating a half a million new people a year since the mid-1970s, the pace and scale of urbanization defies comprehension. There are newly sprouted areas *within* Mexico City that, by themselves, are larger than all but the very largest North American cities—for example, the city-within-a-city, Netzalhualcoytl. In the 1950s, "Netza" was an inhospitable, dried-up lake bed, with a population of a few thousand squatters. Today it is a teeming urban zone of nearly 3 million inhabitants—only slightly less populous than Los Angeles or Chicago and more than twice the size of Detroit or Dallas.[19]

How, one might well ask, can an unplanned urban agglomeration such as Netza mushroom from virtually zero to nearly 3 million in about the time that a single individual grows to adulthood? What social, physical, economic, and political processes turn so much rocky lake bed into so many houses, roads, postal routes, water lines, jobs, and school districts?

It has now become commonplace to respond that this vast *ad hoc* urbanization is carried out "by the people."[20] In Mexico, it is certainly incorrect to say that this urbanization is carried out "by the state" (much less by the formal construction industry); but, on the other hand, the by-the-people argument can easily be overstated to underplay the state's direct participation in the process.

First, the vast "self-built" city does not refer to a sea of carton shacks and sheet-metal hovels like those of Lima, Guayaquil, or Lagos.[21] Neither does it suggest highly self-sufficient efforts at mutual help, led by non-governmental organizations, in which neighborhood construction crews have cooperatively built each others' homes after work and on weekends.

The actual situation is more complicated. Over the past twenty years, most poor Mexico City neighborhoods have been built by individual homeowners who purchased (extralegally) rather than squatted (illegally) upon property at the edge of the central city. These families toil year after year to upgrade the value and quality of their living space. They struggle with lawyers and the bureaucracies to legalize their property titles. Working as fast as the availability of cash and family labor permits, they proceed wall by wall, room by room. Occasionally they benefit from cooperative labor arrangements; sometimes they contract commercial builders; more often they purchase materials and services from within the informal sector. When looking down upon a typical poor neighborhood from, say, the rim of the valley surrounding the megacity, one sees tens of thousands of iron reinforcement rods sticking out of concrete posts. It is as if each new surface remained unfinished—each piece like a child's Lego blocks, laying a pattern for the next (and next and next) piece to be added.[22]

No family can provide everything that goes along with a house. As families manage household construction, neighborhood groups form, reform, hybridize, and affiliate with non-neighborhood groups in order to reach out to the public sector for water, sewers, electricity, garbage removal, pavement, schools, teachers, health posts, mail service, phones, buses, parks, municipal markets, and police protection.

In Mexico, this process not only encourages but *demands* organization. What is needed is a years-long effort in which individuals within constantly shifting alliances make contacts, learn the ropes, ask, barter, and demand services from various extensions of the public sector. For its part, the state's ability to grant or deny these requests in exchange for loyalty is one cornerstone of the PRI's sixty years of political control.[23]

The hundreds of millions of individual actions, collective actions, and transactions with the state add up to create the urban fabric. One result is new neighborhoods, and these inevitably merge together to make up new zones of the Lego-like city under construction. But to see *just* the physical result would be to seriously misread the essence of the process; for, as described below, there is also a newly created social, political, and cultural fabric that is as new as the massive sprouting of neighborhoods.

The Urban Popular Movement and the Politics of Housing

Over the past two decades, corresponding to the physical "massification"[24] of the megacity, an intricate web of organizations, activists, and neighborhood institutions has evolved that corresponds to the new physical webs. This social web is thick, centerless, and has no simple point of origin. Its intertwined strands wind back not just to the neighborhoods, but to opposition political parties, the PRI, the public sector, the Catholic Church, the universities, foundations, charities, and foreign private voluntary organizations.

The descriptive term used in Mexico—and elsewhere in urbanizing Latin American cities[25]—to describe this phenomenon is the "urban popular movement" (*movimiento urbano popular*, or MUP). The term is generally used generically—as in "civil rights movement" or "labor movement."[26] It is a movement that has no single leader, no unified ideology, and no agreed-upon plan for political action (although many individuals and organizations energetically seek to provide that).

The Mexican urban popular movement is generally described as having its geographic roots in the industrial and border cities of the country's north.[27] Its political roots are in the *aperatura democrática*, the "democratic opening" in which the administration of Luis Echeverría (1970–76) sought to relegitimize the PRI after the violent repression of the student movement in 1968. In particular, Echeverría recognized the volatility of the outlying settlements. His "populist" administration devoted considerable political and technical resources to the rapidly growing population of urban poor, creating government agencies to increase the housing stock and to legalize property titles.

Throughout the 1970s, many student and leftist activists also turned their energies to organizing the urban poor.[28] As the enrollment of the National University (UNAM) shot up in the late 1960s and

1970s, an increasing proportion of students came from the poor and urban middle class. They had family roots in the *barrios*, technical skills, political commitment, and practical knowledge.[29] Meanwhile, labor bosses generally controlled the new, state-generated housing, and local PRI leaders manipulated the legalization of land titling and provision of utilities.[30] An intensely bitter competition developed between the state and the party on the one hand, and the students and independent political parties on the other—with neighborhood people shrewdly playing all options while constantly complaining about the sellouts and false promises of the various *semicaudillistas* who represented them.

President José López Portillo (1976–82)—like his predecessor—tried to reassert control over the increasingly unruly urban popular movement. He created his own plethora of government-sponsored, barrio-level community organizations; centralized the existing array of urban agencies; launched ambitious new attempts at city planning; and in 1981 created Fondo Nacional de Habitaciones Populares (FONHAPO), a low-income housing authority with substantial financing from the World Bank.[31]

FONHAPO represented a curious blending of the government's standard approach to housing (i.e., providing low-cost, highly subsidized finished units to those who knew how to ask), the World Bank's ideas on progressive slum upgrading,[32] and the know-how of key activists from the Mexican urban NGO community[33] on how to provide low-cost housing.

In essence, FONHAPO created, and then enlarged, a second financing "window" within the public housing programs of Mexico. The established window was largely allocated to state and municipal employees, labor organizations, and politically important subgroups. The new "social sector" window opened up credit to barrio associations, cooperatives, and community groups.[34]

Looked at from the community point of view, the differences between the public and social sector approaches were night and day. Practically, FONHAPO transferred considerable power to local groups by allowing them to solicit their own credit, participate in design, select their own technical assistance, and contract directly for construction services (thus circumventing a major source of graft and shoddy construction).

FONHAPO was almost immediately flooded by requests for local projects, ensnared in partisan politics, besieged by the old guard, tangled by bureaucracy, confronted with technical limitations, and frustrated by community organizations that were more adept at political maneuvering than at actually building houses. One would not wish to overstate the degree to which FONHAPO actually reformed the public sector's approach to low-cost housing.[35] Nevertheless, at a minimum it created a powerful new housing model and deepened the incentives for local people to become better organized.

Frequently, groups that were unsuccessful at obtaining concrete goals such as FONHAPO loans quickly disappeared. But perhaps more often, the "social energy" of failed efforts was "transformed and mutated"[36] into new organizations and larger collective actions. By the early 1980s, federations of urban popular organizations became increasingly effective in taking on larger city-wide issues—for example, organized resistance to forced relocations due to road construction or unified opposition to cutbacks in food, transportation, and education subsidies.[37] In 1981, the generic urban popular movement (or rather, a part of it) formalized as CONAMUP, a confederation of urban activist organizations. CONAMUP itself became one of several *coordinadoras* that make up the Mexican independent (i.e., non-PRI) left.[38]

The Earthquake and its Organizational Aftermath

On September 19 and 20, 1985, two fierce earthquakes struck the central zone of Mexico City. Approximately 2 million people—living in 300,000 housing units—reside in the *colonias* affected by the earthquake. Government figures put the death toll at 5,000 and estimated that 40,000 people were injured and 350,000 people were left homeless.[39]

The public visibility and political force of the urban popular movement was frequently said to be waning in the mid-1980s.[40] But by all accounts, it came alive after the earthquake. Within a day or two, organizations throughout the affected areas mobilized to prevent landlords and government officials from using the disaster to evict low-income tenants. Refusing government attempts to disperse them to relocation sites,[41] they camped out by their damaged or destroyed homes, and demanded that the government provide adequate temporary shelters that did not require separation from neighborhoods.

With astonishing speed and political acumen, a vast coalition of *damnificados* (earthquake victims) united to bring pressure to bear.[42] As a direct result, on October 11, 1985, the first of several presidential decrees was issued that led to the expropriation of over 4,000 damaged lots in 70 central city neighborhoods. Reconstruction funds were allocated by the World Bank—in large measure through institutional links created by FONHAPO—to finance a program known as Renovación Habitacional Popular.

The Coordinadora Unica de Damnificados (CUD) unified scores of neighborhood organizations. By refusing to bargain separately, by legal maneuvering, and with deft manipulation of the media, the organized earthquake victims were successful in wresting innumerable concessions from the government—and then maintained unrelenting pressure to force compliance with what was promised. In May 1986, an extraordinary event occurred: the signing of a Concertación Democrática—a kind of "social pact" in which the president of Mexico and the heads of virtually all relevant government agencies formally agreed to a set of reconstruction ground rules laid out by CUD, the barrio groups, foreign funders, university groups, and local housing NGOs.[43] This agreement became the essential blueprint that was actually carried out by the World Bank-financed reconstruction program.[44] Whenever the government dragged its feet, pressure was applied. In May 1986, for example, CUD announced that tens of thousands of still-homeless earthquake victims would link hands around Aztec Stadium during the internationally televised World Cup Soccer championship. This was called off at the last minute as a crash construction program begun in April began to show visible results.

In light of the construction of nearly 50,000 units and major repair of another 40,000 units[45]—more or less on time and approximately within budget—the Mexican government, the Bank, and the urban popular movement have each proudly proclaimed "their" success in the reconstruction effort. Whichever combination of versions and credits one chooses to accept, it is undeniable that when compared to the post-earthquake reconstruction in Managua in 1972 or Guatemala City in 1976, Mexico managed to build rapidly a remarkable number of reasonably low-priced units that were not giveaways[46] and did not ride roughshod over the preexisting character of the city.

Yet while the government is now pleased to discuss the success of its reconstruction program (especially in light of an ongoing presidential election campaign), the barrio associations are far from satisfied. They angrily point out that the government's housing program has touched only the tip of the "damnificado problem." From their point of view, the reconstruction program, at best, has simply brought the low-cost housing effort back to the starting line. What about the situation *before* the earthquake? What about legal protection for renters facing evictions? What about enforcement of housing codes? What about expropriating abandoned property and non-taxpaying properties for building sites?[47] What about new credit to renters and property owners willing to renovate rental units? What about an agency-by-agency review of all government housing to see who is building what for whom and at what cost? What about rewriting of building codes, property tax laws, and regulations governing landlord-tenant-state relationships? What about the creation, on the periphery of the city, of new "territorial reserves" upon which to build new low-cost housing?

Not surprisingly, the Coordinadora Unica de Damnificados has declined as a political force as increasing numbers of earthquake victims have been re-housed. But at the same time, a new configuration of associations[48] has reformed and is aggressively pressing the post-earthquake agenda.

The "leader" of the post-earthquake movement is Superbarrio, a Robin Hood-like *lucha libre*[49] wrestler whose true identity is unknown (and unimportant). Dressed in his yellow tights, red cape, and SB-emblazoned superhero wrestler's mask, Superbarrio seems to appear everywhere at once ("where the people are struggling, there I am . . . where there is injustice, . . ." etc.).

Superbarrio's sworn adversary is the bureaucracy, the greedy land-lord, the political boss, and the state. He leads street protests of tens of thousands of people; and because he loses his superstrength when cut off from the sight of the people, he forces the bureaucracy to negotiate on the street (in front of television cameras and reporters) and stead-fastly refuses to negotiate in more dignified closed-door sessions.

The Mexican press, naturally, loves Superbarrio and avidly follows his every move. In August 1987, for example, when Superbarrio an-nounced he would wrestle his archenemy Catalino Creel[50] in front of the National Cathedral, the government angrily rejected the unseemly location for a wrestling match. The government's willingness to allow the match (and if so, where) became an issue for negotiation and the subject of innumerable political lampoons. Agreement was finally reached to hold the match behind the Cathedral. However, in the wee dawn hours before the match, the ring was stolen—prompting taunts, accusations of fraud, government theft, and new waves of street protest.

By creating a media hero who symbolizes the *lucha*—or strug-gle—of the poor and is squared off against the government, the barrio associations have managed to create considerable excitement and a "cause" that partially substitutes for the momentum lost after the earthquake period. In some respects, the good-humored, unpredictable Superbarrio brings to mind the Yippie tactics of the 1960s American protest movement. But even more so, he is a figure in the most ag-gressive, highly confrontational, direct-action organizing tradition of Saul Alinsky. Superbarrio breaks all the established rules of negotia-tion (and gets farther as a result), cleverly uses the media, creatively applies public anger and humor, and generally refuses (with 10,000 or so observers behind him) to take no for an answer and go away.

Because of his capacity to embarrass the government, Superbarrio negotiates and commands reluctant attention at the highest levels.[51] Meanwhile, the barrio organizations have forced concessions and put on the table an enormous range of sensitive issues that are at the very heart of the future urban policy debate.

At the moment, Superbarrio is energetically running for presi-dent; but in a year or so, he will doubtless retire. The point is not

Superbarrio, but *organization itself*. In the constantly changing Mexican urban movement, individual organizations rise and die and new organizations rise, phoenix-like, from their ashes. What is more permanent is a still-amorphous but nonetheless very real bartering structure through which the poor can independently engage the state.

Mexico City as a Glimpse into the Future

Returning now to this essay's central question—"What is not the same about the urban poor?" and, more specifically, "Are there new ways for donors to think about urban poverty?"—one can certainly argue that Superbarrio has done more for the interests of the Mexican urban poor than have many roomfuls of World Bankers with the best of poverty-oriented sensibilities.[52] Yet even if this is so, the case of Mexico City need not necessarily preview the future of other Latin American cities—much less the future of non-Latin American cities, or of the rural poor.

Certainly social movements that rise in cities are nothing new on Latin America's landscape. But, on the other hand, the tendency to respond "plus ça change, plus c'est la même chose" may cause us to overlook something that *is* genuinely new: the *scale* of mobilization among the urban poor, the *magnitude* of social energy that it has captured, and the *certainty* that the poor will increasingly be negotiating in their own behalf.

As discussed at the outset of this essay, development donors are looking for new ways to renew poverty lending. In thinking about cities, they are perhaps at a watershed, genuinely baffled about what to do. One "new approach" propounded by virtually all donors is an "expanded role" for non-governmental organizations. But role to do what? By whom?

Development donors could take a giant conceptual step forward if they troubled themselves less about what that role could or should be and started paying considerably more attention to what that role actually is. Even though donors do not yet find themselves in forehead-to-forehead negotiation with urban popular movements, they are nonetheless indirectly confronting new configurations of political forces and significant social reorganizations. Largely through politics, the poor are entering the "policy dialogue" uninvited; and as a result, the character of poverty lending is sure to change as the 1990s unfold. In part, donors need new sociological understanding; in part they need practical skills to act upon what they learn; and in part, they need to prepare themselves to be pushed far harder than they have been in the past. That is the lesson of Mexico City.

Notes

[1] The annual urban growth rate of the Third World is approximately 3.5 per cent per year. See Rafael Salas, *The State of World Population 1986* (New York: United Nations Fund for Population Activities, 1986), p. 2. For urban growth rates of individual countries and regions, see *World Development Report 1987*, Table 33, p. 266 (Washington, D.C.: The World Bank, 1987).

[2] United Nations, Department of International Economic and Social Affairs, *Estimates and Projections of Urban, Rural and City Populations 1950–2025* (New York: United Nations, 1985), p. 147.

[3] Salas, op. cit., p. 39.

[4] Janice E. Perlman, "Megacities and Innovative Technologies," *Cities* (May 1987), p. 129.

[5] UNICEF estimates that in the very poorest countries (which are ranked and classified according to mortality rates of children under the age of five years), 35 per cent of the urban population, in contrast to 65 per cent of the rural population, lives below the absolute poverty level. In slightly less poor countries, the average urban rate is 30 per cent, in contrast to 45 per cent in rural areas. *The State of the World's Children 1988* (New York: Oxford University Press for UNICEF, 1988), Table 6, pp. 74–75.

[6] Perlman, op. cit., p. 130. The emphasis here is on the word "explicitly." Obviously, much non-targeted, non-urban aid also affects urban people.

[7] Inclusion of $3.2 billion in Economic Support Funds would bring AID's total budget to $6.1 billion (FY1987). To put urban expenditures into better perspective: AID's housing guarantee program (its main Third World urban activity) totaled about $147 million worldwide, which is roughly equivalent, for example, to what private developers spent to renovate the rundown Willard Hotel in downtown Washington, D.C.

[8] "IBRD and IDA Cumulative Lending Operations by Major Purpose and Region, June 30, 1987," *The World Bank Annual Report, 1987*, p. 158.

[9] An excellent discussion of the relative trends in rural and urban poverty is to be found in "Human Settlements," *World Resources 1987*, (New York: Basic Books for World Resources Institute and International Institute for Environment and Development, 1987), pp. 25–38.

[10] For discussions of urban bias in national development projects, see, for example, Michael P. Todaro and Jerry Stilkind, *City Bias and Rural Neglect: The Dilemma of Urban Development* (New York: The Population Council, 1981); Judith Tendler, *Rural Projects Through Urban Eyes: An Interpretation of the World Bank's New-Style Integrated Rural Development Projects*, Staff Working Paper No. 532 (Washington: The World Bank, 1982); and Michael Lipton, "Urban Bias and Food Policy in Poor Countries," *Food Policy*, November 1975 (see Costa Rican case study, for example).

[11] Governments throughout the Third World have experimented widely with measures to stem cityward migration—through closed city policies, dispersion policies, and rural or regional development policies. These measures have generally been most aggressive in centrally planned economies (in Cuba, for example). While migration flows have in some cases been at least partially controlled, reviews of the literature generally confirm that these measures have had little overall success in slowing the growth of primate cities. See, for example, Janice Perlman and Bruce Schearer, "Migration and Population Trends and Policies and the Urban Future" (paper presented at the U.N. Fund for Population Activities (UNFPA) International Conference on Population and the Urban Future, Barcelona, Spain, May 1986).

[12] Many colleagues may strongly disagree with this grim assessment of the state of the art. My conclusion is based on interviews with urban development workers, personal experience, and a review of recent documents. The general conclusion is also reinforced, I believe, by the recent work of the World Bank Urban Poverty Task Force (unpublished memos, 1987). On a more positive note, great institutional enthusiasm currently exists for the notion that the informal sector is an underharnessed alternative "engine" for urban growth. That idea ranges well beyond the scope of the present paper; however, I concur with Portes, Castells, and Benton, who find many of these wishful claims to be sociologically naive, ideologically motivated, and thoroughly untested by empirical data. (Alejandro Portes, Manuel Castells, and Lauren Benton, eds., *The Informal Economy: Studies in Advanced and Less Developed Countries* (Baltimore, Md.: Johns Hopkins University Press, forthcoming).

[13] See Michael Cohen, "The Challenge of Replicability: Towards a New Paradigm for Urban Shelter in Developing Countries," *Regional Development Dialogue*, Vol. 4, No. 1 (1983); Stephen K. Mayo and David J. Gross, "Sites and Services—and Subsidies: The Economics of Low-Cost Housing in Developing Countries," *The World Bank Economic Review*, Vol. 1, No. 2 (January 1987); Johannes F. Linn, "Urban Housing: Land, Services,

and Shelter," in *Cities in the Developing World: Policies for their Equitable and Efficient Growth*, (Oxford and New York: Oxford University Press for the World Bank, 1983).

[14] The point I wish to emphasize here is not that public institutions do not know how to build houses (they do), but that they do not know how to build houses in a fiscally sustainable manner faster than the poor's growing need for houses.

[15] Two especially useful summaries of urban policy issues are George Tolley and Vinod Thomas, eds., *The Economics of Urbanization and Urban Policies in Developing Countries* (Washington, D.C.: The World Bank, 1987) and Johannes F. Linn, *Cities in the Developing World: Policies for their Equitable and Efficient Growth*, (Oxford and New York: Oxford University Press for the World Bank, 1983).

[16] Ricardo Jordan, "Population and the Planning of Large Cities in Latin America" (paper presented at the International Conference on Population and the Urban Future, sponsored by UNFPA, Barcelona, Spain, May 19–22, 1986; cited in Brown and Jacobson, op. cit.).

[17] By the turn of the century Latin America is projected to be 77 per cent urban. North America will be 78 per cent urban; Europe, 79 per cent; East Asia, 79 per cent; and the Soviet Union, 74 per cent. In contrast, China will be 40 per cent urban; Africa, 42 per cent; and South Asia, 35 per cent). Carl Haub, *1986 World Population Data Sheet* (Population Reference Bureau), cited in Brown and Jacobson, op. cit., p. 40.

[18] *Estimates and Projections of Urban, Rural and City Populations, 1950–2025*, op. cit.

[19] The comparison is city to city, not including suburbs. For brief descriptions of the growth of Netzahualcoyotl, see Carlos Velez-Ibanez, *Rituals of Marginality: Politics, Process, and Culture Change in Central Urban Mexico, 1969–1974* (Berkeley, Calif.: University of California Press, 1983), pp. 31–38.

[20] The by-the-people argument is enunciated most powerfully in J.F. Turner's two well-known books, *Freedom to Build* (with Robert Fichter) (New York: Macmillan, 1972) and *Housing by People* (New York: Pantheon Books, 1976) and the many writers that have expanded upon his fundamental insights. See, for example, John Friedman, "The Right to the City," in *Development Dialogue*, Vol. 1 (Uppsala, Sweden: The Dag Hammarskjold Centre, 1987).

[21] In 1985–86, Mexico City gained considerable notoriety in the international press for the large number of people living in makeshift burrows in a hillside garbage dump. The earthquake of 1985 also, literally, blew the lid off abysmal housing conditions—for example, the scores of families who were revealed to be squatting in abandoned warehouses; and the *azoteros*, primarily maids and service employees living camped out on the roofs of the government-owned Tlateloco housing project, renting the government-owned space from their middle-class bosses. Nevertheless, in fairness such conditions are not the norm in Mexico City. The seas of tin and tarpaper shacks of Lima, La Paz, Guayaquil, or Guatemala City are, for the most part, the exception rather than the rule in Mexico City.

[22] "Legal" occupation means the residential property is fully in compliance with building and zoning codes, and the property purchase was duly recorded and taxed. "Illegal" occupation means that squatters found an empty spot and moved in; someone else owns the property; it probably meets no health or public safety codes; it does not meet zoning or construction regulations; it is not taxed or legally served by municipal services. "Extralegal" occupation—by far the more common case—does not imply legal defiance or assume the risk of forceful eviction. The property was purchased from somebody who bought it from somebody else who probably did not have full legal right to sell it (most commonly, urbanized, former communally owned *ejido* land on the outskirts of the city, often purchased by speculators and sold quickly in small plots). The title and property boundaries may be obscure. The building may violate several codes and owe back taxes (yet it would not be torn down as a result). More than one party may claim the property. Legal adjudication may be necessary to clarify ownership for sale or inheritance, establish a basis for taxation, or clear the way for installation of services. Building a well-served, secure home that will be fully saleable in the future (the less legal, the less the house is likely to be worth on the market) is not just a physical process; it involves paperwork, lawyers, visits to officials, much waiting, and the ability to pull strings. It is commonly estimated that about 60 per cent of Mexico City property is in some ways "extralegal."

[23] The ruling party in Mexico—the Partido Revolucionario Institucional—is known everywhere as "the PRI." For a good discussion of the politics of low-income housing in Mexico City, Bogota, and Valencia (Venezuela), see Alan Gilbert and Peter Ward, *Housing, the State and the Poor: Policy and Practice in Three Latin American Cities* (Cambridge: Cambridge University Press, 1985); and Gilbert and Ward, "Community Participation in Upgrading Irregular Settlements: The Community Response," *World Development*, Vol. 12, No. 9 (September 1984), pp. 913–922.

[24] The English translation "massification" is borrowed here from the Mexican journalist/urbanist, Angel Mercado, who has articulately explored the social-cultural dimensions of massificacion. See, for example, "Las Masas, Protagonistas del Futuro," *La Jornada* (April 10, 1985), p. 15.

[25] For articles on urban popular movements in Brazil and Chile, see Scott Mainwaring, "Urban Popular Movements, Identity, and Democratization in Brazil," *Comparative Political Studies*, Vol. 20, No. 2 (July 1987), pp. 131–159; Alexandrina Sobreira de Moura, "Brasilia Teimosa: The Organization of Low-income Settlement in Recife, Brazil," *Development Dialogue*, Vol. 1 (1987), pp. 152–129; Renato R. Boschi, "Social Movements and New Political Order in Brazil," in John D. Wirth, Edson de Oliveira Nunes, and Thomas E. Bogenschild, eds., *State and Society in Brazil: Continuity and Change* (Boulder, Colo.: Westview Press, 1987), pp. 179–212; and Fernando Kusentzoff, "Urban and Housing Policies under Chile's Military Dictatorship, 1973–1985," *Latin American Perspectives*, Vol. 14, No. 2 (Spring 1987), pp. 157–186.

[26] In contrast to the generic term "MUP," the term "CONAMUP" (Confederación de los Movimientos Urbanos Populares), as described below, refers to a formal membership organization. One researcher/activist interviewed for this study estimates that about 2 million people nationwide consider themselves part of MUP. He estimates that about 700,000–800,000 persons in Mexico City consider themselves part of MUP, including about 70,000 "core activists," whose participation transcends the neighborhood groups. CONAMUP is another matter; Ramirez estimates that in 1986 it had 100,000 member families—mostly in Mexico City, the northern states, and Oaxaca. Juan Manuel Ramirez Saíz, "Asentamientos Populares y Movilización Social," *El Día*, Special Supplement (June 1987), p. 22.

[27] The Monterrey "Tierra y Libertad" land invasions of the early-to-mid-1970s. See Manuel Castells, *The City and the Grassroots* (Berkeley, Calif.: University of California Press, 1983), p. 197; and Pedro Moctezuma, "Apuntes sobre la Política Urbana y el Movimiento Popular en México," *Sociológica*, Vol. 2, No. 4 (Summer 1987), pp. 133–142.

[28] Javier Farrera, Efren Rodriguez, and Gloria Tello, "El Movimiento Urbano Popular en el Valle de México," *Cuadernos de Dinámica Habitacional*, Vol. 4/82 (Mexico City: Centro Operacional de Vivienda y Poblamiento, A.C. (COPEVI), 1982), pp. 27–28; and Ramirez Saíz, op. cit., p. 22.

[29] Traditionally, an overwhelming proportion of Mexican intellectuals and political leaders have lived in Mexico City and have come from the upper classes; see Roderic A. Camp, *Intellectuals and the State in Twentieth-Century Mexico* (Austin, Texas: University of Texas Press, 1985), especially pp. 73–98. However, with the "massification" of UNAM in the 1970s, a much wider swath of students from working-class backgrounds emerged in positions of intellectual and political leadership. A very large number "paid their dues" through on-the-ground organizational work among the vast poor and working-class communities that fed the public university system.

[30] Farrera, Rodriguez, and Tello, op. cit., p. 55.

[31] FONHAPO does not itself build houses. In principle, it is a fiduciary mechanism that lends for construction. FONHAPO is essentially a public trust fund (a *fideicomiso*), administered by the state-owned Banco Nacional de Obras y Servicios Públicos (BANOBRAS) and operating within the Secretariat of Urban Development and Ecology (SEDUE).

[32] World Bank thinking on low-cost housing in the 1970s—of which FONHAPO is in part a reflection—is well captured in Michael Cohen, *Learning by Doing: World Bank Lending for Urban Development, 1972–1982* (Washington, D.C.: The World Bank, 1983).

[33] The most notable is FONHAPO's current director, Enrique Ortíz, who served a 20-year apprenticeship in the Christian Left and co-founded and directed CENVI, the best-known Mexican housing NGO.

[34] In 1981-82, over 90 per cent of FONHAPO's loans went to public sector entities to finance finished housing, i.e., not to what it refers to as the "social sectors." By 1985, however, lending to the "social sectors" accounted for 67 per cent of FONAHAPO's portfolio. Adjusting for size of loans, roughly half of all FONHAPO loans are now going to public sector entities; half are going to non-governmental community associations and cooperatives; and a very small segment to the traditional "private sector" (source: Departamento de Planificación, FONHAPO). It should be stressed that Mexico's larger "low-cost" housing entitities—for example FOVI and INFONOVIT—continue to provide housing in the traditional way.

[35] One public official I interviewed in 1985 estimated that FONHAPO provides, at most, about 10 per cent of public sector financing for house construction and upgrading.

[36] I refer here to a concept that is eloquently developed by Albert O. Hirschman in *Getting Ahead Collectively: Grassroots Experiences from Latin America* (New York: Pergamon Press, 1984); see especially Chapter 4, "The Principle of Conservation and Mutatation of Social Energy." For further application of Hirschman's concept of social

energy, see Norman Uphoff, "Drawing on Social Energy in Project Implementation: A Learning Process Experience in Sri Lanka" (paper prepared for presentation at the annual meeting of the American Society for Public Administration, Boston, Massachusetts, March 30, 1987).

[37] Barry Carr, "Introduction," in Barry Carr and Richardo Anzaldua Montoya, eds., *The Mexican Left, the Popular Movements, and the Politics of Austerity*, Monograph Series 18 (San Diego, Calif.: Center for U.S.-Mexican Studies, University of California, 1986), pp. 1–18.

[38] For accounts of the history of CONAMUP, see Ramirez, Mercado, Moctezuma, Hernandez, and Carr and Anzaldua, op. cit.. Other *coordinadoras* are CNTE, a dissident group in the teachers' union, and CNPA, an independent peasant movement. For a description, see Ana Maria Prieto, "Mexico's National Coordinadoras in a Context of Economic Crisis," in Carr and Anzaldua, op. cit., pp. 75–94.

[39] Unofficial church and non-governmental sources estimate that the dead and injured probably totaled at least two to three times these official estimates. The World Bank estimates $4–$6 billion in damages and 115,000 housing units destroyed or badly damaged. See "Recovering from Sudden Natural Disasters," *The Urban Edge*, Vol. 10, No. 10 (December 1986), pp. 1–2.

[40] For accounts of government repression against CONAMUP in the 1982–85 period, see Pedro Moctezuma, op. cit., pp. 141–142; Ricardo S. Hernandez, *La Coordinadora Nacional del Movimiento Urbano Popular: Su Historia 1980–1986* (Mexico City: Equipo Pueblo, 1987), pp. 52–59; and Ramirez Saíz, op. cit., p. 22.

[41] Most government officials and city planners strongly favor "de-concentration" of the central zone of Mexico City. In general, this means moving the poor to more peripheral areas and using high-value, central-zone real estate for sleek commercial development, tourism, or administrative functions. The resident poor vigorously oppose these efforts. For this reason, the most pressing question to be resolved immediately after the earthquake was whether the government would finally be able to "rationalize" the city. (The best-known example of this conflict is the barrio of Tepito, where an estimated 100,000 people live in twelve large square blocks (*manzanas*) just eight blocks from the city's downtown *zócalo*. Tepito is a thriving beehive of informal sector commerce. For years, its residents have stubbornly resisted all city attempts to alter their residence, distinctive culture, or highly successful economy. Even though Tepito was physically devastated by the earthquake, its residents unified immediately to resist pressures to be relocated.

[42] For description and analysis of the Coordinadora Unica de Damnificados (CUD), see Alejandra Massolo, "Que el gobierno entienda, lo primero es vivienda," *Sociologia* (April-June 1986), pp. 195–238, and Juan Manuel Ramirez Saíz, "Organizaciones Populares y lucha política," *Cuadernos Políticos* (January-March, 1986), pp. 48–55.

[43] Virtually all elements of the urban popular movement—with the exception of the strident left—signed and participated in the *concertación*. The *concertación* was reproduced widely in all newspapers, discussed at length by the electronic media, and reproduced in its entirety as a wall poster that appeared everywhere in the affected areas of the city.

[44] Key provisions of the *concertación* are that: Benefiting families will receive their house and lots for debts not to exceed 2.8 million pesos (about $4,700 at the then prevailing exchange rate); houses will be a standard 40 square meters (from about 10 alternative floor plans); mortgages will be paid in a maximum of 8.5 years in monthly installments not to exceed the equivalent of 30 per cent of the legal minimum wage (that is, an annual interest rate of about 18 per cent).

[45] Reported in "Mexico City: A Remarkable Recovery," *The Urban Edge*, Vol. 11, No. 8 (October 1987).

[46] Houses built under the reconstruction program generally followed the preexisting *vecindad* (neighborhood) model and provided families with about 40 square meters. The government and World Bank cite construction costs of $4,080 per unit, with the expectation of eventual 50 per cent cost recovery ("Mexico City: A Remarkable Recovery," op. cit.). However, some private voluntary organizations charge that the government has misrepresented its actual costs and absorbed subsidies in order to drive non-governmental competition out of the reconstruction process. One knowledgeable source estimates that the government's true cost could be no less than about $6,500 per unit.

[47] Because of strict rent control applied since the end of World War II, it is not generally profitable to rent out properties to tenants. Neither is it profitable to maintain units. On the other hand, the appreciation of land for commercial sites maks central-zone properties extremely valuable. Landlords often discontinue maintenance of their properties in order to force out their tenants. They also discontinue payment of property tax, or pay out-of-date assessments. The barrio associations argue that such non-taxpaying, semi-abandoned, unsanitary properties in the central city that are being held for spec-

ulative purposes that are not in the "social interest" therefore should be expropriated by the state in order to provide building sites for the second phase of the National Reconstruction Program.

[48] In 1987, the most forceful element within the urban popular movement was the Asamblea de Barrios, a confederation that drew from the *damnificado* movement, from poor people living in central zones not affected by the earthquake, and from militant barrio associations in the outlying zones.

[49] The words "lucha libre" literally mean "free struggle," but the sense of the term is "no holds barred"—an apt metaphor for the *lucha* of city life. As in the United States, wrestling is more a matter popular theater than serious sport. For a detailed description of the exploits of Superbarrio, see "Superbarrio: Magical Realism in Ciudad Gotham," *Mexico Journal*, No. 32, May 23, 1988.

[50] The wrestling opponent Catalino Creel is a takeoff on Catalina Creel, a well-known, tightfisted, villainous landlady who appears on a popular daytime soap opera.

[51] In a July 14, 1987 open letter to President Miguel de la Madrid, for example, the Asamblea de Barrios recounted their meetings with senior officials in various housing and legal agencies. The letter demands more money and credit for low-cost housing construction and repair, expropriation of lands belonging to landlords who evade taxes and housing regulations, and legalization of property titles for homeowners in peripheral zones. The president necessarily was forced to respond—prompting new rounds of meetings with the senior officials.

[52] Although one can and should argue that Superbarrio's presence, for better or worse, also has a least something to do with past roomfuls of World Bankers (and others) with poverty-oriented sensibilities.

Chapter 8

Women, Poverty, and Development in the Third World

Mayra Buvinić and Margaret A. Lycette

A case can be made for considering the gender dimension of anti-poverty strategies 1) if the poverty of women differs from that of men in degree or kind, or 2) if women's economic contributions are distinctive and make a difference in the welfare of poor developing-country households. In the first instance, anti-poverty strategies need to be adjusted or tailored to the poverty of women; in the second, they need to strengthen women's economic achievement in order to improve family welfare.

The evidence gathered during the past decade on women's participation in economic development suggests that the case can stand on both counts: Although women's poverty in developing countries is not intrinsically different from that of men, their share of poverty is disproportionately large. In addition, women's economic contributions to households appear to be more important in periods of economic contraction than in stages of economic prosperity. They are also more critical among low-income than high-income families, and they are central to ensuring the nutritional welfare of infants in poor families.

To help illuminate the design of anti-poverty policies, this chapter summarizes evidence on women's share of poverty in developing economies and on their contributions to developing-country households. It goes on to examine the effectiveness of past and current development interventions in meeting the needs of poor women. We then review briefly how development action was structured in the past decade to address women's poverty; what lessons have been learned; and what the impact of the changed development agenda in the mid-1980s has been on women's poverty and on development programs for women. We conclude with recommendations for addressing the gender dimension in Third World poverty.

Women's Share of Poverty

The relative intensity of women's poverty is apparent from data on: 1) the income of households that are headed by women, and 2) the productivity and earnings of women's work in developing countries. This section reviews the evidence related to these measures and describes some of the factors that explain why income tends to be lowest in women-headed households and why women's work is less productive than men's work and the lowest paid.

The Poverty of Women-Headed Households

The incidence of households headed by women is increasing rapidly in the Third World. In Africa in the 1980s, the seasonal migration of males seeking work abroad or in domestic urban labor markets has resulted in large numbers of rural households headed by "left behind" women. From one-third to one-half of all rural households are at any one time headed by women in, for example, Botswana, Kenya, and Zambia. In the Arab, Islamic countries of North Africa, the male exodus has created women-headed households on a large scale, even though this household category is scarcely recognized in the applicable family law. In Latin America and in the Caribbean region, steady rural-to-urban migration of young women since the 1960s—combined with marital abandonment and unstable unions—has led to a heavy incidence of households headed by women in the urban areas.

The available data show that in rural Africa, in the Commonwealth Caribbean territories, and in urban Latin America, women-headed households are poorer than those jointly headed or headed by men. In Latin America, comparative analyses of the earnings of household heads show that the type of occupation, rather than age or education, explains most of the differential earnings between male and female heads. Female-headed households also are poorer because they have fewer secondary earners and more dependents to support than male-headed households. The pattern is the same in the English-speaking Caribbean. Similarly, in Africa, comparisons of male and female household heads reveal no significant differences as to age and education. Instead, women-headed households are poorer because they have fewer resident working members than male-headed households, but more dependents and smaller landholdings. It is also true that these households are much less likely to have access to productive services such as agricultural extension and credit for more explicitly gender reasons. In any event, in Latin America, the Caribbean, and Africa, female-headed households are on average distinctly worse off.[1]

The situation in Asia is more hopeful in that poverty does not seem to be concentrated on women-headed households. Evidence from India, Nepal, Sri Lanka, Taiwan, and peninsular Malaysia indicated that women-headed households are not found disproportionately among the bottom deciles of the household distributions of per capita income and expenditure.[2] This is probably due to the fact that in Asia—in contrast to Africa and Latin America—few women of prime reproductive age have sole responsibility for the care of young children and the extended family household is more common. Even in Asia, however, a substantial number of women, often widows, do head households, especially among the lower castes.[3]

Women's Earnings

Women-headed households are not the only cases of poverty among women—nor should they be the only ones targeted for gender-oriented interventions. Women in male- and jointly-headed households contribute to family income through both unremunerated home labor and production for income, and the low compensation some of them receive keeps their households' incomes in the poverty zone.

To a large extent, the poverty of women (including heads of households) is related to the type of work women do and the meager returns they obtain for it. Their lower earnings are a direct function of their limited access to capital and modern technologies. Women perform low-productivity, labor-intensive work both as homemakers and income earners. The result is overwork and low pay for women and harder times for their families.

Moreover, the poorer the country, the more hours women work. In parts of East Africa, for example, women work sixteen hours a day doing housework, caring for children, preparing food, and raising 60–80 per cent of the food for the family. In Burkina Faso, women have only a little more than one hour a day in which to perform personal care, undertake community responsibilities, and engage in leisure activities.[4] In fact, in all regions women devote significantly more time than men to a combination of work for income and home maintenance, food preparation, and childcare. As the demand for child-rearing time and for cash income increases over the household life cycle, women's work hours increase and leisure decreases.[5] The burdens of poverty are aggravated when women, out of need, seek work in the marketplace and, because of their lack of assets, undertake low-productivity work in agriculture, in the informal non-agricultural sector, or in the lowest paid sectors of the modern economy.

Table 1. 1980 Distribution of Economically Active Population by Sector

	Agriculture		Industry		Services	
	% males	% females	% males	% females	% males	% females
Latin America and Caribbean	38	15	28	20	34	66
Asia	63	71	17	13	21	16
Africa	64	78	15	6	21	17

Source: International Labour Office, *Economically Active Population, 1950–2025,* Vols. I, II, III, and V (Geneva: ILO, 1986).

In agriculture, because of limited access to credit and modern technologies and services, women's work is labor-intensive and yields very low economic returns. This has been documented for countries as disparate as Cameroon, Indonesia, and Peru.[6] Women wage laborers in agriculture are hired for lower-paid agricultural tasks and/or are paid less than men for similar work. In Sri Lanka they receive only 66–75 per cent of the male wage, while in Honduras they are paid about 70 per cent of the male wage for performing the same tasks in tobacco cultivation.[7]

In industry and services, women tend to be clustered in low-skilled jobs with little potential for training or advancement. While the proportion of women among unskilled industrial workers is less than 30 per cent in developed countries, it is higher than 50 per cent in some Asian and African countries. In Latin American countries, women workers tend to be concentrated in lower-status occupations in the service sector rather than in industry. In Brazil, Chile, and Peru, for example, over 50 per cent of economically active urban women work in services—a low-wage sector in those countries.

Unable to gain better-paid, formal sector employment, increasing numbers of women have turned to self-employment in the informal sector—either as a supplement to formal sector earnings or as their sole source of support. In much of the Third World, the informal sector rivals formal employment as a source of jobs for both men and women. In Bombay and Jakarta, for example, as well as in many African and Latin American cities, 50 to 60 per cent of the labor force is employed in the informal sector, which is often the fastest-growing segment of the economy. Informal sector employment tends to be labor-intensive and to have low output per worker. This is reflected in the close association between informal employment and lower average earnings, particularly for women. In Kenya in 1978, for example, 41 per cent of informally employed women—compared to 13.8 per cent of men—had incomes of less than 199 shillings.[8] In Bolivia, 48 per cent of the self-employed in La Paz in 1983 were women, and their average weekly earnings were 70 per cent of those of men.[9]

Even if much of women's increased participation in product and labor markets yields low economic returns, it often makes a crucial difference to family well-being.

The Economic Contributions of Poor Women

Three indicators of the importance of women's earnings in low-income developing-country households are their proportional representation in household budgets, their role in promoting child nutritional status, and their importance in periods of economic crisis.

Women's Earnings in Low-Income Households

Studies have repeatedly shown that the earnings of adult women are proportionately more important in poor families than among the better off. In Indonesia, women and girls of poor landless families, unlike those of upper-income families, devote almost as much time to wage labor as do men and boys. In the Peruvian Sierra, women from landless peasant households provide 35 per cent of the total number of family labor days devoted to agricultural production, while women from the middle and rich peasantry provide only 21 per cent. Moreover, it is mainly the women in poor near-landless and smallholder households who resort to wage labor or artisan activities to supplement family incomes; in so doing, they are adversely affected by the differential returns to male and female labor.[10]

Women's Earnings and Child Nutrition

Joanne Leslie's 1987 critical review of fifty empirical studies on the relationship between women's market work, infant feeding practices, and child nutrition demonstrates that children of higher-income-earning mothers are nutritionally better off than children of lower-income earners. Efforts to raise women's incomes are critical[11] to the provision of high-quality foods for infants and children.

In the case of women heads of households it is possible that the additional meager income from market work may not compensate for the time lost in child (and self) care, especially since these women may have little access to alternative child caretakers. Nevertheless, evidence for rural Africa suggests that children may actually be nutritionally better off in households headed by women. This is largely because women heads of households have more control over income, and resources controlled by women are more likely to be allocated to family food expenditures.[12] In Kenya, for example, female-headed households (controlled for land size and household composition) allocate a greater proportion of income toward supplying high-calorie foods than do male-headed households.[13]

Women's Earnings in Periods of Economic Adversity

As happened during the Great Depression in the United States, adverse economic conditions in developing economies in the early 1980s seem to have increased the participation of poor women in formal and informal labor markets to help compensate for the loss in real family incomes. In rural Africa, poorer women farmers and nearly landless women have responded to economic contraction and food insecurity by increasing the time they devote to farming marginal lands and to low-productivity informal sector activities.

In Latin America, during the economic crises of the early 1980s, women's labor force participation rates generally increased more than those of men, leveling off or declining during periods of relative economic recovery. In Chile, for example, despite a long-term downward trend in women's labor force participation, women's activity rates in the lowest quintile of household incomes increased sharply—from 18 per cent to 22.4 per cent—during the economic crisis of 1974–75. Over the same period, the participation rates of women in the higher quintiles of the income distribution declined.[14]

From the foregoing, it is clear that attempts to expand women's economic opportunities and increase their earnings should be a preferred anti-poverty strategy. The next sections examine problems such efforts must overcome and make some recommendations for policy reform.

Constraints on Gender-Related Reforms

Five major constraints have to be addressed in poverty-alleviation strategies that are intended to focus in whole or in part on the particular economic and social needs of women.

1. Perhaps the most important of these constraints is the virtually universal responsibility of women for household production chores such as childcare, food preparation, and provision of water and fuelwood or other sources of cooking fuel. The dual burden of home labor

and production for cash income has far-reaching implications for women's ability to invest the time often required to participate in and benefit from development programs.

2. Women's educational attainment in developing countries is severely limited, both relative to men and in absolute terms, in most world regions. Only in Latin America are there virtually identical enrollment rates for girls and boys through the secondary school level. Even in this region, however, functional literacy and numeracy rates among women—especially in rural areas—are still low. Until the educational imbalance between women and men is reduced, it will be impossible for adequate numbers of women to be trained for skilled occupations or to participate in development programs that depend on participants' ability to read and write.

3. Cultural dictates regarding the sexual division of labor in agriculture, formal employment, and, perhaps to a somewhat smaller degree, informal employment, can effectively bar women's participation in what often are the more lucrative areas of economic activity. Such dictates are reflected in, and in turn contribute to, biases regarding the extent, quality, and type of education available to women. Other biases regarding, for example, the types and levels of women's asset ownership and the "protection" of women, must also be dealt with in the design of many development programs, as such cultural factors often determine when and in what circumstances women can attend a training center or meet collateral conditions for loans.

4. Some of the restrictive cultural norms are enshrined in laws. In many countries, laws prohibit a woman's participation in education or family planning programs without the consent of her husband or father. More important, laws regarding title to land or housing can determine whether or not women—even women who head households—are able to participate in housing or credit programs; and protective labor laws may result in women being denied the chance to work and be paid for overtime or to work at all in certain occupations in which late night shifts are common.

5. Because of the factors cited, women are over-represented in the most marginally productive occupations and are among the smallest operators and producers. The scale of women's economic activities, in and of itself, increases the difficulty of reaching women through development programs.

These constraints translate into sectoral policy and program concerns and point to the need for alternative approaches in poverty-alleviation programs that hope to incorporate women. For example, women who operate micro-enterprises face particular constraints in access to credit. First, they may lack access to information about credit programs, especially when the latter are sponsored by organizations to which women do not belong. Because women are less educated than men, they are less likely to be able to fill out loan application forms. Collateral requirements, based on land or property ownership, are another serious constraint, since women seldom hold title to such assets. And in loan programs that accept business ownership as collateral, women may miss out because their businesses are too small or are not formally registered.

Women farmers typically face similar problems. Lack of title to land can block their access to agricultural credit, services, and inputs. In addition, women farmers rarely have direct contact with agricultural extension agents; and when they are reached, their limited education may prevent them from using agricultural information effectively. A study of six rural Peruvian communities revealed that 88 per cent of women farmers had never been offered any agricultural extension services or advice, although 67 per cent expressed strong interest in agricultural and livestock training.[15]

Women's access to vocational training is also inhibited by many factors. Low-income and rural women especially are often precluded from participation in such programs by educational prerequisites, timing conflicts between instruction hours and inflexible work and family responsibilities, as well as distance and lack of cheap transport.

Moreover, when women do gain access to training, the effectiveness of the programs often is diminished by sex-biased curricula. Women's training typically concentrates in such traditionally female areas as cosmetology, hairdressing, and typing, while men predominate in such higher-paying areas as machine tool operation and motor vehicle mechanics.

Finally, because of their household responsibilities, women choose courses of short duration, which generally do not lead to high-paying jobs. In Argentina, for example, a recent survey found that 95 per cent of the students in short-term training programs were women, while 92 per cent of those in long-term training were men.[16]

A Decade of Experience

NGOs, donors, and governments all have had their greatest successes in addressing the constraints on and improving the opportunities for women in development in projects focused on the informal sector. Evaluations by USAID, the Canadian International Development Agency (CIDA), The Ford Foundation, and the United Nations Development Fund for Women (UNIFEM) all suggest that small-scale credit projects and micro-enterprise projects (designed to assist the smallest and most informal business, such as shoe repair, fruit and vegetable vending, home-based bakeries, bicycle repair, etc.) have been able to reach a relatively large number of women beneficiaries and have provided credit or technical services that have increased women's business income. These projects have of course faced obstacles—the chief problem being an overall policy environment skewed against female small-business operators. Currently there is debate over which project characteristics maximize the success of these interventions.

In recent studies, Tendler and Liedholm and Mead[17] identify the better-performing projects as those run by specialized agencies that have a narrow focus on a particular task and that are set up to provide the single "missing ingredient" (e.g., credit) instead of providing integrated services or executing multiple tasks. In the better-performing projects, clients carry out familiar tasks or easily mastered new ones, are not required to engage in collective production, and undertake an economic activity for which there are assured supplies and an established demand.

On the other hand, a substantial number of micro-enterprise projects in the last decade have been run by organizations that have provided integrated services for poor women, such as training in numeracy, basic accounting, and inventory control; technical assistance with marketing strategies and with determining when expansion is appropriate; and human-development components focused on consciousness-raising and building self-reliance. Many of these projects have promoted group-run enterprises on the premise that, because of women's multiple responsibilities and inferior status in society, projects with combined objectives and a multifaceted approach are more effective than projects that have only an economic goal and provide a single service.[18]

Regardless of which approach has been taken, it is important to note that the focus in these micro-business projects has been on *women themselves* rather than on women as members of households to which assistance is being targeted. Agricultural development and integrated rural development projects, on the other hand, generally have been targeted on improving the welfare of farm and landless *families*, and these ventures have been much less successful in improving women's economic opportunities. Often attempts to raise yields and to market more of crops that the "household" produces have increased the demand for women's unpaid labor, diminished the time women have for producing food for consumption, and increased the welfare of households less than their gains in cash income might suggest. In Mali, for example, men have been successful in increasing their production of maize, producing a surplus to process for cash income. But the grinding of maize—traditionally women's labor—is extremely difficult and time-consuming, and some women are refusing to undertake such work, for which they receive no remuneration, at the expense of activities that will provide direct sustenance for the family.[19]

The record on job training and vocational education projects for poor women is quite mixed. In the experience of USAID, vocational education as a tool for employment generation has had relatively poor payoffs. A review of these interventions shows that training opportunities have been more or less equal for women and men (although women have been taught more traditional, less employable skills), and that no project has had difficulty attracting applicants. However, many of these projects failed because the demand for labor was ignored or misjudged. In a USAID/Women In Development review of projects, it was pointed out that job training projects for women often failed because salaried employment was not available and the trainees lacked capital to set themselves up in business.[20]

A comparison of USAID-sponsored evaluations of a successful pilot training project for poor women in Morocco and an unsuccessful training and advisory center for poor women in the Dominican Republic indicates success in this area to be related to the nature of the implementing agency and the type of training provided.[21] The Morocco training project was carried out by technically qualified training and job development centers attached to the Ministry of Equipment of the Government of Morocco, while the Dominican Republic project was implemented by a non-governmental organization with no technical capacity in the area of job training. In addition, most of the training in the Dominican Republic effort took place in traditionally female tasks with low employment potential, while the Morocco scheme trained women in non-traditional areas such as drafting, electricity, and electronics and in employable female work areas such as secretarial work and commercial accounting. At the time of the evaluation, 75 per cent of the women trainees in the Morocco project had been placed in jobs; in the Dominican Republic project, 89 per cent of the women trainees were unemployed one month after training completion. These evaluations suggest that training projects for women can be effective if they are implemented by qualified agencies and train women in skills for which there is demand.

From Projects to Policy

As emphasized in other chapters of this volume, anti-poverty strategy in the 1980s, in its preoccupation with structural adjustment, has been shifting from an emphasis on projects to one on policy. This implies, on the one hand, a need to shift emphasis in women-in-development programs from the project toward the policy level, while on the other hand, such sectoral and project interventions as remain must be designed to complement policy actions in ways that ensure that women contribute to, and benefit from, structural reform.

For example, agriculture—the largest productive sector in many developing countries—is typically targeted by short- and medium-term structural adjustment programs that seek to increase production of exports or import substitutes in order to improve a country's balance of payments. One element of a structural adjustment program may be, for example, measures to increase price incentives for the production of export crops. Since women provide substantial amounts of unpaid labor to the production and transformation of household crops controlled by the men of the family, such measures may shift some of the time women have been spending on self-provisioning activities, requiring them to work more hours, recruit the help of their children, or accept a decrease in their real incomes. Each of these options may have a negative impact on the family, on national food security, and on the long-term success of structural adjustment policies. Stepping up export-oriented production at the expense of locally grown food may cause a dysfunctional dependence on food imports.

There may be a case, therefore, for *balancing policy reform with effective sectoral strategies for raising the productivity of women's work in agriculture* through, for example, the provision of improved technology. Agricultural extension efforts must be effective in assisting women to improve food production while allowing them to shift more of their labor to export production.

Policy reform and structural adjustment should, and can, benefit women if, for example, they include some features that encourage the relative expansion of the informal micro-enterprise sector in which women play such a major role. As economies pass through periods of austerity, demand for the goods and services provided by the informal sector may rise relatively. In addition, moves to deregulate production and reduce licensing and other requirements on producers may permit easier entry to this sector for women. Further, if the liberalization of credit markets reduces the need for credit rationing, women's access to credit may be improved.

It must be noted, however, that women micro-entrepreneurs face important constraints as small operators. Their capacity to export is likely to be very weak in the absence of marketing cooperatives or other such mechanisms. Their limited access to production information and technology will curb their ability to compete with the formal sector over the long run. Meanwhile they have fewer resources to help them through adjustment's transition phase when production costs rise and before increased revenues can be generated. Thus assistance with marketing, price information, and new technologies will be needed to encourage women entrepreneurs to respond to the price incentives of adjustment.

Conclusions and Recommendations

Given the degree of poverty among women in developing countries and the importance of their economic contributions to households, it is clear that anti-poverty strategies must be designed to address the social, legal, and economic constraints that women face.

An effective strategy for accomplishing this goal should include, first, a focus on women themselves rather than on women as members of households or families. Because there are critical differences in the types of work men and women perform, and in the ways in which they utilize income received, development interventions aimed at the household or family are not effective in alleviating women's poverty nor, in most cases, that of the children for whom women are almost universally responsible. Conversely, programs focused on women, when they are effective in raising women's productivity and income, produce benefits for family well-being.

Micro-enterprise interventions have been successful in reaching women largely because they have been designed to improve entrepreneurial, rather than family, income. Agricultural projects, however, must be reoriented to smallholders and should rely on a farming systems approach that takes into account women's roles as farmers and resource managers. Improvements in women's education and training will depend on the introduction of flexible class timing, incentives for parents to release girls from home production, and the removal of traditional biases regarding "appropriate" training for women.

At the policy level, the need to consider gender implications is becoming increasingly clear. Structural adjustment and other policy reform programs worldwide have produced a number of unforeseen problems because the role of women in various economic activities was not taken into account. To be effective, such reforms must be structured to assist women, not only men, to respond to price and other incentives. Similarly, broader changes in legal, financial, and educational systems must be undertaken in order to genuinely enhance women's social and economic contributions to development in the long term. There is a need to examine carefully, for instance, the ways in which legal inheritance patterns or protective labor legislation can reinforce women's disadvantaged economic position. Financial policies that encourage biases against, or reduce the profitability of, the types of borrowing that poor women seek must be revamped in order to maximize the productivity of women's work. And educational policies and funding must be changed to reflect the very high social and economic returns to women's primary education and literacy.

In essence, policymakers and development practitioners must consider gender differences, and the implications of development interventions for women, at each stage of policy and project development and for all social and economic sectors. Failure to do so may mean not only bypassing women in poverty-alleviation efforts, but perhaps even increasing their relative poverty.

Notes

[1] For Latin America and the Caribbean, see Mayra Buvinić, Nadia Youssef, and Barbara Von Elm, "Women-Headed Households: The Ignored Factor in Development Planning," (Washington, D.C.: International Center for Research on Women, 1987). For Sub-Saharan Africa, see Mari H. Clark, "Women Headed Households and Poverty: Insights from Kenya," *Signs*, Special Issue on Women and Poverty, No. 10 (Winter 1984), pp. 338–354.

[2] P. Visaria, "Poverty and Living Standards in Asia: An Overview of the Main Results and Lessons of Selected Household Surveys," in *Living Standards Measurement Study Working Paper*, No. 2 (Washington, D.C.: The World Bank, 1980).

[3] Andrea M. Singh, "Rural-Urban Migration of Women Among the Urban Poor in India: Causes and Consequences," *Social Action*, No. 28 (October-December, 1978), pp. 326–356.

[4] B.G. McSweeney, "Collection and Analysis of Data on Rural Women's Time Use," *Studies in Family Planning*, No. 10, 1979, pp. 379–383.

[5] Joanne Leslie, Margaret Lycette, and Mayra Buvinić, "Weathering Economic Crisis: The Crucial Role of Women in Health," in David E. Bell and Michael R. Reich, eds., *Health, Nutrition, and Economic Crisis: Approaches to Policy in the Third World* (Boston, Mass.: Auburn House Publishing, 1988).

[6] For Cameroon, see Jeanne Koopman Henn, "Feeding the Cities and Feeding the Peasants: What Role for African Women Farmers?" *World Development*, Vol. 11, No. 12 (December 1983), pp. 1043–1055.

[7] For Sri Lanka, see Rae Lesser Blumberg, "Females, Farming and Food: Rural Development and Women's Participation in Agricultural Production Systems," in *Invisible Farmers: Women and the Crisis in Agriculture* (Washington, D.C.: U.S. Agency for International Development, Office of Women in Development, 1981), pp. 24–102. For Honduras, see Mayra Buvinić, "La Productora Invisible en el Agro Centroamericano: Un Estudio de Caso en Honduras," in Magdelena León, ed., *Las Trabajadoras del Agro* (Bogotá, Colombia: Asociación Colombiana para el Estudio de Población), pp. 103–114.

[8] Nwanganga Shields, *Women in the Urban Labor Markets of Africa: The Case of Tanzania*, World Bank Staff Working Paper No. 380 (Washington, D.C.: The World Bank, 1980).

[9] Roberto Casanovas, "Los trabajodores por cuenta propia en el mercado de trabajo: el caso de la ciudad de La Paz," in Daniel Carbonetto et al., *El Sector Informal Urbano en Los Paises Andinos* (Ecuador: Instituto Latinoamericano de Investigaciones Sociales and Centro de Formación y Empleo para el Sector Informal Urbano, 1985).

[10] For Indonesia, see Gillian Hart, "Patterns of Household Labor Allocation in a Javanese Village" (Revised version of paper prepared for the A/D/C/-RTN Workshop in Household Studies, Singapore, August 3–7, 1976). For Peru, see Carmen Diana Deere, "The Allocation of Familial Labor and the Formation of Peasant Household Income in the Peruvian Sierra," in Mayra Buvinić, Margaret Lycette, and William Paul McGreevey, eds., *Women and Poverty in the Third World* (Baltimore, Md.: Johns Hopkins University Press, 1983).

[11] Joanne Leslie, "Women's Work and Child Nutrition in the Third World" (Report prepared for the Carnegie Corporation of New York and the Rockefeller Foundation, International Center for Research on Women, 1987).

[12] Joachim Von Braun and Eileen Kennedy, "Commercialization of Subsistence Agriculture: Income and Nutritional Effects in Developing Countries," Working Papers on Commercialization of Agriculture and Nutrition, No. 1 (Washington, D.C.: International Food Policy Research Institute, 1986).

[13] Joel Greer and Erik Thornbecke, *Food Poverty and Consumption Patterns in Kenya* (Geneva: International Labour Office, 1986).

[14] Osvaldo Villanvicencio Rosales, "La Mujer Chilena en la Fuerza de Trabajo: Participación, Empleo, y Desempleo (1957–1977)" (Masters thesis, Universidad de Chile, Santiago, Chile, 1979).

[15] Carmen Diana Deere and Magdelena León, *Women in Andean Agriculture: Peasant Production and Rural Wage Employment in Colombia and Peru* (Geneva: International Labour Office, 1982).

[16] Libbet Crandon and Bonnie Shepard, "Women, Enterprise, and Development: The Pathfinder Fund's Women and Development: Projects, Evaluation and Documentation (WID/PED) Program" (Report prepared for USAID/PPC/PDPR, Chesnut Hill, Mass., The Pathfinder Fund, 1985).

[17] Judith Tendler, "What Ever Happened to Poverty Alleviation?" (Paper prepared for the Mid-decade Review of The Ford Foundation's Programs on Livelihood, Employment, and Income Generation, March 1987); Carol Liedholm and Donald Mead, "Small Scale Industries in Developing Countries: Empirical Evidence and Policy Implications" (U.S. Agency for International Development, Washington, D.C., 1987).

[18] United Nations Development Fund for Women (UNIFEM), "Development Cooperation with Women: The Experience and Future Directions of the Fund" (Report prepared for UNIFEM, United Nations, Department of International Economic and Social Affairs, New York, 1985).

[19] Virginia Caye and Lisa McGowan, "Report on Gender Issues Consultancy" (Report prepared for USAID/Mali, International Center for Research on Women, 1988).

[20] Alice Stewart Carloni, "Lessons Learned from 1972–1985: The Importance of Gender for AID Projects" (draft, U.S. Agency for International Development, Washington, D.C., 1985).

[21] For Morocco, see Margaret Lycette, "Industrial and Commercial Job Training for Women: 608–0147, Morocco," International Center for Research on Women, Washington, D.C., 1985. For the Dominican Republic, see Elizabeth Dore, Robert H. Girling, and Rebecca Reichmann, "A Mid-Course Evaluation of Training and Advisory for Women (APEC/CENAM) in Santo Domingo, the Dominican Republic" (Report prepared for USAID/Dominican Republic, International Center for Research on Women, 1983).

Chapter 9

Poverty and Adjustment in the 1990s

Richard Jolly

For development in the Third World, the 1980s have been years of extreme polarization. In the dynamic exporting countries of Asia, as well as in the large low-income countries, growth has been rapid. In China and India, which account for half of the Third World's population, growth of GDP *per capita* in 1980–85 was double that of 1965–80—the result of an acceleration of GDP growth and a decline in population growth rates.

In contrast, for most of Africa and Latin America, the 1980s have been a development disaster. Average per capita income since 1980 is estimated to have fallen by a quarter in Africa and by a tenth in Latin America. Long-run development goals have given way to the economics of survival, with the emphasis on debt servicing, domestic cutbacks, and austerity. Gradually, structural adjustment has replaced the initial emphasis on stabilization—but it is taking place at very low levels of growth and, even after recent initiatives on debt, with extreme uncertainty as to whether per capita growth will be resumed.

In terms of poverty and the poor, this increasingly contrasting situation has had differing effects in various parts of the world. In Asia, there is some evidence that poverty has been declining with growth, depending on the extent to which poverty-focused measures have been deliberately incorporated in development policy. "Redistribution with growth" policies will remain as important in the 1990s as they were in the 1970s and 1980s for determining the speed and extent to which the numbers in poverty decline. In Africa and Latin America, the challenge is different. Most countries in both continents are caught up in a massive process of restructuring, but a process within such severe external constraints that little margin exists for improving general living standards. Thus further decline or stagnation has become the order of the day.

Stagnation should not, however, be overstated. As in the 1930s, widespread stagnation does not mean the total absence of elements, or even sub-sectors, of growth; and, in terms of human progress and welfare, a measure of restructuring is taking place within the social sectors that has dramatically accelerated some of the basic elements of primary health care, notably immunization, diarrhea disease control, low-cost water schemes, and social mobilization for community action.

Nevertheless, there is increasingly clear evidence that in many parts of Africa and Latin America, poverty has been worsening. This is hardly surprising, given that per capita incomes have fallen so much. But *in addition*, the poor in general and vulnerable groups in particular have been bearing the brunt of adjustment in many countries of these regions.

In urban areas, this is typically the result of a fall in real household incomes. Families are caught between employer reluctance to increase wages and rapidly rising prices—with food prices often rising fastest. At the same time, social services have been cut, often disproportionately. The consequence has been widespread declines in both incomes and standards of health and education services, with the poorer families hit hardest. Since poorer families typically have larger numbers of children, the sequence of events has frequently ended up with children, the most vulnerable of all, suffering the most.

In the rural areas, especially in Africa, where many peasant farmers grow most of their own food, the impact of rising food prices (and rising agricultural prices in general) can be quite different. For farmers who are net food producers, rising food and agricultural prices raise incomes. Many adjustment programs in Africa have been trying to achieve just this, and in some cases they have succeeded. But the favorable effects of rising agricultural prices on the rural-urban terms of trade often have been offset by rising costs of transport and increasingly difficult access to markets and by declines in the availability and quality of health, education, and other basic services. Moreover, the severity of drought in many countries over several years in the 1980s has often dealt a blow to farmer incomes from which it may take several years to recover *even* with higher prices.

The Human Dimensions of Adjustment

It is in this context that adjustment policies need to be considered. Initially, these policies were narrowly focused on the *economic* dimensions of adjustment with little, if any, serious attention to the social sectors or to the human dimensions of adjustment. The formal neglect of these issues in the preparation of most adjustment programs was compounded by the narrow range of decisionmakers and institutions typically involved in formulating the policy. In general, this was a small group in the ministry of finance and the central bank—often working in great confidentiality and relating primarily to a visiting group of experts from the World Bank and IMF. This was in sharp contrast with the development planning mode of the 1960s and 1970s, in which most ministries of government had played some part in a process that was considerably more open, both politically and administratively. Add to this the overwhelming focus on macroeconomic variables of adjustment and the short time horizon within which adjustment had to be planned (and in theory implemented), and one can readily see how the subtle and decentralized process and sectoral details of effective anti-poverty planning got neglected.

Fortunately, by 1986 or so, sufficient evidence and pressures over growing poverty and social neglect were beginning to build up, and a process of rethinking was set in motion within the World Bank and the Fund. The Bank issued several statements on the importance of monitoring the impact of adjustment policies on vulnerable groups and declared itself ready to "help to develop compensatory programmes, targeted on the affected groups as required." At the July 1986 session of the U.N. Economic and Social Council, the Managing Director of the IMF likewise explicitly acknowledged the importance of giving attention to social concerns in making adjustment policy, stating that "the forms of adjustment that are conducive to growth and to protection of human needs will not emerge by accident. They have to be encouraged by an appropriate set of incentives and policies. They will also require political courage." This was apparently the first public statement of this kind by the IMF.

It would be false modesty not to refer to UNICEF's part in this. In 1983, UNICEF had undertaken a first study, *The Impact of World Recession on Children*,[1] and thereafter had increasingly advocated the need and economic logic of adjustment policies giving specific attention to such vital concerns as protecting the nutritional status, health, and education of children and of other vulnerable groups. Particularly important in mobilizing wider support was a meeting in April 1986 of the subcommittee on nutrition of the United Nations Administrative Committee (UN-ACC). This meeting—with the participation of donor and recipient countries and most of the relevant U.N. agencies, including the World Bank and the IMF—was expressly devoted to the subject of "adjustment and nutrition." It concluded by issuing a statement that the "nutrition objectives for the poor [should] form an explicit part of adjustment policies and programmes. . . ."

Adjustment with a Human Face

In 1984, UNICEF itself had launched (initially at the suggestion of the IMF) country studies in Sri Lanka and Ghana, in both cases setting up a small team of government and non-governmental specialists to assess how vulnerable groups had been affected and how adjustment policies might be modified or supplemented to offset the negative human consequences. These studies provided a starting point for discussion and a process of interaction with policymakers and representatives from other international agencies and donors, leading to the incorporation of poverty-focused measures within the adjustment process. Building on these and other country experiences and case studies, UNICEF issued in 1987 a two-volume study, *Adjustment with a Human Face*, an analysis of the actions required for "protecting the vulnerable and promoting growth" as an integral part of a broader approach to adjustment.[2]

This comprehensive study set out the need for governments and international agencies to state unambiguously that protection of the poor and vulnerable should be one of the important and integral objectives of adjustment policy. It also identified five crucial elements of policy for a more satisfactory adjustment process:

1. More expansionary fiscal and monetary macroeconomic policies aimed at sustaining levels of production, employment, and general human needs satisfaction over the adjustment period, which should be lengthened to 5–10 years. While domestic efforts at improving the efficient use of existing resources should not be spared, the international community will also need, in many countries, to help mobilize additional finance for this more expansionary approach.

2. The introduction of "meso and targeted policies"[3] to ensure that a fair share of the inputs for economic growth (i.e., foreign exchange, credit, land, water, skills, scarce materials, etc.) is channelled to the poor on equitable conditions.

3. A restructuring of production to give greater emphasis to generating income and productive employment for the poorer sections of the population—especially to benefit small-scale farmers and the landless, urban informal workers, and women. Indeed—as the International Labour Organisation (ILO) had clearly shown in the 1970s—any meaningful poverty-alleviation strategy has to aim at increasing the incomes, employment, and productivity among these groups if it is to succeed.

4. A restructuring of government expenditures on health in favor of greater cost-effectiveness and expansion of services for the poor. This would entail, for instance, restraining expenditures on high-cost urban hospitals while expanding expenditures on primary health care and such basic health needs as immunization.

5. Special support programs—often of limited duration—to protect the basic health and nutrition of the most vulnerable low-income groups during adjustment. Public works employment schemes and food subsidies are examples of such policies.

UNICEF's *Adjustment with a Human Face* study also identified the need for three changes in the modalities of preparing adjustment programs:

- Broaden the group of national and international analysts and policymakers involved in the decisionmaking on adjustment so as to bring in those with knowledge and expertise on the many human dimensions of the process;
- Set up a broader approach to monitoring, including continuous monitoring of the human situation, especially of living standards, health, and nutrition of low-income groups during adjustment;
- Establish a longer time horizon over which the adjustment program is planned, implemented, and supported internationally.

A schematic presentation of the adjustment with a human face approach is given in Figure 1, which also shows how its characteristic elements contrast with those of orthodox structural adjustment policies.

In April 1987, the World Bank issued "Protecting the Poor during the Process of Adjustment." This document was originally prepared for the Development Committee, to serve as the basis for their discussion of the impact of adjustment measures on the poor and of how adjustment policies might be supplemented or modified to protect the poor during adjustment. This document and *Adjustment with a Human Face* have many elements in common. Both accept the need for adjustment; both accept the need for targeting the poor and vulnerable; and both recognize the need for extreme economy if realistic programs are to be prepared and implemented at a time of severe constraints.

But there are also certain differences. The Bank paper essentially concentrates on how to *add* compensatory measures focused on the poor to *existing* adjustment programs—and indeed is at pains to protect the latter from any disruption. It also does not recognize, or explore, the extent to which the unqualified promotion of free market policies may, in fact, conflict with the targeting and the deliberate interference with the market needed to support employment, the informal sector, and protection of vulnerable groups. (Some of these "interferences" may in fact be necessary to offset non-competitive biases in the actual operation of existing market forces, especially in monopolistic situations). In

Figure 1. A Comparison of Orthodox and "Human Face" Approaches to Adjustment

Orthodox Approach:	"Human Face" Approach:
OBJECTIVES	
• Reduce inflation.	• Accelerate growth, with an emphasis on growth of production and incomes among low-income groups; concern with inflation, but inflation not an overriding priority.
• Reestablish equilibrium in the balance of payments.	• Reestablish the equilibrium in the balance of payments.
• Promote growth.	• Protect the poor and vulnerable.
POLICIES	
• *Restrictive* "demand management" policies (fiscal, monetary rate, wage).	• *More expansionary* "demand management" policies (fiscal, monetary rate, wage); more active search for foreign exchange required—related to that management policy.
• *Untargeted* "supply expansion" policies (exchange rate, interest rate, producer prices).	• *Targeted* (on the poor) "supply expansion" policies (exchange rate, interest rate, production prices).
• No specific policy.	• *Support for small-scale production*—urban informal sector, small farmers, women, and the landless.
• *Generalized "institutional reform" policies* toward privatization and export-orientation.	• No specific policy.
• No specific policy.	• *Restructuring of social expenditure* toward low-cost, basic education, primary health care, and other basic mass-coverage services.
• No specific policy.	• *Additional focused support for those affected by adjustment.* — Public works employment programs. — Food stamps-supplementary feeding-nutrition support programs.
MODALITIES	
• Short duration (1–3 years).	• Longer duration (5–10 years).
• Monitor primarily financial targets.	• Also monitor economic growth and human conditions.
• Policies generally designed *only* by Ministry of Finance, Central Bank, IMF/World Bank.	• Policy design *also* by Ministry of Planning, Health, and Education, and ILO/UNICEF/UNDP/IFAD/etc.

contrast, *Adjustment with a Human Face* calls for more expansionary macro policies and underlines the need for restructuring policies in the productive and social sectors, as well as the need for *meso* policies to help direct more attention and resources to poor and vulnerable groups in general.

By the end of 1987, a model of what the two approaches might mean in practice had emerged in the form of Ghana's "Programme of Action to Mitigate the Social Consequences of Adjustment."

Protecting the Poor and Vulnerable During Adjustment: The Case of Ghana

The Ghana case provides probably the most useful operational example of the international agencies working with a country to develop a program of human recovery linked to adjustment. Already in 1983, the Ghana government had recognized that "improving the living standards of the rural populace and the working classes generally is, in the final analysis, the very essence of the Economic Recovery Programme and the ultimate standard by which its success will need to be judged"[4] The economic difficulties of the late 1970s and early 1980s had serious consequences for the living standards of many Ghanaians—especially for their health and nutritional status and for access to education by lower-income groups. The sacrifices involved were, in many cases, crushing. It was recognized that economic recovery would "need to address issues related to rehabilitating the country's human capital through programmes targeted at specific vulnerable groups, the up-grading of our local training and retraining capability as well as increased expenditures and improved policies in the health and education sectors."[5]

Nevertheless, the first phases of Ghana's Economic Recovery Programme, launched in April 1983, essentially concentrated on the economic aspects of adjustment, with little direct attention to the human dimensions. In early 1985, however, UNICEF embarked with the government of Ghana on a study of how the welfare of children and other vulnerable groups in Ghana had changed throughout the period of severe economic decline that the country experienced both before and during the process of adjustment and, in particular, on what priority actions could be taken to protect nutritional and other basic needs during this difficult phase. Initially a report on Ghana was prepared by a small team commissioned by UNICEF and comprising Ghanaian experts from the Ministry of Finance, the Ministry of Health, the Department of Economics from the University of Ghana, and the UNICEF representative, together with three outside economic consultants. This report was prepared in draft and reviewed by the government. After various changes were made to take account of government comments, it was issued as a UNICEF report in September 1986.[6]

In parallel, UNICEF drew attention to this study when it participated in the Consultative Group meeting on Ghana in November 1985—in the first phases of the World Bank's Structural Adjustment Lending missions and in a special meeting on the human dimensions of adjustment convened and chaired by the government in July 1986. The latter meeting, which brought together, among others, a key advisor to the President, the Minister of Finance, and representatives of the World Bank and UNICEF, proved to be the decisive point of change. Thereafter, the need to develop a strong program of special action to support vulnerable groups in the course of adjustment was accepted by all parties and became a focus of specific action.

In September 1986, a sectoral meeting on education and health was held in Vienna, co-chaired by the World Bank and UNICEF and attended by Ghana's major donors as well as by three NGO representatives. Later that year, UNICEF, the World Food Programme, and the ILO prepared for an inter-agency mission to program support for the human-focused elements in the adjustment effort. This mission, postponed for timetabling difficulties, later was absorbed (at the Bank's initiative) in the larger, World Bank-led inter-agency mission of July 1987. Meanwhile, in April 1987, UNICEF had itself commissioned a consultant to update the recommendations of its 1986 report and to prepare specific program proposals.

All of these initiatives and developments were brought together at the Consultative Group meeting of donor agencies in Paris in May 1987, when the World Bank, with the agreement of the Government of Ghana, proposed an inter-agency mission to prepare a "Programme of Actions to Mitigate the Social Costs of Adjustment" (PAMSCAD).[7] This mission—led by the World Bank and comprised of the World Food Programme, the ILO, the World Health Organization (WHO), the U.N. Development Programme (UNDP), the International Fund for Agricultural Development (IFAD), and the Overseas Development Administration (of the United Kingdom) as well as UNICEF—prepared an initial report in July, which was substantially revised within the World Bank and circulated to the involved agencies in October. Discussion on the PAMSCAD draft—involving the Ghana government and the concerned agencies as well as the World Bank—was held in Ghana in October and November and resulted in a final PAMSCAD program proposal of $84 million, mostly to be spent over the two-year period 1988–89. This amounted to about 6–8 per cent of the estimated annual cost of international support for Ghana's economic adjustment program. The foreign exchange component is about $38 million—some 40 per cent of the total PAMSCAD program—with some $11 million projected to be provided in the form of food aid.

Five main criteria were adopted for including projects within the PAMSCAD program. Each project component had to show:

- A strong poverty focus;
- High economic and social rates of return or, when this could not be quantified, evidence of cost-effectiveness and support for deepening the social dimensions of adjustment;
- Modest institutional requirements to ensure speedy implementation;
- Avoidance of "any distortions" to the wider goals of the Economic Recovery Programme;
- High visibility to enhance confidence in adjustment.

The Ghana PAMSCAD program provides a model that can greatly help to protect the poor and vulnerable in the course of adjustment and ensure that the adjustment process helps build structures for long-term development and recovery that emphasize poverty eradication.

This said, the program is not without weaknesses as a model. In the first place, PAMSCAD in Ghana has followed the introduction of the stabilization and structural adjustment program by several years instead of being an integral element of that larger program from the beginning. By implication, this means it has been constructed as an *addition* to the economic adjustment program, and has, by design, avoided "any distortions to the wider goals of the Economic Recovery Programme." While the avoidance of "any distortions [itself a pejorative word] to the wider goals" is perhaps acceptable, one fears that the authors of the phraseology may really have meant to proscribe any and all changes in the other basic elements of the broader adjustment program. Since poverty relief and eradication require a shift of income, production, and social services toward the poor and vulnerable, it is difficult to imagine that some modifications in the basic elements of the original adjustment program will not be required.

Second, by limiting itself to the short run, the PAMSCAD program may neglect the wider needs of poverty-focused development over the longer run. In the mid-1970s, "redistribution with growth" was a strategy expressly designed to combine growth with structural changes for poverty-focused development over the longer run. If PAMSCAD programs neglect the longer run, one is left only with hopes for "trickle-down" from market-oriented growth for the long run. And there is much experience to show the inadequacies and failures of trickle-down alone.

Finally, it is not clear how far the PAMSCAD model will prove effective in supporting the community-focused, low-cost, local-resource-using participatory approaches that are needed for poverty eradication. In principle, several such elements are built into the

Figure 2. Basic Elements of the Ghana Programme of Actions to Mitigate the Social Costs of Adjustment (PAMSCAD)

Type of Project		Cost ($ millions)
1. **Community initiative projects**, in which communities would identify and implement projects to rehabilitate socio-economic infrastructure and generate employment (e.g., schools, health posts, water-sanitation projects, agricultural infrastructure rehabilitation).		$ 7.0
2. **Employment-generating projects**, comprising:		36.6
	(i) Food-for-work, public works projects, especially in the North of Ghana, for employment creation, income generation, and infrastructure rehabilitation;	2.6
	(ii) A priority public works project, focused on urban slum upgrading and urban infrastructure rehabilitation with an urban demonstration program for stimulating low-income housing developed by the private sector;	17.0
	(iii) Labor-intensive feeder road project;	3.4
	(iv) Credit schemes for small-scale enterprise and small farmers;	2.0
	(v) Credit for small-scale farmers;	3.0
	(vi) Rehabilitation of secondary schools, plus improvements in sanitation;	6.0
	(vii) Income generation for women through provision of basic inputs, with a strong training component;	1.8
	(viii) Support for small-scale mining.	0.8
3. **An information strategy and compensation for redevelopment of public service employees** declared redundant. This included:		18.6
	(i) Redundancy payments to enable redeployment in self-employment;	6.0
	(ii) Small amounts for improving counseling and placement services;	10.0
	(iii) Training toward self-employment.	2.6

Type of Project		Cost (*$ millions*)
4. Basic needs projects:		16.4
(i) Low-cost water and sanitation, including 2,000 hand-dug wells and 6,000 demonstration ventilated pit latrines in 1,500 rural communities;	5.0	
(ii) Essential drugs, linked to primary health care (PHC) services and community financing;	6.0	
(iii) Supplementary feeding-nutrition education, targeted on 15,000 children through existing nutrition rehabilitation centers;	3.6	
(iv) Deworming program for primary school children;	0.6	
(v) Improvement of local shelter, to be used for improved local building materials and rural shelter rehabilitation.	1.2	
5. Strengthening education activities, including:		11.2
(i) Paper commodity aid for printing primary school exercise and textbooks. A modest element of cost recovery will be used to pay printing, with the balance of funding raised going to a primary education development fund for rural areas;	9.6	
(ii) Creation of initial food stock to start a revolving fund for bulk purchase of food for boarding schools at the secondary school level.	1.6	
6. Monitoring, follow-up, and evaluation of the PAMSCAD program, with strong element of strengthening capacity for district and sub-district planning, to be funded by UNDP.		
Total Cost		$89.8
Less contributions from local cost recovery and other contributions		−5.8
Total Net Cost		$84.0

program, notably in the community initiative projects, which are to be supported by block grants to villages and sub-district-level groups. This is certainly one necessary condition for effectiveness—but not a sufficient one. Community control with widespread participation is also needed if the poor are to benefit. Otherwise such projects may simply be captured by local elites or local bureaucrats, with the poor left outside and local power structures reinforced.

Adjustment and Poverty Reduction in the 1990s

Without major initiatives on debt and/or commodity prices, the international context creating much of the current crisis of development is likely to extend well into the 1990s. The tight constraints on foreign exchange availability and thus on economic growth therefore are likely to continue—especially in the African and other poorest countries, and quite possibly also in Latin America and the Caribbean. Adjustment policies will also remain a dominant preoccupation—and so, therefore, will the need for combining poverty-focused measures with adjustment policies, both in the short run and in the longer run.

This will make increasingly important the widespread application of "adjustment with a human face" policies by governments and by international agencies. Each of the elements earlier set out will retain its relevance, though no doubt with adaptation and development in the light of experience and further analysis. The need for poverty eradication (and more balanced human development in general) means nothing less than that the objective of eradicating poverty be brought into the full range of economic and social policymaking in the fields of adjustment, finance, debt, and development planning. Micro and sectoral policy and grassroots approaches, however important, will never on their own be sufficient to tackle poverty in the long run. The broader aspects of macro, financial, and fiscal policy must provide the resources and space in which micro, sectoral, and grassroots approaches can flourish.

Notes

[1] Richard Jolly and Giovanni Andrea Cornia, eds., *The Impact of the World Recession on Children* (London: Pergamon Press, 1985). Also available in French and Spanish.

[2] Giovanni Andrea Cornia, Richard Jolly, and Frances Stewart, eds., *Adjustment with a Human Face* (New York: Oxford University Press, 1987).

[3] Meso policies encompass a category of policies between macro and micro or sectoral policies. Meso policies are often neglected, but they in fact have a vital impact on the poor

and vulnerable. Tax or credit policies, for example, are frequently analyzed in terms of their macro impact, when what matters for adjustment with a human face is how the tax or credit policy changes will affect the poor and vulnerable.

[4] Kwesi Botchwey, Provisional National Defense Council, Secretary for Finance and Economic Planning, "Overview" to *Progress of the Economic Recovery Programme 1984–86 and Policy Framework 1986–88* (Accra, Ghana, 1985.)

[5] Ibid.

[6] UNICEF, *Ghana: Adjustment Policies and Programmes to Protect Children and Other Vulnerable Groups* (Accra, Ghana: UNICEF, 1986). A later summary version of this paper was incorporated as Chapter 4 in Cornia, Jolly, and Stewart, *Adjustment with a Human Face*, op. cit., Vol. 2, pp. 93–125.

[7] The Government of Ghana, Programme of Actions to Mitigate the Social Costs of Adjustment (PAMSCAD), November 1987.

Chapter 10

The Changing World of Northern NGOs: Problems, Paradoxes, and Possibilities

Thomas W. Dichter

Throughout the diverse ranks of development professionals, there is a growing consensus about the importance of grassroots projects and of participation in them by non-governmental organizations. Not only are NGOs being given an ever greater role as project implementors, but mainstream development theorists have come to echo their views—a "first" in the short history of development.

Both NGOs and the major official development organizations now seem to agree that (for example):

- Structural adjustments are necessary in the Third World;
- The involvement and participation of the poor in alleviating their poverty is essential;
- Indigenous and appropriate technology is key;
- "Trickle-down" is slower than we thought;
- The development project time-frame must be lengthened;
- Policy dialogue is necessary;
- Ignoring the political realities at the top is folly for those who would work at the bottom; and
- The formation of local organizations and the catalytic role of assisting organizations at the grassroots is a key to sustainability.

But NGOs, like other development organizations, do not always act on what they know. Worse, what is known is not based on much hard data, and NGOs increasingly face a dilemma: They are being asked to take on more and more although they are not, in truth, certain what will work over the long haul, or, even if they are certain, they remain woefully short of the skills needed to accomplish the tasks. They are also being joined (sometimes petitioned) by indigenous NGOs, which have grown rapidly, often filling in gaps left open by government. Altogether, this means new opportunities and a great challenge ahead. But the risks are also great, especially given the NGOs' tendency to shortchange reflection in favor of action.

To move ahead successfully, reflection is needed. NGOs must, in fact, not only look closely at the realities of their situation, but also face some different dilemmas—the toughest being, perhaps, the public airing of their private doubts. Moreover, even while the NGOs' main-stream development partners—the U.N. Development Programme (UNDP), the African Development Bank, the World Bank, and USAID among them—call for a greater NGO role, they do harbor private doubts about the capacity, the seriousness, and the very mindset of NGOs. This "insider's" look at the (largely) Northern NGO sector raises a few such doubts itself. This is deliberate. We need a frank self-examination, and we also need the help, understanding, and construc-tive criticism of our partners in the larger development endeavor. Calling for such help is, of course, a risk. Not only is development now an industry, but it is also one under great pressure. And what industry wants a poor press?

As an industry, the development endeavor has come to have a life of its own—one that is to some degree independent of its market. A stake has arisen in maintaining the "profession." When, therefore, we see past efforts as too heavy-handed, too fast, or too massive, and when we recognize that what appears to work is often less involving of "us" as professionals and more of "them" as participants, there may be a certain discomfort with the implication that we, the professional prac-titioners, may not need to be as involved as we like to think. We face just this sort of conflict of interest when, for example, we begin to single out the "informal sector" within urban economies as a model of development, as is the current trend. Has not the informal sector, by definition, grown and prospered without our or anyone else's intervention?

Questions like these become more difficult as the industry grows. Right now, between 10 and 15 per cent of development assistance funds generated by the OECD member nations is channeled through the Northern NGOs. U.S. NGOs are growing and want to continue to grow. The stakes, too, grow; NGOs are now more supply-driven than de-mand-driven.[1]

As a sub-industry within the greater development endeavor, NGOs are more conditioned than ever to see themselves as important. We get, and appreciate, some good marks for our ability to reach the poor, for our independence, for our smallness, flexibility, cost-effectiveness, and all-around ability to "deliver the goods"—whether actual goods, such as food, or moral and social goods, such as political empowerment and better nutrition. These claims, however, are not very well founded, as Tendler and others have said for at least six years.[2] In almost all cases—even the best work of the most development-oriented NGOs— the reality is less rosy than reports indicate. Yet at a time when the development industry is under great pressure, realities are not always trumpeted. The facts about Africa have raised questions (however unfairly) of performance. Where did all that money go? What did it accomplish?

To answer the skeptics, Northern NGOs who struggle for growth, and in some cases for survival, look for successes. A few "star" projects that show promise after a few short years of existence are cited. Even though there are thousands of NGO development projects now under way in the Third World, the same four or five "stars" are trotted out at conferences and seminars as proof of new paradigms of successful development. Worse yet, the best cases are brought to the public relations table far too soon. Most successes are pilot projects and have not stood the test of either time or replicability. And those who praise them, even those outsiders who seemingly have no stake in NGOs, frequently are too kind. More often than not, the evaluators of many promising projects are co-opted by the project designers, and their sharing of the myths and hopes is such that a willingness to suspend disbelief becomes significant. As a result, project evaluators often do not fulfill the promise of rigorous testing with which they enter the process.

Inside U.S. NGOs

This chapter presents one insider's view of where NGOs now stand— some trends and signs, along with what they suggest (given in no particular order).

U.S. development-oriented NGOs are worried. By means of staff retreats and through an increase in internal meetings and the use of outside consultants, we are trying to restructure and reshape our- selves. We are going through painful, and in some cases wrenching, processes of transition from, for example, food aid and relief to develop- ment, and from horizontal, and rather uniform, integrated rural devel- opment to a more vertical, sophisticated, and technically skilled ap- proach that takes both "top" and "bottom" into account.

We have rushed to borrow terms and concepts "wholesale" from the corporate world. For the past two or three years, NGO staffers have suddenly begun talking about "positioning," "management information systems," "strategic planning," "product," and the like. We are trying to professionalize staff, grapple with governance issues, and restructure ourselves. Some large NGOs have discovered that they have no articulated statement of mission or purpose. Some are scrambling to clean up their accounting, and others, strikingly, are now doing budgeting and financial planning for the first time. But major weaknesses remain. On the accounting side, for example, few NGOs have a developed cost-accounting system.

This infusion of business practices is also leading to internal strife and confusion. Changes toward structured management, whether of the more hierarchical sort or of the more participatory sort, are not always going over well in organizations that for years operated with a very loose management style, marked by collegiality and often consensual decisionmaking—or, at the other end of the spectrum, marked by charismatic leaders who made all decisions. In some organizations, new executives are being recruited from the business world, and their ways of running things are generally more exacting.

These things are taking place quietly as far as outsiders are concerned. But internally, there is tension because NGOs recognize that they do not always live up to their image and, more problematically, that some changes are taking place not because NGOs believe in them but because they amount to good public relations. Those who study the rise of different industrial sectors talk about the "growth maturity" stage as one marked by a growing attempt to differentiate within an industry, to position parts of an industry, and to engage increasingly in public relations activities and lobbying activities both directly and through trade associations. This is where the U.S. NGO community is now.

Within the Northern NGO community, however, our efforts to differentiate ourselves from one another are rather primitive. It is significant that many NGOs can talk about their "mission," yet do a very poor job of describing what they actually do to outsiders. This is not for lack of print. More and more is being written by NGOs to describe their work. But descriptions are often "boilerplate" and so much like what everyone else is saying that claims to being unique in the field are a bit naive. As happens in other industries in the growth maturity stage, a shakeout occurs when the "market" cannot absorb so many makers of the same type of product.

Unlike the corporate industries, however, NGOs are decidedly not in business to grow and achieve greater "market share," but to help others grow. Our commitment has been to ultimately drive ourselves out of business. Hence, to the extent that we strive to improve our management, as well as to professionalize and change the way we run our organizations, we should be doing so to improve our performance in the field and to have greater impact in alleviating poverty, rather than to improve our "donor base." Most important, these trends—entered into rapidly with half an eye on public relations and getting a larger piece of the pie—get seriously in the way of our learning.

How we learn is in fact highly problematic. At present we have no real data—no systems to measure our work. While studies are now being undertaken, they are largely not the work of NGOs themselves. Ironically, moreover, those NGOs who now do attempt to quantify and examine their own work still defend their right to maintain that what they do cannot be quantified.

We have made some methodological compromises as well. As we have grown, so has our tendency to follow fads—some of our own creation. For the 1980s, the best example is the rise of "enterprise development"—occasionally still called income generation. Now that it is fashionable and there is much money to be spent on it, many U.S. organizations are suddenly very involved in it.

Another fad involves "smallness" in development, which has been so overdefined that now the trend is to see which approach can lay claim to being the smallest; hence the clamor over the micro sector. Ideologically, NGO purity is now defined as being able to say that one works definitively with the poorest of the poor.

Yet many U.S. NGOs who have been doing development-oriented work since the 1970s know by now that there really are no easy answers, and that most fads eventually fade. Indeed, most lessons learned by NGOs are of the "it depends" sort. Some agencies tacitly acknowledge that they are not really sure what method works, but that they do now know that competent and committed staff make a difference. Others recognize that we always underestimate the time a project takes. Also, we have come to see that no development, even grassroots development, works well in isolation. A "systems" approach is called for, as are well-run organizations. To effect these changes, middle-range approaches, ones capable of leveraging impact, seem to work; but these kinds of lessons, because they are not the current fad, are little discussed.

Finally, NGOs in the United States are struggling especially with their own dependency: fearful of being too tied to AID, yet afraid to wean ourselves. (There are now over 200 U.S. NGOs registered with AID, or about one-third of all NGOs engaged in overseas development work.) In the case of those who have not taken government money, there is erosion of the lines between what is and what is not public money. The few who remain "pure" are showing smaller incomes. A very few, largely those with more international donor bases and with a sponsorship type of appeal, are showing embarrassing surpluses of money and are literally not ready to use it effectively. Yet, in practical terms, it would be financial suicide to deliberately slow down or turn off the flow on the grounds that absorptive capacity is limited.

In a word, there is a gap between the NGOs' image and the new call for their larger role on the one hand, and their capacities on the other. We are understandably ambivalent about the course we are on. We are worried. We feel we are good, but we cannot prove it. We would like a chance to "upscale," to extend the benefits of our work, to have greater impact (our biggest failing of all is that even when we do demonstrably good work, it affects very few people), but are not sure we can, or should, handle it.

Recognizing our clout, we are for the first time aware of our numbers, and these are significant: At least 2,500 Northern NGOs with a Third World focus exist in the donor countries.[3] Ten per cent of this total (about 200 organizations) have annual budgets of $1,000,000 or more. And the sector is growing—with tens of thousands of people on our payrolls.

Northern NGOs in the Larger "Third Sector" Context

The above is an insider's description of the U.S., not the Canadian or the European, NGO scene. But recent research indicates that some of the tensions occurring in the U.S. context may eventually surface in some European NGOs.[4] For the moment, however, European NGOs do not feel the pressure that we do. They enjoy more consistent partnerships with their donors, both official and individual, than do U.S. NGOs. These donors, moreover, are not yet inclined to be very critical and are listened to with great care. In the throes of its first postwar wave of charitable giving, the European middle class in countries like Holland now has enough affluence so that a large market can be counted on by many organizations. Indeed, public advocacy and interest in development is greater in Europe than in the United States.

Finally, there are new entrants upon the scene, particularly from southern Europe (especially Italy) and Japan. These countries have large untapped reserves of public and private funding without a highly developed national NGO base to tie them to. Eager to carve out sectors, these new actors are positioning themselves to maximize their input and resources.

More broadly, the entire non-governmental "third sector"—from private voluntary organizations to universities, churches, research centers, and those in existence to work for poverty alleviation in the Third World—is increasingly fluid. The lines between public and private, between governmental and non-governmental, and even between the profit and the non-profit firm are becoming blurred.

Both functionally and structurally, many non-governmental and governmental organizations resemble each other. Voluntary organizations, in the United States at least, have been steadily moving toward professionalization and inevitably a degree of bureaucratization. Consequently, they are now less in service to the individual member and are catering more and more to three constituencies: 1) larger donors, sometimes the government, 2) "targeted" beneficiaries, and 3) the agenda of their own professional staffs. Many NGOs are now engaged in what has been called "government by contract," and a revolving-door phenomenon has become common whereby the staffs in government and the staffs in private agencies are often the same people, although they move back and forth from the one sector to the other in serial fashion. A term coined by Alan Pifer of the Carnegie Corporation in 1967 has caught on to allude to this and has been widely used in Britain: "QUANGO," the quasi-non-governmental organization.

Southern NGOs

A major new player—the indigenous NGO—has entered the world of development endeavor. Variously referred to as voluntary development organizations, grassroots support organizations, and indigenous or local NGOs, these Southern NGOs are a major new organizational phenomenon in development history.

Yet there are almost no reliable statistics on this movement. The few organizations that track NGO activity, such as the United Nations NGO Liaison Office and the UNDP Division for NGOs, do not have accurate information. The tracking is done through "umbrella" organizations, and many NGOs are not registered with them. Furthermore, definitions of NGOs differ: Many registered NGOs, formed for tax or other purposes, are not active. Finally, the number of organizations seems to be growing so rapidly that the information that is collected is out of date as soon as it is published. If local NGOs are considered as an undifferentiated lot, their numbers—perhaps upward of a million—are staggering. And even if we consider only indigenous NGOs that are devoted in their countries to a role analogous to that of the largest international (Northern) NGOs, it would seem not unreasonable to estimate that they number 20,000 to 30,000.

Instead of guessing at numbers, it may help to give a sample of NGO types and their numbers in a select group of countries.[5] Among those organizations or entities that can be counted as development NGOs are:

Crafts co-ops (tens of thousands worldwide)
Agricultural co-ops (tens of thousands)
Indigenous irrigation organizations (the Philippines)
Village forestry associations (Korea)

  Squatter neighborhood-improvement associations in Latin
   America (at least 20,000)
  Small farmer development groups in Nepal (2,100)
  Local Development Associations in Yemen (130)
  Christian Base communities in Brazil (80,000)
  Self-help housing groups in Colombia (700)
  Non-governmental development organizations in Peru (450)
  Non-governmental development organizations in India (24,000)
  Non-governmental development organizations in
   Bangladesh (600)
  "Technology institutions" in Africa (711)
  Savings clubs in Zimbabwe (5,700)

Numbers aside, these NGOs can be roughly seen as a pyramid. The largest number of organized groups—those which are educational, religious, cultural, linguistic, age-related, or socially based—is at the broad base of the pyramid. In the next layer of the pyramid are economically based groups: co-ops, savings clubs, etc. Further up, in a still narrower slice of the pyramid, are the groups with an explicit welfare or charity orientation. And finally, at the pyramid's top, is the smallest group: indigenous NGOs of relatively recent founding whose stated purpose is development at the local level.[6]

Northern and Southern NGOs Working Together: Paradoxes and Possibilities

The future of indigenous NGOs cannot be predicted. But they are now riding a rising wave and have become increasingly articulate. At the March 1987 London conference sponsored by *World Development* and the Overseas Development Institute, Southern NGOs challenged Northern NGOs to, in effect, "back off" and help the Southerners establish themselves as the lead practitioners in the field. The challenge had a certain logic; we were asked to put our money where our rhetoric lies. If, as the Southerners observe, we claim that we are in business to "work ourselves out of a job," then why not get started? In fact, the very feeling that Southern NGOs have of being the outsiders (even though they are the people we are trying to help) suggests how closed a shop Northern NGOs have become: To give up aspects of control of our development process is to give up market share.

  The rise of the Southern NGO is a positive phenomenon. Not only are development assistance-oriented Southern NGOs filling a gap in countries where the public sector has failed, but there is growing evidence that in many instances they may be a stabilizing influence.

As such, they have the potential to foster change that will be sustainable—in contrast to the poor record of direct implementors of assistance from the North in this regard.[7]

Even when Northern NGOs are clear about the positive impact of indigenous NGOs, however, their own rapidly changing status makes it hard for them to know how to work with Southern partners. For example, the large bilateral agencies, the UNDP, the World Bank, and others want Northern NGOs to play a larger role in development—to play both a facilitating and an institution-building role, as well as to take on still heavier responsibility for actual delivery and practice. But Southern NGOs ask that we play a *less* direct role and spend more time as educators, advocates, and supporters of the Southern agenda—that we in effect be brokers, facilitators, catalysts, and, not least, funding channels.

Not only are Northern NGOs torn between these two different demands and definitions of their role—they have their own private demons as well. We are not sure, as acknowledged earlier in this discussion, that we have figured out how to be effective as deliverers of assistance, especially as promoters of sustainable, cost-effective poverty alleviation. Yet we are being asked to play a larger role in grassroots development—a craft we may have pioneered but are only just beginning to learn seriously. The ironies multiply: We now are asked to teach lessons that we are ourselves still in the process of learning. Given our newfound respectability and visibility, we are of course quite reluctant to get off center stage. As a result, we continue to try to set agendas and even to create a poverty-alleviation orthodoxy that our Southern brethren are encouraged, in the name of autonomy, to follow.

Obviously, we need to slow down. Before launching ourselves as teachers, we need time to assess what does and does not work and, not least, to review our own subculture.

Northern NGOs: Our Past Culture and Future Possibilities

Until about ten years ago, most Northern NGOs were made up of concerned amateurs, often from a religious background. Our organizations generally relied on volunteer or low-paid staff who worked hard at the grassroots and showed a populist, if not radical (even militant) political bent. Much of the time these staffs felt culturally uncomfortable with elites, whether from government or business, and to the extent that NGOs had ties with them, these ties (as ties with traditional power) were an embarrassment.

We were "do-gooders" but not afraid to work. We could stay in the field for long periods of time, learn the languages, and deliver limited services. Largely predisposed toward people-orientation, we were able to work well with small groups and communities; and we achieved some small successes, the impact of which may be greater than our detractors think.

We were out there, forced to compromise by the realities of the field. We very much played things by ear, often listening so fully with open heart to people's needs that we were overwhelmed with the massiveness of the task and tried to give away too much, too soon, and too readily. We wanted to solve all problems at once and thus became enamored of the idea of integrated rural development in the most horizontal sense.

We tried, moreover, to tackle empowerment as a *prerequisite*, rather than as an outcome, of development. By doing so, we neglected the "nuts and bolts," and some of the unpleasant politics, of development. Politically, we sidestepped the job of linking policymakers at the top to data gleaned from the grassroots; and practically, we shortchanged some old-fashioned bases of good management: leadership, vision, solid administrative and accounting systems, and rigor in data collection.

None of this should surprise us. We are a young profession and often did not see the forest for the trees. Nor were we sophisticated about foreign aid and development assistance, well versed in economics, or initially possessed of solid technical skills. Given our empowerment orientation, moreover, we often deliberately shunned structures that encouraged rigorous measurement, clear decisionmaking, and even planning or budgeting. But now the habits of day-to-day crisis management and the ethos of the grassroots are not enough. Even as we undergo rapid change, and professionalization, we struggle with the legacy of our subculture's origins and biases. Part of that struggle, indeed, is recognizing how much we have been in the thick of things without the time (or, sometimes, the inclination) to look at our own history or the research and interdisciplinary work that—however incomplete—is available.

During this decidedly transitional stage, we Northern NGOs need encouragement to do our own research in order to truly approach a "lessons learned" stage. We must also work to establish some norms and standards that are quantitative in nature. However difficult and distasteful this work proves, it will nonetheless allow us to better answer, first for ourselves, questions about how well we do. If, for example, we were to discover that 15 per cent of all our projects have been sustained for more than five years, or that 35 per cent of projects produced positive, but wholly unintended, results, we would be better able to accept that there is no "state of the art" in grassroots development. Such a combination of effort, research, reflection, and examination of performance would create an atmosphere in which, probably for the first time, learning lessons would be possible. We would then be in a much better position to give the kind of help for which Southern NGOs have asked us.

Effective, self-aware help is our goal. To meet this goal—returning to a key point made at the start of this chapter—Northern NGOs need to use their major multilateral and bilateral supporters as rigorous sounding boards for their work. Those who talk now about a larger role for NGOs must learn to be tough on us.

What, finally, does the future of the Northern NGO look like? It seems that, in time, a sorting out will occur and the sector will mature. If, hopefully, a division of labor is recognized as sound, then two kinds of Northern NGOs may survive intact in the next decade: 1) the small or medium-size, sector-focused NGO that has solid technical skills and a track record of success, and 2) the larger NGO that is able to catalyze, to wholesale rather than retail development in various forms, and to play a policy dialogue and development education role.

The first type would be akin to a "development boutique" and might specialize in unorthodox approaches, "surgical" interventions, pilot and experimental projects, and regional concentration. Such an organization might deliberately practice what has been called "unbalanced development" and make an asset out of the regrettable historical fact that not all problems can be—or are—solved in integrated ways. Usually there is progress on one aspect of a related set of problems first—and then, later, on others. It would have international funding, but a national staff, and be very businesslike in its approach—being, among other things, selective and able to say "no."

The second type, the broker NGO, would play a multitude of roles: a policy role, a data-gathering role, a facilitation role. It would be committed to research and to the documentation of learning, as well as to policy analysis. Such NGOs would function as "connective tissue" between institutions in society that are related to development. This complex set of tasks will require new kinds of leadership and new kinds of donor relationships.

At the same time it is possible that the old relief and food aid NGOs may revert back to their original roles. In a development industry where the division of labor is the hallmark, their role would again make sense.

For the most part, all the necessary ingredients for an effective aggregation of the players in development are present, perhaps for the first time. In the whole of the development industry, as well as in the developing world, there is nothing missing. Everything needed is present. Perhaps what is needed now is a balancing—an articulation of the parts. That will take time.

Notes

[1] In Europe also, growth is apparent. On growth and competitiveness among European NGOs, see Nigel Twose, "European NGOs: Growth or Partnership?" in *World Development*, Vol. 15 (Autumn 1987), pp. 7–10.

[2] See Judith Tendler, "Turning Private Voluntary Organizations into Development Agencies: Questions for Evaluation," AID Program Evaluation Discussion Paper No. 12 (Washington, D.C.: USAID, April 1982.)

[3] The Northern countries that are members of the Development Assistance Committee of the Organisation for Economic Co-operation and Development.

[4] See Anne Gordon Drabek, ed., "Development Alternatives: The Challenge for NGOs," special issue of *World Development*, Vol. 15 (Autumn 1987).

[5] The author is indebted to Dr. Julie Fisher, Technoserve consultant, for compiling these data.

[6] Certain preconditions must exist for the development of some of these sectors; and the whole pyramid will be found in only a few countries—India being one of them.

[7] See Julie Fisher, *The Alternative Revolution: Development Organizations of the Third World*, forthcoming; and Willard R. and Vivian R. Johnson, *Relations Between Governments and Volunteer Development Organizations in Selected West African Countries* (Cambridge, Mass.: MIT, Center for International Studies, 1988).

Chapter 11

Aid for the Poor: Performance and Possibilities in India

S. Guhan

Evolution of Anti-Poverty Policies in India

India's size, its share in world poverty, its importance among aid recipients, and the receptive policy environment it offers for direct anti-poverty programs make the Indian case of special interest and significance in any consideration of the role of external aid in poverty reduction. The second most populous country in the world, India accounts for about one-seventh of global population, for over a fifth of the population of all developing countries, and for nearly a third of that of all low-income countries. In terms of per capita income ($270 in 1985), India is among the poorest countries, and it accounts for about 40 per cent of the world's "absolute poor."

In terms of aid volume, India heads the list of recipients, with a current share of about 7 per cent of overall new official development assistance (ODA) transfers; in per capita terms, however, aid flows to India amount to less than $2 a year (1985), compared to the average of over $7 for all developing countries. Although net external assistance has remained a very low proportion of GNP—only about 1 per cent—there is no doubt that aid to India (including food aid) has over the years significantly contributed toward promoting development and averting distress. There is also no doubt that it will be required in sizable measure for sustained growth and poverty alleviation in the decades ahead.

As Robert Ayres has pointed out, "poverty alleviation was not invented with McNamara's Nairobi speech of 1973."[1] Among aid recipients, nowhere is this truer than in the case of India, the World Bank's leading borrower. International thinking on development, donor policies, and India's own development priorities all evidenced some convergence toward the late 1960s on the need to pursue direct anti-poverty approaches along with, and as a part of, traditional growth-oriented development. The emergence of the "redistribution with growth" approach has been well documented at the levels of the development and donor communities.[2] Yet the endogenous evolution of India's anti-poverty policies and programs has not received similar attention. It is worthwhile to trace it here, at least in summary, since external intervention has to operate within the possibilities and constraints of domestic policy, even while attempting to enlarge or overcome them.

Although social justice is a primary objective of the Indian Constitution and of the country's development plans, it was only toward the end of the Second Plan (1956–61) that the government explicitly took note of the distributional issues by setting up a Committee on Distribution of Income and Levels of Living under the chairmanship of P.C. Mahalanobis. As early as 1962, the problem of absolute poverty and the need to eradicate it was the theme of an influential paper, prepared in the Perspective Planning Division of the Planning Commission, that received much attention among academics, policymakers, and politicians.[3] While the elimination of absolute poverty was presented in this paper as the goal, radical redistribution was not considered feasible, desirable, or likely to succeed in reducing poverty. The paper concluded that there was no real alternative to attempting the highest possible rate of overall economic growth and combining it with redistributive taxation for financing the social consumption needs of the poor.[4]

A distinct shift from this purely growth-oriented approach to poverty reduction occurred in the late 1960s. The Fourth Plan (1969–74) for the first time included specific programs for rural employment; for the development of dry farming areas; and for the benefit of small farmers, marginal farmers, and agricultural labor. The Fifth Plan (1974–79) continued and enlarged some of these programs. It also included a national minimum-needs program, comprising elementary education, environmental improvement of urban slums, nutrition interventions for mothers and pre-school and primary-school children, and rural health, water supply, roads, electrification, and housing for landless laborers. The Sixth Plan (1980–85) took a distinct further step by including two types of programs for the "direct" alleviation of poverty: (a) rural public works programs, such as the National Rural Employment Program (NREP) and the Rural Labor Employment Guarantee Program (RLEGP); and (b) a set of programs—with the Integrated Rural Development Program (IRDP) as the core—seeking to assist "target group" households below the poverty line through

Table 1. Outlays for Poverty-Oriented Sectors in India's Seventh Plan (1985–90)

Sector	Outlay (Rs. billions)
Agriculture	105.74
Irrigation	169.79
Rural Development	90.74
Special Area Programs	31.45
Social Services	293.50
Total	691.22

Source: Government of India, *Seventh Five Year Plan, 1985–90.*

various kinds of asset transfers so as to lift them above the poverty level on a sustained basis. The current Seventh Plan (1985–90), which continues the same set of direct programs, contains substantial allocations for sectors having a proximate or direct salience for poverty reduction (Table 1). Altogether, they amount to Rs. 691 billion, or over 38 per cent of the public sector plan of Rs. 1,800 billion.

In summary, from the beginning the pursuit of growth has been the major plank of anti-poverty policy, supplemented with fiscal redistribution, better regional balance, and encouragement to smaller entrepreneurs in industry, agriculture, and the tertiary sectors. Since the late-1960s, sizable resources have been allocated for the provision of minimum needs and for a set of programs aimed at income and employment generation for the poor. It is worth noting that the accent on growth in the 1950s and early 1960s coincided with a period of sustained improvement in the GNP, while the mutation of the emphasis to "growth with social justice" since the late 1960s paralleled the emergence of a variety of factors such as a deceleration in the growth rate, widening regional and inter-class disparities following the "green revolution," and the belief that a progressively higher level of development ought to permit larger resources to be devoted to welfare and poverty alleviation.[5] Throughout, however, *major structural changes have been ruled out.* The redistribution of assets (especially land), or incomes, or consumption to the poor have been deemphasized as policy objectives. And to the extent that these objectives have found a place in state policies, they have largely remained at an aspirational or rhetorical level, with implementation lagging far behind.

The Planning Commission's paper of 1962 calculated that a sustained rate of growth in GNP of 7 per cent per annum would be required during 1966–76 to assure at least the third poorest decile of a minimum income (Rs. 20 per capita per month). Due to various constraints, Indian plans confined themselves to annual growth rate *targets* of 5–6 per cent, while the actual long-term growth trend in India has been only of the order of 3.5–4 per cent per annum. This rate, while not striking, compares very favorably with growth in the colonial period. Nor is this rate insignificant as a long-term trend rate in a country of India's size, regional variation, and dependence on predominantly rain-fed agriculture. Nevertheless, the "trickle-down" expectation has not been fulfilled because a) there has not been much that could trickle, and b) given entrenched inequalities in assets and incomes, the trickle has not turned out to be sufficiently fast or downward.

Anti-Poverty Aid in Review

In the context of India's slow GNP growth, a persistent post-independence population increase of around 2 per cent a year, and an unwillingness to undertake redistributive measures, direct anti-poverty programs have attracted a great deal of attention in India. Clearly they cannot provide a panacea, but clearly also it is necesary to maximize their impact—especially in ways that strengthen both growth and redistribution. To explore how external aid can contribute to this process in the current Indian context, we must first examine the extent to which aid has been available for anti-poverty sectors, and then assess its actual impact on poverty alleviation.

In a broad sense, aid can help relieve poverty to the extent of its impact on growth and the latter's impact on poverty reduction. Since our specific concern, however, is with aid that is "poor-oriented" in more *direct* ways, we must try to identify the *components* (in terms of sectors and projects) and the *scale* of aid's anti-poverty portfolio. For this purpose, the aid-absorbing sectors may be grouped in two categories. The first of these—hereafter referred to as the "traditional aid sectors"—includes transportation and telecommunication, power, energy (oil, gas, coal, and lignite), and industry (including mining). The second category comprises irrigation, agriculture, and social services (urban development, water supply, sanitation, health, family planning, nutrition, and education), which, as a first approximation, can be taken to be more directly "poor-oriented." Official data published by the Reserve Bank of India provide a broad sectoral distribution of multilateral and bilateral loans and credits up to 1974, and a disaggregated project/program listing for 1974–79 and each of the years beyond

1979–80. The data indicate that up to 1974—that is, roughly until the mid-1970s—the traditional sectors claimed nearly 83 per cent of bilateral and multilateral official lending taken together; irrigation and agriculture about 6 per cent; and social services barely 1 per cent.

Table 2 shows the shifts in the distribution of aid in the late 1970s and early 1980s in favor of the more poverty-oriented sectors. Irrigation and agriculture had distinctly improved their share to about 26 per cent (from 6 per cent pre-1974), and the social services edged up to 5 per cent—although the traditional aid sectors continued to dominate, with a share of 67–68 per cent in both periods. The share of irrigation and agriculture in *multilateral* lending declined between the late 1970s and the early 1980s, while the share of these sectors in *bilateral* lending improved to a countervailing extent. Multilateral lending for social services remained at around 7 per cent in both periods, representing a small improvement from 4 per cent in the past. The share of social services in bilateral lending is still less than 1 per cent. Some shifts within the traditional sectors are also of interest. In multilateral loans, there was a sharp drop in industry's share between the late 1970s and early 1980s; and this, along with the decline in the share of irrigation and agriculture, has been redeployed to increase the shares of power and energy.

Multilateral lending has been of crucial importance to India, both overall and in the poor-oriented sectors. Almost all such aid comes from the World Bank group in the form of IBRD loans and IDA credits. In overall aid authorizations, the share of multilateral lending has sharply increased—from under 20 per cent prior to 1974 to nearly 60 per cent in the late 1970s and close to 70 per cent in the early 1980s. The multilateral channel contributes 80–85 per cent of lending for irrigation and agriculture and over 90 per cent of that for social services. The World Bank, which also chairs the Aid India Consortium,[6] thus plays a key role in terms of aid volume, coordination, pace-setting, and policy dialogue. It is accordingly useful to take a closer look at the sectoral distribution of IBRD/IDA (hereafter World Bank) lending to India.

Table 3 gives the figures for World Bank lending in three periods; up to FY 1970, FY 1971–FY 1980, and FY 1981–FY 1987. It shows the significant increase in the share of the Bank's poor-oriented portfolio in the 1970s (from 8 per cent to 46 per cent) and its distinct decline in the 1980s (from 46 per cent to 34 per cent). The decline is mainly linked to the share of agriculutre, which fell by nearly half, from 20 per cent in the 1970s to 11 per cent in the 1980s. The share of irrigation has continued at around 16 per cent in both periods. Social services, which previously received no lending at all, claimed a share of over 9 per cent in the 1970s and 7 per cent in the 1980s—mostly for urban development and water supply.

Table 2. Sectoral Distribution of External Lending to India (Rs. billions and percentages)

Sectors	1974–79						1979–85					
	Multilateral		Bilateral		Total		Multilateral		Bilateral		Total	
	(billions)	(%)	(billions)	(%)	(billions)	(%)	(billions)	(%)	(billions)	(%)	(billions)	(%)
Transportation and Telecommunication	4.0	10.4	0.4	1.5	4.4	6.6	10.0	12.3	3.0	8.2	13.0	11.0
Power	6.8	18.0	1.8	6.4	8.6	13.1	24.0	29.4	5.8	16.0	29.8	25.3
Industry[a]	8.7	23.0	21.1	75.4	29.8	45.2	7.2	8.8	19.2	52.9	26.4	22.4
Energy[b]	1.1	3.0	0.1	0.4	1.2	1.9	9.2	11.3	1.8	4.8	11.0	9.3
Food, Agriculture, and Irrigation[c]	14.4	38.0	2.4	8.7	16.8	25.6	25.2	30.9	6.2	17.2	31.4	26.7
Social Services	2.9	7.6	0.2	0.8	3.1	4.7	6.0	7.3	0.3	0.9	6.3	5.3
Debt Relief	–	–	1.9	6.8	1.9	2.9	–	–	–	–	–	–
Total	37.9	100.0	27.9	100.0	65.8	100.0	81.6	100.0	36.3	100.0	117.9	100.0

[a]Includes industrial imports.
[b]Oil, gas, coal, and lignite.
[c]Includes sectors allied to agriculture and fertilizer imports. Food loans exclude PL 480 aid.

Source: Calculated from data in Reserve Bank of India, *Report on Currency and Finance, 1984–85*.

Table 3. Sectoral Distribution of IBRD/IDA (World Bank) Lending to India ($ millions and percentages)

Sectors	Up to FY 1970 ($ millions)	(%)	FY 1971-FY 1980 ($ millions)	(%)	FY 1981-FY 1987 ($ millions)	(%)
Traditional Sectors						
Transportion and telecommunications	992	37.3	903	10.8	1,944	12.0
Power	265	10.0	1,797	21.4	4,719	29.0
Industry	1,124	42.3	1,672	20.0	1,906	11.7
Energy	55	2.1	50	1.8	2,109	13.0
Poverty-Oriented Sectors						
Agriculture and irrigation	219	8.3	3,081	36.6	4,442	27.3
Urban development and human resources	—	—	795	9.4	1,149	7.0
Total	2,655	100.0	8,298	100.0	16,269	100.0

Source: The World Bank.

The discussion of sectoral shares of course indicates trends in terms of relative priorities, not absolute amounts. The volume of World Bank lending for the broad poor-oriented portfolio of irrigation, agriculture, and social services has nearly doubled from about $400 million per annum in the 1970s to about $800 million in the 1980s. In real dollars, the increase is much smaller but positive. In sum, the 1970s witnessed a distinct shift in external lending to India from all sources in favor of uses—including irrigation, agriculture, and social services—that can rather loosely be described as "poor-oriented." The share of this group of uses, which went up to about 30 per cent of overall external lending in the late 1970s, remained at around that level in the 1980s. Over 80 per cent of lending in this category has been for irrigation and agriculture. In the 1980s, the shift of multilateral lending out of agriculture has been compensated for by an increased share in bilateral lending for that sector. And the volume of multilateral aid available for the poor-oriented portfolio has seen some increase in real terms in the early 1980s.

What are the likely near-term trends in the share and volume of aid availability for anti-poverty uses? Clearly the prospects are not encouraging for any significant growth in real ODA, or its multilateral component, on which India depends in such large measure. Added to this is the certainty of a decline in India's share in World Bank/IDA lending on account of competing claims from Sub-Saharan Africa and China. We then have to take account of a continuing shift in donor[7] as well as recipient priorities toward aid allocations to industry, power, and other forms of energy. India's adjustment to the second oil shock of the late 1970s is likely to be prolonged and difficult;[8] in such a context, investments that can *directly* contribute to a better external balance will naturally have the highest priority. Industry, infrastructure, and energy are also sectors with strong natural advantages in terms of aid-giving and aid-absorption. Projects in these sectors are import-intensive. They also can be packaged in larger loans, and they are easier to process and more amenable to swift disbursement, making for greater "efficiency" in the resource transfer process than projects in the poor-oriented sectors.

If all this points to a shrinking share for the anti-poverty portfolio, some countervailing factors—and these should not be ignored—suggest that this may not happen, at least to any alarming extent. Anti-poverty aid has firmly entered the agenda of both bilateral and multilateral aid programming in the last fifteen years or so. It has helped in mobilizing support for aid-at-large with the public, legislatures, and NGOs in donor countries, and it has become very much a part of the rhetoric of the international community. Moreover, much of it is local currency financing that, although slow-disbursing, provides the recipient with valuable, freely usable foreign exchange. Thus strong "mutual interests" are likely to firm up the share for the anti-poverty portfolio while its real volume will, of course, depend on that of overall aid available to India. As it is, this share (around 30 per cent and about $800 million per annum in World Bank/IDA lending) is not insignificant. Nor is the proportion of anti-poverty aid to anti-poverty outlays in India's own developmental plans (about 7 per cent) negligible at the margin.

So much for aid volume and proportions. These being what they are—and likely at best to remain about the same—a further set of questions needs to be answered. What do we know about the *impact* of anti-poverty aid on poverty? How poor-specific has it been? And, in light of the answers to these questions, on which sectors and what kinds of projects should it, in future, be concentrated?

Trends in poverty have been the subject of a wide-ranging and continuous debate in India.[9] The discussion has included questions such as whether it is appropriate to use any specific nutrition-related poverty line at all, and if so, what it should be; the inadequacies of the data base; and a host of methodological issues involved in estimating the level and trends in the proportion of the poor. Rich and complex as the debate has been, a fair amount of consensus can be discerned in the basic conclusions that have emerged. Between the late 1950s and the early 1980s, the rural poverty proportion in India has tended to fluctuate between about 55 per cent and 40 per cent, depending on the impact of weather conditions on agricultural output. Meanwhile, there has been an increase in the numbers of the absolute poor. Although there is evidence that the rural poverty ratio declined somewhat between the late 1970s (1977–78) and the early 1980s (1983), the extent of the decline is debatable, and it is too early to conclude that it represents a trend. Finally, no definitive statements are possible on whether, and to what extent, the decline in recent years is attributable to direct anti-poverty programs. This all-India picture of course needs qualification at the state level, where there are significant variations in both levels and trends in the poverty ratio.

In the face of such agnostic conclusions, very little can be said on the impact of aid on poverty at a macro level except that "but for aid, poverty might have got worse." Such aid as has been available to India has supported what growth has taken place. Aid also has helped to avert crises. And aid cannot be blamed for the inadequacies in commitment and implementation of domestic policies in relation to growth and redistribution.

Table 4 shows the breakdown of the anti-poverty category of sectors and projects that have received World Bank/IDA lending. Of the 140 projects in the portfolio for which Bank lending was committed in 1971–87, 108 relate to irrigation and agriculture, with these two sectors accounting for nearly 80 per cent of anti-poverty aid. In the

Table 4. The World Bank's Anti-Poverty Lending Portfolio to India ($ millions and percentages)

Sector	FY 1971-FY 1980			FY 1981-FY 1987		
	Number of Projects	Amount ($ millions)	(%)	Number of Projects	Amount ($ millions)	(%)
Irrigation	16	1,395	36.0	26	2,671	47.8
Agriculture	46	1,686	43.5	20	1,771	31.7
Urban development and water supply	11	684	17.6	15	1,028	18.4
Population	2	67	1.7	2	121	2.1
Education	1	12	0.3	—	—	—
Nutrition	1	32	0.9	—	—	—
Total	77	3,876	100.0	63	5,591	100.0
Annual Average	8	388		6	799	

Source: The World Bank.

agricultural sector, about 60 per cent of aid went to agricultural credit, with extension and social forestry representing other main areas of concentration. Although there are no specific evaluations of the poverty impact of aid-financed projects in India on the model of Uma Lele's for Africa,[10] there are a large number of studies concerning the access of the poor to the benefits of the "green revolution" in general and to those activities (irrigation, credit, dairying, and social forestry) that have been the prime candidates for aid financing.[11] The specific question of the poverty impact of aid for the agricultural sector has been most recently researched in some detail by Lipton and Toye with reference to the high-yielding variety (HYV) technology in India that has been supported and promoted by credit, irrigation, and extension (both aid-financed and other).[12] Their final conclusion, supported by much other evidence on the subject, is that while HYV technology is in principle "poor-specific," in practice the more affluent farmers have been able to capture most of the incremental gains accruing from it because of their better access to land, credit, subsidies, agricultural extension, and irrigation (especially private irrigation in the form of credit-financed tube wells). In their words,

> Modern varieties are, as such, a "poor-specific" technology; but they enter a power context in which their gains are largely diverted to help the rich. The answer has to be redistribution of agriculture-linked assets, and of work chances, towards the poor. . . . Since India . . . has not significantly reduced the share of its workforce in agriculture (of about 70 per cent), it is plainly central to get assets and/or labor income to its *agricultural* poor.

Some Future Possibilities for Interaction

It thus seems that not much of the (limited) aid available for the poverty-oriented portfolio has proved to be particularly poor-specific. It is in this context that this paper will sketch ways in which, within the possibilities that offer themselves in India, improvements could be sought in the focus and poverty impact of aid.

The intention in scoping out these options is not so much to evolve a blueprint for programming anti-poverty aid to India as to illustrate possibilities for a much better interaction of aid with India's policies, priorities, and programs. For this to happen, several considerations would have to be harmonized. In the Indian context of limited aid availability, a very large-scale poverty problem, and an extensive range of ongoing domestic anti-poverty programs, effective external intervention will require a selective focus on a few areas of strategic priority.

The chosen areas will have to be ones in which aid practices and predilections—projectization, institution-building, policy reform, cost recovery—can be useful. Preferably the chosen areas would be in sectors with which donors have acquired some degree of familiarity. "Additionality" of effort on the recipient's part could be induced by aiming aid at activities that but for the stimulus and incentive of external resources are likely to be neglected. Most important, aid would have to be made much more poor-specific, which would entail concentration in sectors, projects, and programs that have a strong capacity for reaching the poor.

Asset Transfers and Employment

First on such an agenda could be the interlinking of aid with the two major sets of programs in India that aim at asset transfers and wage employment for the poor: 1) the Integrated Rural Development Program (IRDP), which finances—through a combination of loans and subsidies to households under the poverty line—a variety of income-earning assets, such as irrigation wells, milch cattle, draught animals, other livestock, poultry, carts, and facilities for small-scale occupations in production, trade, and services; and 2) the National Rural Employment Program (NREP) and the Rural Labor Employment Guarantee Program (RLEGP), which seek to provide wage employment on minor irrigation works, land reclamation, soil conservation, afforestation, rural roads, and small buildings. In their present form, these progams date from around the beginning of the 1980s and continue to receive substantial budgetary allocations. Although a number of evaluations of the IRDP and of the rural employment programs have shown up various deficiencies in these programs and have raised questions concerning their impact on poverty reduction,[13] there is no question that, taken together, these programs represent an unprecedented, massive, and sustained anti-poverty effort not paralleled anywhere else in the world. Despite the fact that so far aid has not been sought or offered for these programs, there are ways in which external assistance could usefully interact with them to improve their impact.

One possibility would be to use agricultural credit to finance the acquisition of land by IRDP beneficiaries. Neither traditional aid-financed agricultural credit nor the IRDP, as it operates now, enables the poor to buy land, which is in many ways the most basic asset that they would like to possess. In India, legislation has been notoriously unsuccessful in effecting land redistribution: As of the mid-1980s, it has been possible to redistribute only about 1 per cent of the cropped area and no more than 20 per cent of the estimated "surplus" under the land ceiling laws. Even with the best will (which, given India's political economy, is not likely to be forthcoming), it would be quite impossible, short of a political upheaval, to bring back to the books land that has been stashed away in evasion or avoidance of the ceiling laws, which have provided many loopholes for such sequestering. It might, however, be possible to stimulate and facilitate natural market processes through which land tends to get transferred from the rich to the poor. Such processes may not be taking place on a large scale, but they are not absent; with increasing modernization, urbanization, and industrialization, there is in many parts of India some movement of traditional landowning households to towns and to non-agricultural vocations, with a tendency for landed assets to be converted into investments in professional education, urban property, industrial shares, and financial assets. At the same time, there is some increase in the bargaining power of tenants and some accumulating surpluses with small peasants and rural craftsmen that need to be strengthened and supplemented. In this situation, if conventional agricultural credit could be meshed with IRDP to promote land purchases by the poor, a definite fillip could be given to natural market-oriented processes of land redistribution.

The second respect in which the IRDP could be strengthened relates to one of its present major drawbacks: the lack of essential support services. The large-scale transfer of assets, notably milch cattle, to the poor is very inadequately supported with ancillary supplies and services (feed at low cost, immunization and veterinary services for cattle, insurance, marketing of milk, and so on) that are vital for translating these rather vulnerable assets into dependable streams of income. This is not surprising since, while IRDP lending was extended country-wide virtually overnight in 1980 by utilizing the substantial rural coverage of nationalized banks, the financing infrastructure was not accompanied by correspondingly extensive facilities for common and support services. The creation of the latter—given the manpower, equipment, transport, construction, and other needs involved—will be an expensive and time-consuming process. And aid can make critical inputs for speeding it up.

More generally, it is important to integrate direct anti-poverty programs into the growth process by creating and enlarging home markets for poor-specific activities of various kinds, enabling consumption expenditures of the non-poor to benefit rural poor producers with minimum intermediary siphoning-off. This would essentially involve a threefold approach. *First*, household-level activities that are, or can be, financed under the IRDP in different sub-sectors—such as dairy, sheep farming, poultry, pisciculture, horticulture, sericulture, small-scale production, and handicrafts—will have to be knit together in each case in area-specific projects that provide (as appropriate) for support services such as credit, input supply, disease control, quality upgrading, design inputs, and marketing. *Second*, professionally managed producer cooperatives will have to be encouraged and sustained. *Third*, it is necessary to stimulate demand for the products and services that are generated from the assets created by the IRDP in urban, semi-urban, and the more prosperous rural areas; in fact, without such demand promotion, IRDP has often resulted in a fallacy of composition, whereby the new beneficiaries tend to compete with each other and with existing producers in the same limited markets.

Similarly, concentrating employment programs on specifically defined areas can avoid diffuseness and, if combined with land consolidation, generate useful jobs in, and linked to, activities such as field irrigation, soil conservation, and afforestation.[14] When implemented by *local* authorities, as is the case in West Bengal, such rural works have a large participatory dimension. Area-specific, micro-level planning can provide an integrative and coordinating framework for diverse rural employment activities. In all this, project-oriented approaches that are a part of aid practice can make a logical contribution.

Urban Development Services

Urban development, which has been a sub-sector of concentration in World Bank/IDA lending, includes a wide cross-section of investments, including provision of developed housing sites along with civic services, slum improvement, transportation, roads, water supply, sanitation, and income-generating activities for the poor. Although in India the level of urbanization (about 24 per cent of total population in 1981) and its growth (about 4 per cent a year in 1971–81) are not high by Third World standards, the pattern of urbanization is such that there is much need and scope for intervention.[15] As much as 60 per cent of India's urban population lives in agglomerations of 100,000 or more. There were 216 centers in 1981—twelve with a population of over a million. The largest among them—Calcutta (9.2 million), Bombay (8.2 million), Delhi (5.7 million), and Madras (4.3 million)—are among the world's biggest cities, with two more—Bangalore and Ahmedabad— expected to cross the 5 million population mark by the year 2000. Urban development, as is well known, is expensive; many of its components, notably water supply, get postponed—with the resulting neglect leading to even more costly and lumpy investments later on. Even the routine maintenance of essential civic services such as water supply, sanitation, roads, street lighting, transport, and traffic control has suffered much neglect in India. The situation in the slums, where 30 to over 40 per cent of the people in the biggest cities of India live, is appalling.

There are several ready reasons why urban services are excellent candidates for aid. High percentages of the poor can be reached in urban projects[16]; slum improvement, for instance, is highly poor-specific. Aid can absorb some of the costs of urban housing and transport, the lack of which contributes in good measure to urban poverty. And water supplies and sanitation directed toward the poor can have multiplier effects in reducing morbidity and infant mortality. External interaction can help in reasonable and appropriate cost recovery, induce "additionality," transfer international experience, and encourage inter-agency coordination that, without some external insistence, gets stymied by entrenched departmentalism. Finally, the urban environment in India is much better equipped with non-governmental organizations than the rural one. It is also much more amenable to the participatory involvement of beneficiaries: People in urban areas live closer together, are more aware and literate, and are less riven by caste barriers.

Nutrition

Nutrition is a sub-sector that raises a different order of issues. Supplementary feeding for pregnant and nursing mothers and for young children is a critical intervention that can have significant multiplier effects in reducing mortality, avoiding permanent damage to child health, and inducing a decline in fertility. It is readily combinable with immunization of mothers and children, family planning advice, and health education. The World Bank has financed a pioneering project in this sector in the state of Tamilnadu, the Tamilnadu Integrated Nutrition Project (TINIP), which targets pregnant and nursing women and children of six months to three years of age. The program provides immunizations, vitamin A, and diarrhea management, along with short-term supplemental nutrition for children with faltering growth. Pregnant women receive pre-natal care, tetanus immunization, food supplements, and health education. Preliminary evaluations indicate that in several districts the project has been able to *halve* the proportion of severely malnourished children—from about 20 per cent to under 10 per cent—in 3–5 years. TINIP has proven to be the most cost-effective scheme of this kind and compares very favorably with two other large-scale nutritional interventions in India, the Integrated Child Development Scheme (ICDS) and the Chief Minister's Noon Meal Scheme (CMNS) in Tamilnadu. Both of these programs are much more loosely targeted—especially the latter, which covers more than 8 million children up to age fifteen at a unit cost nearly three times that of TINIP.[17]

The central issue in nutritional interventions is targeting, as these programs tend to consume large *recurring* expenditures that have a high opportunity cost (in that they reduce the availability of funds for complementary interventions in, for example, primary health care, water supply, and sanitation). Unless these expenditures are kept at sensible levels, they are not likely to be sustainable in the long run. Technical, administrative, and budgetary aspects argue for precise targeting, but populist politics in many Indian states (for example, Tamilnadu, Andhra, Pradesh, Karnataka) has led to nutritional interventions that are high-cost and hard to sustain. Striking the right balance in targeting between premature (or immature) welfarism and narrow technicalism is difficult but necessary. Per Pinstrup-Andersen sums up the dilemmas succinctly:

> ... perfect targeting should not be attempted. There is a point beyond which increases in administrative costs, including the cost of identification of target households, exceed the cost savings from further reducing benefit leakages to non-target households. Furthermore, as a program gets more narrowly targeted, the risk of excluding target households increases due to insufficient information. Finally, a program narrowly targeted on the poor is likely to have little political support in all but the most enlightened societies and if implemented may have a short life. . . .[18]

The TINIP itself supplies an interesting lesson. Close and cost-effective targeting in the TINIP has not been able to prevent the Tamilnadu state from opting in addition for the massive, loosely targeted, and very expensive Chief Minister's Noon Meal Scheme. Thus, while the World Bank scheme has demonstrated a good model of a *nutrition* intervention, its impact on *public policy* has not been equally successful: While the battle (of nutrition) is being waged, the war (on waste) would appear to have been lost. The moral is that, in a populist democracy, targeting cannot be too narrow; and the higher input costs entailed by wider coverage may get offset to some extent by savings in administrative delivery costs. If, then, it is not possible to restrain *overall* costs below an acceptable level, attention will have to shift to achieving some element of cost recovery through community participation and to maximizing benefits by supplementing nutrition with immunization and health education. It will be very worthwhile to extend the TINIP-type scheme to many other states in India—with such adaptations as may be necessary to make it not only technically sound and fiscally viable, but also administratively robust and politically sustainable under local conditions.

Participation and "Wholesaling"

Participation by beneficiaries or local communities or non-governmental organizations (NGOs) in the planning, implementation, and monitoring of projects has attracted much attention. There is, moreover, a growing literature on methodologies for organizing participation as well as on the gains to be expected and the problems involved in securing and sustaining it.[19] Participation is of vital importance not only for improving micro-efficiency at the project level, but even more for stimulating *processes* that favor mobilization, replication, and self-reliance across the entire range of anti-poverty efforts.

India has had a history of experiments in "community development" linked to *panchayati raj* institutions (i.e., statute-based, democratically elected local bodies at the level of cities, districts, sub-districts (*taluks*), groups of villages (*panchayat samithis* or unions), and villages). NGO activity, particularly in health and education, has a long history. The cooperative movement in India is also extensive and long-standing. Yet with all this, India has not succeeded in providing a hospitable environment to local effort; and this indeed is one of the serious failures of Indian planning and political evolution. At worst, politicians and bureaucrats tend to be hostile to local bodies, cooperatives, and NGOs; at best, they treat them with benign neglect. There are, however, some signs of change. NGOs have grown greatly in number in recent years and are involved in diverse fields—not only in health and education, but also in rural development, environmental concerns, tribal welfare, women's issues, civil liberties, legal aid, and other issues. Effective decentralization to local bodies is also re-entering the agenda in the wider contexts of relations between the central government and the states and of multi-level planning. Some state governments, notably those of West Bengal and Karnataka, have recently implemented a good measure of such decentralization, while traditional arrangements for the devolution of resources and responsibilities to local bodies continue in many other states. Renewed attention is also being given to revitalizing and strengthening credit, production, marketing, and consumer cooperatives.

Externally aided projects can stimulate and support these trends in concrete ways in rural development, employment programs, urban services, and nutrition—in all of which there is obvious scope for participation involving communities, local bodies, cooperatives, and NGOs. *First*, resources and responsibilities under projects could be routed through *local* bodies and cooperatives recognized in formal terms as agencies in the project implementation chain. *Second*, programs could be worked out at the level of districts, with the higher-tier bodies at this level treated as the agencies for "retailing" individual sub-projects and activities to lower-tier levels such as *panchayat* unions and *panchayats*—with a beginning being made in states (such as Karnataka) where an institutional framework for the purpose is in existence. *Third*, and in similar fashion, associations of NGOs operating in different locations/sectors could be utilized for intermediating assistance to smaller and dispersed NGOs. *Fourth*, project design could aim at establishing a variety of complementary relationships between NGOs and state-run facilities and activities.

The issue of "wholesaling" versus "retailing" aid is related to the general theme of participation. Individual loan size in the anti-poverty portfolio is typically around 50 per cent of loan size in lending for transport or energy or industry.[20] Such lending also typically involves much more staff time at the various project cycle stages (for example, identification, appraisal, and supervision). Altogether, moving a given amount of money via anti-poverty projects is therefore some three to four times as demanding—for donors and recipients alike—as lending for infrastructure and industry. The obvious answer, in this situation, is to *wholesale* loans to national, state-level, local, and NGO agencies and, in the process, involve their participation.

In the Indian context, participation need not boil down to a simple issue of "top-down" versus "bottom-up." It is possible and necessary to involve a *variety* of institutions—parastatals, cooperatives, local bodies, NGOs—that lie in the large middle between the national and state level on one hand and the "grassroots" on the other. Many of these might need strengthening to come up to the reasonable expectations of external lenders, but the process of upgrading them, and in some cases even constituting them, will happen only if the decision is made to use them for intermediation. Painful and time-consuming as this process might turn out to be, it could have a high payoff not only in reducing time and costs involved in lending, but, equally important, in creating agencies that can replicate worthwhile elements in aided projects in identical or similar *domestically* financed programs, which will continue to account for the bulk of the anti-poverty budget in India.

Clearly all this will call for a willingness on the part of donors to take reasonable risks and to learn through trial, error, and retrial. This, however, is not likely to happen under current procedures for project selection and appraisal, which take place through short visits (of two to six weeks) by staff and consultants from aid agencies. Instead it would require continuous interaction with anti-poverty research, analysis, and action across the wide and diverse canvas of India. Resident missions of the World Bank as well as those of major bilateral donors would have to be considerably strengthened for the purpose— strengthened not just in numbers, but with involved, imaginative, and intelligent souls prepared to venture out from their rather incestuous expatriate circuits into the confusing world of Indian reality in order to keep themselves continuously well informed of data, evaluation, research, emerging needs and possibilities, and the strengths and weaknesses of organizations, governmental and otherwise. Thus the donor organizations, too, will have to "decentralize" and "participate" if anti-poverty aid is to be something more than transactions in periodic aid-programming between the Indian bureaucracy and outside money-movers.

Notes

[1] Robert L. Ayres, *Banking on the Poor* (Cambridge, Mass.: MIT Press, 1983), p. 9.

[2] See, for instance, Hans W. Singer, "Poverty, Income Distribution, and Levels of Living: Thirty Years of Changing Thought on Development Problems" in C. H. Hanumantha Rao and P.C. Joshi, eds., *Reflections on Economic Development and Social Change: Essays in Honor of Prof. V.K.R.V. Rao* (New Delhi: Allied Publishers, 1979); Paul Streeten et al., *First Things First: Meeting Basic Human Needs in Developing Countries* (New York: Oxford University Press, 1981); and Robert L. Ayres, op. cit.

[3] Government of India, Planning Commission, *Implications of Planning for a Minimum Level of Living* (New Delhi, 1962).

[4] Referring to this paper and to its author, Paul Streeten (op. cit., p. 23) points out: ". . . Pitambar Pant anticipated many features of the basic needs approach. But, since he believed with Pareto in the similarity of income distributions in all societies, minimum needs had to be met by general economic growth. He postulated this growth to be much higher than the five-year-plan target, which, in turn, was higher than actual growth. Moreover, he regarded the poorest 20 per cent as unreachable by economic growth."

[5] Internal political developments also played a part. In 1969 Indira Gandhi, then Prime Minister, initiated a major split in the ruling Congress Party on the basis of a "socialist platform" that included nationalization of commercial banks and the introduction of some direct poverty-alleviation programs.

[6] The group of multilateral and DAC-member bilateral donors assisting India that meets annually with Government of India representatives to discuss the Indian economy's performance, problems, prospects, and needs.

[7] We have drawn attention to such a shift in the case of India in recent years. For overall trends in World Bank lending, see Sheldon Annis, "The Shifting Ground of Poverty Lending," in Richard E. Feinberg, ed., *Between Two Worlds: The World Bank's Next Decade* (New Brunswick, N.J.: Transaction Books in cooperation with the Overseas Development Council, 1986).

[8] Montek S. Ahluwalia, "Balance-of-Payments Adjustment in India, 1970–71 to 1983–84," in *World Development*, Vol. 14, No. 8 (August 1986).

[9] See T.N. Srinivasan and P.K. Bardhan, eds., *Poverty and Income Distribution in India* (Calcutta: Statistical Publishing Society, 1974); Montek S. Ahluwalia, *Rural Poverty in India: 1957–58 to 1973–74* (Washington, D.C.: The World Bank, 1978); and John W. Mellor and Gunvant M. Desai, *Agricultural Change and Rural Poverty: Variations on a Theme by Dharm Narain* (New York: Oxford University Press, 1986).

[10] See Uma Lele, *The Design of Rural Development: Lessons from Africa* (Baltimore, Md.: Johns Hopkins University Press, 1975).

[11] See, for instance, Francine R. Frankel, *India's Green Revolution: Economic Gains and Political Costs* (Princeton, N.J.: Princeton University Press, 1971); Keith Griffin, *The Political Economy of Agrarian Change: An Essay on the Green Revolution* (New York: Macmillan, 1974); P.K. Bardhan, "India" in Hollis Chenery et al., *Redistribution With Growth* (Cambridge: Oxford University Press, 1974); S.D. Tendulkar, "Rural Institutional Credit and Rural Development: A Review Article," *Indian Economic Review*, (January-June 1983); H.W. Blair "Social Forestry: Time to Modify Goals," *Economic and Political Weekly*, July 16, 1986; D.M. Chandrasekhar et al., "Social Forestry in Karnataka: An Impact Analysis," *Economic and Political Weekly*, June 13, 1987; A. Vaidyanathan, *Irrigation and Agricultural Growth* (Indian Society for Agricultural Economics, 1987).

[12] Michael Lipton and John Toye, *Does Aid Work in India?* (New York: Methuen, forthcoming).

[13] For an overview, see N. Rath, "Garibi Hatao: Can IRDP Do It?" *Economic and Political Weekly*, February 9, 1985.

[14] For a blueprint, see B.S. Minhas, *Rural Poverty, Employment and Growth: An Agenda for Action* (New Delhi: Indian Statistical Institute, 1970).

[15] Two recent World Bank studies of interest are Edwin S. Mills and Chaytor M. Becker, *Studies in Indian Urban Development* (Washington, D.C.: The World Bank, 1986), and K.C. Sivaramakrishnan and Leslie Green, *Metropolitan Management: The Asian Experience* (New York: Oxford University Press for the World Bank, 1986).

[16] Robert L. Ayres (op. cit., p. 152) notes that several urban projects financed by the World Bank had an anti-poverty component of more than 90 per cent.

[17] K. Subbarao, "Interventions to Fill Nutrition Gaps at the Household Level: A Review of India's Experience" (Institute of Economic Growth, New Delhi, 1987, mimeographed).

208 AID FOR THE POOR IN INDIA

[18] Per Pinstrup-Anderson, "Nutrition Interventions," in Giovanni Andrea Cornia, Richard Jolly, and Frances Stewart, *Adjustment with a Human Face*, Vol. 1 (New York: Oxford University Press, 1987).

[19] See Michael M. Cernea, ed., *Putting People First* (New York: Oxford University Press, 1985).

[20] In 1981–87, average World Bank/IDA loan size in the anti-poverty sectors was about $70 to $100 million, compared with an average size of $200 to $250 million in infrastructure, energy, and industry.

Chapter 12

Sub-Sector Planning and Poverty Reduction: A Donor View

Joseph C. Wheeler

How can we better organize to reduce poverty? In somewhat stylized terms, I will speak of development activity taking place at four levels: macroeconomic, sector, sub-sector, and project. Examples of "sectors" would be agriculture, health, or education; "sub-sectors" would be agricultural research, children's innoculation, or primary education; examples of "projects" would be an agricultural research center, a clinic, or a teacher training institution.

In the past several years, macroeconomic structural reforms have very appropriately been the subject of intense debate and action. As a result, the rhetoric—and to an increasing extent the action as well—has greatly improved on such matters as fiscal policy, exchange rate policy, privatization, and pricing policies. At the other end of the spectrum, at the project level, many donor institutions—both public and non-governmental—are proffering increasing amounts of aid. Sound planning at the sector and sub-sector levels is needed to link the project interventions with the macro policy—and to bring cohesion to the development process. But these middle levels are often a zone of anarchy.

The sectoral policy gaps promote a myriad of *ad hoc* decisions at the project level. Governments lack information needed for informed judgments. Objectives are unclear. Assumptions are unrealistic. Activities are uncoordinated. People engaged in similar activities do not talk to each other. Donors overlap with other donors; collectively, they advocate conflicting policies, some of which are driven by other than developmental objectives. An ordering of sector and sub-sector policies could pay handsome returns.

Two recent conclusions of continuing discussions on coordination in the Development Assistance Committee of the Organisation for Economic Co-operation and Development are important in this context. First, recipient governments, especially in Africa, need to build their aid management staffs to be comparable in prestige and competence to their planning and finance units. Second, recipient governments can bring more coherence to the development process—and the aid process—by paying more attention to creating strategic plans at the sector and sub-sector levels and to a more precise articulation of objectives.

The development of good sectoral strategies is particularly difficult. Politically, it is hard to reach a consensus on sector-level objectives that are precise enough to have operational meaning. Sectoral planning is also inhibited by the fact that there are usually several ministries of government with pertinent responsibilities. Horizontal coordination among several ministries is difficult in any government. When full sector-level strategy development proves very difficult, perhaps a start can be made by first addressing sub-sector pieces of activity that are more manageable and that excite public interest and participation.

Lessons from Pakistan

In the 1970s I spent eight years in Pakistan leading the USAID mission there. In elaborating the themes of this chapter, I will draw on that experience. Pakistan is generally recognized to be one of the most sophisticated developing countries in terms of planning capacity. It has a good record of overall growth. Agricultural production has increased very satisfactorily, at least in terms of major grains. But Pakistan's record in some other areas relevant to strengthening the poor must be rated as only mediocre. Infant mortality remains over 100 per thousand, and not many more than half of Pakistan's children are enrolled in primary school.

I believe that Pakistan's enormous success in irrigation and agriculture provides an excellent example of sub-sector planning. With the partition of the subcontinent, a dispute had developed over the use of the waters of rivers flowing into the Indus in Pakistan whose origin was in India. With the good offices of the World Bank and the backing of a group of donors, an agreement was reached in 1960 that became a classic in sub-sector planning. Dams were built to store water, and huge connector canals were constructed to pass water from river to river to replace water no longer flowing into Pakistan. Other objectives, such as energy development, flood control, and more effective water regulation were also achieved. While history will demonstrate problems, the overall success of the effort is generally accepted. The Indus Basin Plan became the basis for effective coordination among Pakistan's governmental agencies, and it brought forward billions of dollars in donor contributions.

In the 1960s a major problem of groundwater buildup and soil salinity developed. Scientists prescribed at least a short-term cure in the form of another sub-sector strategy: the lowering of groundwater levels with tubewells. The cure was articulated in a report to President Ayub written by the American scientist Roger Revelle, who has a knack for describing complicated technical processes in terms that capture the attention of leaders. The result was the Salinity Control and Reclamation Program (SCARP)—a program that was neatly broken down into projects so that donors could finance components of a coherent package. Some financed a number of tubewells. Others picked up needed electricity transmission. Over time, through successive efforts, millions of acres were reclaimed.

Subsequent research revealed the main reason groundwater had been building up at rates much faster than had been anticipated. The original assumptions about amounts and location of water losses had been drastically wrong; there was far greater seepage from irrigation channels than had been expected. This research result was so surprising that it became necessary to confirm it by repeating the research over and over again, even as remedial measures were developed. Again, officials sought an articulation of the problem and its solutions that would be clear enough to capture the imagination of the political leadership and the donors. Millions of farmers who had to participate in the solution also had to be convinced that it was worthwhile to invest their own funds. The solutions came in the form of another sub-sector strategy involving: a) new organizational concepts (watercourse assocations); b) new technology (precision land leveling with tractor-drawn, small-scale, locally manufactured equipment and the so-called "pucka nukas," or concrete outlets from watercourses); and c) new credit mechanisms. The package required the participation of different government institutions than had been involved in earlier programs. But the objectives were clear and the technical package was proven. While adjustments have been made on the basis of experience, this sub-sector package has been carried through with a very large measure of success, and a number of other countries have learned from Pakistan's experience.

Economic and technical research led to the development of yet another sub-sector strategy—one aiming to double wheat production. Once it was known what seeds worked, what the plant response was to various fertilizer applications, and what level of return was needed to provide a farmer sufficient incentive to invest in the new seeds and fertilizer, a countrywide strategy was articulated for fertilizer production, imports, and distribution. The prices set for wheat and fertilizer were consistent with market realities. Aid for phosphates imports was critical. This strategy, like the others, required cabinet approval. An initially reluctant prime minister and cabinet adopted it in 1976—and wheat production has doubled since.

Agricultural research was the subject of yet another planning exercise. Donors had come to realize that *ad hoc* assistance to individual province-level research institutions was wasteful. A countrywide approach was needed. Over a period of two or three years, a plan was developed, and a scheme was finally adopted establishing a countrywide priority-setting organization and a national research center to provide a scientific focal point. This was another good example of thinking and talking things through, developing a strategy, and embarking on a sustained process of institution-building. The research strategy provided donors with a framework for coordination under government leadership.

There were other agriculture-related sub-sector strategies in Pakistan in addition to those briefly described above. For example, a rice program comparable to the wheat strategy was also pursued with success. Nationwide sub-sector planning exercises of this kind constitute the building blocks for a full agricultural sector plan. They must be designed to operate within the government budget—which usually means the main activity in the sector must be private and self-supporting, with the government playing a limited organizing, policy-setting, and catalytic role.

In the Pakistan case, the successful agricultural sub-sector strategies had some common features. First, they were designed to include all parts of the country affected by the problem. Thus costs and benefits were evaluated in the context of the whole economy. Sub-sector strategies were either designed to work within established macro-level policies, or the macro-level polices were changed to make their successful implementation possible. Second, the sub-sector strategies were of such importance that top political support was sought and given. This meant that bureaucracies and public information channels cooperated. Third, packages were soundly rooted in years of economic, technical, and social research. While there are risks in any new undertaking, the chances of success were clearly perceived to be high by both technical experts and policymakers. Fourth, in each case the packages were sold in simple and understandable terms—with clearly stated objectives—that were convincing to host governments and aid administrators. Fifth, with the possible exception of the agricultural research strategy, the benefits were immediately apparent, generating strong support for program implementation.

In spite of their several successes, the sub-sector pieces fell short of a full sector strategy. For example, Pakistan has been slow to develop a vegetable oil strategy. It lacks a credible forestry strategy. And agricultural education has not had sufficient support. There are other missing links. Furthermore, macro policies have not always been supportive. The process of planning at the sector level is never-ending, and Pakistan, like any other country, can do still better. Yet the agriculture sector clearly benefited from a series of well-founded sub-sector plans based on sound economics and technology and substantial practical research. The plans gained the highest level of political support. Their implementation has pulled along the sector, and dramatic results have been achieved. Despite the lack of a comprehensive sector-wide plan (beyond the general outline of one contained in Planning Commission documents), the accumulation of sub-sector strategies has taken Pakistan's agriculture a long way.

In contrast, similar successes have not been achieved in health and education in Pakistan. Until recently, decisionmakers did not succeed in carefully articulating countrywide objectives, nor in developing the specific policies and programs needed to make them work. Instead, much of the decisionmaking has been of the "seat of the pants" variety, based on a minimum of serious research and characterized by announcements of unrealistic targets without sufficient effort to think through the policy implications, test out the solutions, or develop the packages that would have a decisive impact on the problems.

In the health sector, the government ran a successful smallpox campaign and was able to mount fairly effective malaria-control programs, but it seemed unable to articulate a well-designed program of interventions that would efficiently reduce child mortality or achieve government goals in reducing the number of births. While progress has been made, and Pakistan has recently carried out successful innoculation campaigns, overall health conditions in Pakistan are far below what they should be for the money spent. Classical errors have been committed. Primary health experiments have been initiated in a minister's district—and fallen apart with the minister's departure from office. Expensive hospitals have been built without consideration of their recurring costs. In the absence of the political and organizational advantages of really bold strategies, the health of the poor has been neglected.

In the education sector, literacy remains under 25 per cent. In the early 1970s, decisionmakers lacked basic information on population, school attendance, dropout rates, and costs. When information did begin to be accumulated, it became increasingly clear that the implied priorities of a decisionmaking process characterized by a myriad of *ad hoc* decisions uninformed by the facts favored special groups, and that poverty alleviation was not given much attention. But as more solid information did become available, policymakers began to see the issues. The government discovered, for example, that it was financing university studies in literature at some one hundred times the student-year cost of primary education. It also became apparent that capital costs for school construction had been favored over recurring costs for school operations and repair.

Although Pakistan has been slow to bring coherent planning to the health and education sectors, there is now promise of a major turnaround. Budget priorities have been changed, and programs have been put in place that may result in substantially improved performance in these neglected sectors.

The Art of Sectoral Planning

Clear Nationwide Objectives

What are the generalizable lessons? I advocate a national-level, sector-by-sector planning effort that starts out with a carefully formulated statement of objectives. Politically, it is very difficult to articulate nationwide objectives without facing up to the problems of the poor. The establishment of clear objectives also disciplines planners to concentrate on what is essential. The statement of objectives needs to be based on a reasonably accurate understanding of the current situation. Putting together the necessary information may take time, and governments and donors alike need to recognize this. The statement of objectives must also take into account budgetary realities. Since government strategy must be modified to fit within financial constraints, policy decisions must be taken on user fees or local government responsibilities. Countrywide planning frequently leads to more reliance on the private sector and local government. With a general strategy articulated, project priorities can be set.

Overcoming Political Obstacles

More often than not the minister of agriculture, health, or education who seeks to develop bold nationwide sector or sub-sector strategies will be discouraged by the intractable nature of the constraints. The right policies take too long to carry out. Political time horizons call for quick results. Cabinet colleagues want expenditures in their districts. Friends, who tend to be landowners or city-oriented people, want policies tailored to their interests: They want agricultural policies that provide them a subsidy, hospitals that serve their families, or higher education facilities that their children can attend for free. The programs they support are usually too expensive in terms of unit costs to be extended to the whole population. The minister, for his part, wants the political visibility that comes with ribbon-cutting ceremonies on new and larger facilities. He gets more benefits from the award of larger contracts than from encouraging small entrepreneurs. Thus the pressures brought to bear against a countrywide strategy that specifically targets the poor—or at least includes the poor among its target groups—are often overwhelming.

Although most development donors are concerned to reduce poverty, they make decisions on what we in the OECD Development Assistance Committee call "official development assistance" with many other factors in the balance. These are well known and I need not dwell on them. In general I am impressed with the high degree of development orientation that the donor community *has* achieved and do not wish to minimize it. But development considerations *do* struggle for position with a set of concerns not unlike those facing decision-makers within developing countries: geo-political factors, commercial interests, the natural human desire to attend dedication ceremonies and get publicity, and short time horizons.

On both sides there are people who work to make the most of development opportunities. I puzzle about how to strengthen their hands. A more rigorous effort in countrywide sector or sub-sector planning might help.

Budgetary Realism and the Need for Priorities

It is easy for a country's sector and sub-sector development plans to lose touch with budgetary reality. By including several times the number of projects that are likely to be affordable, traditional development plans give some satisfaction to short-term political pressures, but lack utility as tools for setting priorities or for establishing policies. Without guidelines for day-to-day decisionmaking, project planning can be reduced to informal deal-making between *individuals*—on the recipient-country side and within the large donor community—with common interests in particular investments. Thus is born many a "white elephant"—an over-designed sports stadium; a high-tech, budget-gobbling hospital; a low-priority road—built without consideration of how it will be run or how the recurring costs will be covered. Many of these projects are born in the minds of cabinet ministers—almost casually: "I am going on a trip. What shall I ask for?" or, if from a donor country: "I am going on a trip. What shall I offer?" Without thought-through countrywide sector or sub-sector plans that have been debated and agreed upon at the cabinet level, it is hard to avoid such *ad hoc* decisionmaking, which (wittingly or unwittingly) slows down the achievement of broad-based literacy, lower child mortality, or increased food production.

It must be admitted that we development practitioners are often deficient in putting to our political masters those alternative packages that both achieve broad-based development and provide political returns as well. On the other hand, there are now many financially and technically feasible sub-sector-level development packages—including the types of packages I witnessed in Pakistan—that have not only been successfully implemented but have also paid good political dividends in both developing and donor countries.

The Useful Role of High-Visibility Campaigns

The most dramatic recent examples of such packages have been those aimed primarily at children, supported by UNICEF, WHO, and their allies. Massive innoculation programs are causing remarkable reductions in childhood diseases in many countries. Campaigns to teach mothers how to use oral rehydration therapy (ORT) to deal with diarrhea are reducing death rates as well. Prime ministers often find it politically possible and useful to mount orchestrated publicity efforts that gain the willing support of both the public itself, which must ultimately take action, and the intervening administrative and private institutions that must provide services. These campaigns are broadly successful because they are relatively simple in design, and the results of the measures they encompass are dramatic enough to be felt or seen by the population—and therefore carry credibility. The technology has been well developed. The costs are low and therefore feasible for both developing countries and donors. Moreover, they concentrate on areas of human need that are not highly sensitive politically, so that everybody can support them without qualification.

Yet the development community is often critical of these politically popular campaigns, even where they produce dramatic results. In my view, we are much too critical. We see the thorns and not the rose. But thorns do sometimes exist and planners need to avoid being overly simplistic. We will not be able to enlist the support of the prime minister for our wheat campaigns or our ORT programs year after year. We need to pay appropriate attention to long-term institutional issues. We should, for example, build immunizations into existing health systems so that they will be provided to children routinely, or, better yet—since efficiently operating rural health systems are almost always lacking—we should design immunization campaigns so that they help create the needed long-term policies, systems, and institutions that will bring health to the poorer sections of our communities on a sustained basis.

Sub-Sector Planning and Donor Coordination

Better sector-level programming in recipient countries can also help the process of aid coordination. It is mind-boggling to consider the problems facing a developing-country official in charge of a sector these days. Not only does the manager get criticized by people like me for not planning things well enough; not only does he or she face the barrage of pressures for projects from all the power centers within the society ("I want a hospital"; "I want a school"; "I want a contract!"); but also there are *all those donors!* There are twenty or more official donors, four or five multilaterals, a family of U.N. agencies, NGOs by the score, and perhaps hundreds of firms—all looking for business. While good sector and sub-sector plans are not going to solve the problem of how to deal effectively with donor representatives, they *can help*. They can provide a policy framework within which donors can be expected to operate. They could also be made a common part of the project paper of each donor operating in the sector.

Strengthening the Information Base

Sector and sub-sector planning is never finished. It might help if recipient-government ministries developed an information-gathering and -analyzing strategy for improving sectoral planning. By dividing the information and analysis they wish to develop into manageable blocks, they could ask project designers to build a module of research or data collection into the project development process—or even into project implementation. In this way, step-by-step sectoral planning could be improved without holding up current efforts. During my experience in Pakistan, I came to realize that the accumulation of the kind of information and experience needed to initiate a major component of a sectoral strategy—such as the irrigation, wheat, reclamation, and research strategies described above—takes several years of effort. The oral rehydration strategy resulted from decades of painstaking research. Prime ministers and cabinets should not be expected to support strategies that have not been very carefully developed.

A Context for Project Planning

In the DAC we have been reviewing our experience in project planning (or, as some call it, project appraisal)—covering the whole process from project identification to project approval by the parties involved. If donors were always exhaustive and serious in their project appraisals, we would not find ourselves building hospitals that countries cannot afford to run, supplying equipment that cannot be operated or maintained, pressing multiple technical assistance teams on the same subject, and insisting on conflicting policies on pricing and cost recovery.

Mistakes such as these can be avoided a lot more easily with proper sub-sectoral and sectoral planning. But even in the absence of such a broader planning framework, project planners can be enjoined to build consideration of sustainability factors into their analysis and to analyze the costs in money and talent if the project were to be replicated countrywide. And it can be insisted that project planners always consult with other donors and clear up conflicts. But the cause of coherence can be greatly helped by good sector and sub-sector framing.

Some Lessons for Donor Cooperation

1. As argued throughout this chapter, countrywide sector or sub-sector planning helps achieve more efficient use of resources. Carefully articulated plans also can help galvanize political and financial support in both recipient and donor countries.

2. Highly focused campaigns that are objective-oriented, simply packaged, and carefully researched—along the lines of the wheat and rice, innoculation, and ORT efforts—can be the "cutting edge" of support for overall sector goals. While such single-focus packages will help with only a portion of the development challenge in any given sector, they can inject enormous energy into the system. And when a program is important enough to capture part of the time and attention of the prime minister, others will support it too.

3. Campaigns focused on a single, major objective should be designed to support the broader and longer-term goals of sector development—for example, by putting into place permanent and sustainable institutions and processes. If such campaigns take money away from other high-priority activities in the sector, they can do long-run damage. If an innoculation program displaces an effective primary health care system, this can be tragic. But if it is designed to strengthen the overall primary care system, it carries an important bonus feature.

4. Donors and host governments should both work harder to improve statistics and to develop measures that trigger constructive political impulses. By giving wide publicity to critical measures of progress, that are accurate but understandable, the development community may be able to get more political support for primary education, public health, and small-farmer agriculture.

5. Donors should use the opportunity that project appraisal presents for helping developing countries strengthen their *sectoral* analysis. Where a sectoral framework is lacking, the project appraisal process should be thorough enough to avoid the classical error of building high-cost projects that cannot be replicated or even fully used. If we

build poverty, equity, and sustainability concerns into the project appraisal process, we can avoid most of those "white elephants."

    6. Finally, donors should stop being shy about publicizing the good things they have helped to achieve. We have as much reason to boast about the progress made as we do to express our anguish about the enormous job that remains. To the extent that our aid supports sectoral programs that are, overall, actually improving life for the disadvantaged portion of society, we should be able to take a little credit. Donors are, after all, part of a recipient-led process that has made dramatic progress over the past four decades.

About the Overseas Development Council

The Overseas Development Council is a private, non-profit organization established in 1969 for the purpose of increasing American understanding of the economic and social problems confronting the developing countries and of how their development progress is related to U.S. interests. Toward this end, the Council functions as a center for policy research and analysis, a forum for the exchange of ideas, and a resource for public education. The Council's current program of work encompasses four major issue areas: trade and industrial policy, international finance and investment, development strategies and development cooperation, and U.S. foreign policy and the developing countries. ODC's work is used by policy makers in the Executive Branch and the Congress, journalists, and those concerned about U.S.-Third World relations in corporate and bank management, international and non-governmental organizations, universities, and educational and action groups focusing on specific development issues. ODC's program is funded by foundations, corporations, and private individuals; its policies are determined by a governing Board and Council. In selecting issues and shaping its work program, ODC is also assisted by a standing Program Advisory Committee.

Victor H. Palmieri is Chairman of the ODC, and Wayne Fredericks is Vice Chairman. The Council's President is John W. Sewell.

Overseas Development Council
1717 Massachusetts Ave., N.W.
Washington, D.C. 20036
Tel. (202) 234-8701

ODC Program Advisory Committee

The Editors

Strengthening the Poor: What Have We Learned? is the tenth volume in the Overseas Development Council's series of policy books, U.S.-Third World Policy Perspectives. The co-editors of this series—often collaborating with guest editors contributing to the series—are Richard E. Feinberg and Valeriana Kallab.

John P. Lewis is Professor of Economics and International Affairs and Director of the Research Program in Development Studies (RPDS) at Princeton University's Woodrow Wilson School of Public and International Affairs. He is simultaneously Senior Advisor to the Overseas Development Council and Chairman of its Program Advisory Committee. From 1979 to 1981, Dr. Lewis was Chairman of the OECD's Development Assistance Committee (DAC). From 1982 to 1985, he was Chairman of the three-year Task Force on Concessional Flows established by the World Bank/IMF "Development Committee" (formerly the Joint Ministerial Committee of the Boards of Governors of the Bank and Fund on the Transfer of Real Resources to Developing Countries.) He has served as a member of the U.N. Committee for Development Planning, of which he was also rapporteur from 1972 to 1978. For many years, he has alternated between academia and government posts (as Member of the Council of Economic Advisors, 1963–64, and Director of the USAID Mission to India, 1964–69), with collateral periods of association with The Brookings Institution, The Ford Foundation, and the World Bank.

Valeriana Kallab is Vice President and Director of Publications of the Overseas Development Council and series co-editor of the ODC's U.S.-Third World Policy Perspectives series. She has been responsible for ODC's published output since 1972. Before joining ODC, she was a research editor and writer on international economic issues at the Carnegie Endowment for International Peace in New York. She was co-editor (with John P. Lewis) of *Development Strategies Reconsidered*; *U.S. Foreign Policy and the Third World: Agenda 1983*; and (with Guy F. Erb) *Beyond Dependency: The Third World Speaks Out.*

Richard E. Feinberg is Vice President of the Overseas Development Council and co-editor of the Policy Perspectives series. Before joining ODC in 1981, he served as the Latin American specialist on the Policy Planning Staff of the U.S. Department of State, and as an international economist in the Treasury Department and with the House Banking Committee. He is the author of numerous books as well as journal and newspaper articles on U.S. foreign policy, Latin American politics, and international economic and financial issues.

Contributing Authors

Norman Uphoff is Professor of Government and presently Director of the South Asia Program at Cornell University, where he has been teaching since 1970 as well as chairing the Rural Development Committee. During this period he has conducted various consulting assignments for the World Bank, The Ford Foundation, FAO, the United Nations, CARE, and Community Aid Abroad. He has also served on the South Asia Committee of the Social Science Research Council and is currently a member of USAID's Research Advisory Committee and the Program Advisory Committee of the Overseas Development Council. Between 1977 and 1982, he directed the Rural Development Participation Project based at Cornell and funded by USAID. Since 1980, he has been involved with USAID projects introducing participatory irrigation management in Sri Lanka and Nepal.

Samuel Paul is an advisor on public sector management in the World Bank's Country Economics Department. Prior to joining the World Bank in 1984, he was a Professor of Economics and Director of the Indian Institute of Management in Ahemedabad. He has also served as a Chief Technical Advisor with the International Labour Organization, and as a Visiting Professor at the Harvard Business School and the Kennedy School of Government at Harvard while on leave from the Indian Institute of Management. He has been a consultant to several international agencies and has published extensively on development and management-related issues. Among his books are *Managing Development Programs: The Lessons of Success* (Westview Press, 1983), and *Strategic Management of Development Programs* (ILO, Geneva, 1984).

Uma Lele is Chief of the Special Studies Division in the Country Economics Department of the World Bank. She is currently completing a wide-ranging program of research on aid and development, which includes the study, "Managing Agricultural Development in Africa" (MADIA). Uma Lele previously has held several positions in research/policy analysis and operational/managerial responsibilities in Asia and Africa regions of the World Bank. She was also Assistant Professor and Senior Fellow at Cornell University. Her books include *The Design of Rural Development: Lessons from Africa* and *Foodgrains Marketing in India: Private Performance and Public Policy*. She has also written numerous journal articles and papers.

Mohiuddin Alamgir is Director of the Policy Review Division of the International Fund for Agricultural Development (IFAD). Previously, Dr. Alamgir held positions as the Research Director of the Bangladesh Institute of Development Studies, Visiting Professor at the Institute for International Economic Studies at the University of Stockholm, Visiting Scholar at the Harvard Institute for International Development, and Senior Economist at Meta Systems, Inc. in Cambridge, Massachusetts. Since 1970, he has served as senior consultant to many major international organizations including the World Bank, FAO, UNCTAD, UNEP, ESCAP, and IFAD. Among his many field assignments, Dr. Alamgir, as a team leader, assisted the Government of Tanzania in the formulation of its National Food Strategy, the Government of Uganda in the formulation of its 10-Year Plan for the 1980s, and the Electricity Generating Authority of Thailand on lignite pricing. He has contributed to numerous international and national conferences and seminars and has

226

published extensively on development, income distribution, food, and poverty issues. Among his books are *Famine in South Asia: Political Economy of Mass Starvation*; *Bangladesh: A Case of Below Poverty Level Equilibrium Trap*; and *The New International Economic Order and UNCTAD IV* (ed.).

Senator Sartaj Aziz is currently Minister for Food, Agriculture, and Rural Development in Pakistan. Prior to taking up his political career in April 1984, he spent twelve years with the U.N. food agencies in Rome. From 1971 to 1975, he was Director of the Commodities and Trade Division of the Food and Agriculture Organization (FAO). He also served as Deputy Secretary General of the U.N. World Food Conference, held in Rome in November 1974. Between 1976 and 1978, he was Deputy Executive Director of the U.N. World Food Council. During this period he also served as Executive Secretary of the Preparatory Commission for the International Fund for Agricultural Development (IFAD), which he joined as Assistant President from the beginning of its operations in January 1978 until his return to Pakistan in 1984. Sartaj Aziz also had a distinguished career in his own country between 1951 and 1971 in the Ministry of Finance and the National Planning Commission. His publications include *Industrial Location Policy in Pakistan* (1968), *Hunger, Politics and Markets* (1975), and *Rural Development—Learning from China* (1978).

Nurul Islam is a Senior Research Advisor at the International Food Policy Research Institute (IFPRI). Prior to joining IFPRI, he was Assistant Director-General, Economic and Social Policy Department, U.N. Food and Agriculture Organization, from 1977 to 1987; and before that, a Fellow at Oxford University (1975–77). Prior to this, he was Minister of Planning, Government of Bangladesh, from 1972 to 1975, Chairman of the Bangladesh Institute of Development Studies, Director of the Pakistan Institute of Development Economics, and Professor and Chairman of the Department of Economics at Dhaka University, Bangladesh. Dr. Islam has served as an expert consultant and member of advisory bodies of the World Bank and several United Nations agencies. He was a founding member of IFPRI's Board of Trustees and also a member of the governing bodies of the International Rice Research Institute and the International Economics Association. His publications include, besides numerous articles on economic development, planning, trade, and agriculture, *Development Planning in Bangladesh: A Study in Political Economy* (1977), *Development Strategy of Bangladesh* (1978), *Aid and Influence: A Case Study of Bangladesh* (with Y. Faaland and J. Parkinson, 1981), and *Foreign Trade and Economic Controls in Development: The Case of United Pakistan* (1981).

Sheldon Annis is a Visiting Fellow at the Overseas Development Council, and is writing a book on the relationship between grassroots organizations and the public sector in Latin America. He is also publishing a book on debt and environmental degradation in Costa Rica. Recently, he was a Visiting Lecturer at Princeton University's Woodrow Wilson School, and prior to ODC, he was Senior Research Officer at the Inter-American Foundation, where, among other responsibilities, he edited the journal, *Grassroots Development*. Dr. Annis has served as a consultant on poverty issues for the U.S. Agency for International Development, the World Bank, and private voluntary organizations. He recently published *God and Production in a Guatemalan Town* (University of Texas Press) and co-edited *Direct to the Poor: Grassroots Development in Latin America* (Lynne Reinner Publishers).

Mayra Buvinić is the Director of the International Center for Research on Women (ICRW). Prior to founding ICRW in 1976, she was a Research Associate at the Office of International Science of the American Association for the Advancement of Science (AAAS). Dr. Buvinić is a trustee of the International Institute for Tropical Agriculture and a member of the Overseas Development Council's Program Advisory Committee. She has been a scholar in residence at the Bellagio Study and Conference Center of the Rockefeller Foundation and is past President of the Association for Women in Development. She is the author of numerous publications on the poverty of women in developing countries, including "Women's Projects in the Third World: Explaining their Misbehavior," and "Weathering Economic Crises: The Crucial Role of Women in Health." She is an editor of *Women and Poverty in the Third World* (with Margaret A. Lycette and William McGreevey), published by Johns Hopkins University Press, as well as *Women's Roles and Population Trends in the Third World* (with Richard Anker and Nadia Youssef). In 1976, she was co-author (with Irene Tinker and Michele Bo Bramsen) of the AAAS/ODC two-volume study, *Women and World Development*. Dr. Buvinić's current research interests include women's responses to recession, the status of women who head households, and trends in development assistance for women in development.

Margaret A. Lycette is Deputy Director of the International Center for Research on Women (ICRW). Before joining ICRW in 1982, she was a project economist for East Asia with the World Bank, and then an international economist specializing in the multilateral development banks at the U.S. Department of the Treasury. She is the author of numerous publications on women's access to credit, education, and low-income housing; and on the importance of women's economic contributions to households during periods of economic crisis in developing countries. She is an editor of *Women and Poverty in the Third World* (with Mayra Buvinić and William McGreevey), and co-author of the World Bank Policy Paper, *Basic Needs in Shelter*. Her current research focuses on the impact on women of user fees in social services and education, and on how structural adjustment programs can be designed to benefit poor women.

Richard Jolly has been Deputy Executive Director of Programmes at UNICEF since 1982. Before this, he was from 1971 Director of the Institute of Development Studies at the University of Sussex. He has combined research and operational work in developing countries during his professional life, beginning as a Community Development Officer in Kenya in 1957. During the 1970s, he participated in ILO World Employment missions to Colombia, Sri Lanka, and Zambia and led, with Hans Singer, the ILO mission to Kenya on Employment, Incomes, and Equality. From this emerged the World Bank/IDS study, *Redistribution with Growth*, of which he was, with Hollis Chenery and others, co-author. Other books he has co-edited include *Disarmament and World Development*; *Rich Country Interests and Third World Development*; *The Impact of World Recession on Children*; and the recent UNICEF study on *Adjustment with a Human Face*.

Thomas W. Dichter is Vice President for Replication and Policy Analysis at Technoserve, an American NGO working in agricultural enterprise development. Before joining Technoserve in 1984, Dr. Dichter served as Peace Corps Director in Yemen, and prior to that, as a policy analyst at the Hudson Institute. A cultural anthropologist trained at the University of Chicago, he has been a consultant to many NGOs as well as to USAID, the World Bank, and the OECD. He is the author of numerous articles on development issues—most recently on the evolution of non-governmental organizations in international development.

S. Guhan has been Senior Fellow in the Madras Institute of Development Studies since 1979. Prior to that, he was Senior Economist in the Independent Commission for International Development Issues (Brandt Commission). In his earlier career in the Indian Administrative Service (1955–78), Dr. Guhan held senior positions in the Ministries of Finance, Planning, and Industrial Development in the Government of India and the State of Tamilnadu, and he was Alternate Executive Director for India in the World Bank (1964–68). He has written extensively on Indian economic problems and has been a consultant to national and international organizations.

Joseph C. Wheeler is Chairman of the Development Assistance Committee (DAC) of the Organisation for Economic Co-operation and Development (OECD). Prior to his election as DAC Chairman, he served as Deputy Executive Director of the United Nations Environment Programme (UNEP) at its world headquarters in Nairobi, Kenya. He served as Deputy Administrator of the U.S. Agency for International Development from 1980 to 1982. Previous assignments with USAID included Assistant Administrator for Near East (1977–79), Director of the USAID Mission to Pakistan (1969–77), Deputy Assistant Administrator for Near East and South Asia (1967–69), and Director of the USAID Mission to Jordan (1965–67). He worked on the establishment of the Peace Corps during its first two years (1961–63). Mr. Wheeler is a Member of the Board of the International Fertilizer Development Center.

Overseas Development Council
1717 Massachusetts Ave., N.W.
Washington, D.C. 20036
Tel. (202) 234-8701

DEVELOPMENT STRATEGIES RECONSIDERED

John P. Lewis and Valeriana Kallab, editors

> "First-rate, comprehensive analysis—presented in a manner that makes it extremely valuable to policy makers."
> —Robert R. Nathan
> Robert Nathan Associates

Important differences of opinion are emerging about the national strategies best suited for advancing economic growth and equity in the difficult global adjustment climate of the late 1980s.

Proponents of the "new orthodoxy"—the perspective headquartered at the World Bank and favored by the Reagan administration as well as by a number of other bilateral donor governments—are "carrying forward with redoubled vigor the liberalizing, pro-market strains of the thinking of the 1960s and 1970s. They are very mindful of the limits of government." And they are "emphatic in advocating export-oriented growth to virtually all comers."

Other prominent experts question whether a standardized prescription of export-led growth can meet the needs of big low-income countries in the latter 1980s as well as it did those of small and medium-size middle-income countries in the 1960s and 1970s. They are concerned about the special needs of low-income Africa. And they see a great deal of unfinished business under the heading of poverty and equity.

In this volume, policy syntheses are proposed to reconcile the goals of growth, equity, and adjustment; to strike fresh balances between agricultural and industrial promotion and between capital and other inputs; and to reflect the interplay of democracy and development.

Contents:
John P. Lewis—Development Promotion: A Time for Regrouping
Irma Adelman—A Poverty-Focused Approach to Development Policy
John W. Mellor—Agriculture on the Road to Industrialization
Jagdish N. Bhagwati—Rethinking Trade Strategy
Leopoldo Solis and Aurelio Montemayor—A Mexican View of the Choice Between Inward and Outward Orientation
Colin I. Bradford, Jr.—East Asian "Models": Myths and Lessons
Alex Duncan—Aid Effectiveness in Raising Adaptive Capacity in the Low-Income countries
Atul Kohli—Democracy and Development

John P. Lewis, guest editor of this volume, is professor of economics and international affairs at Princeton University's Woodrow Wilson School of Public and International Affairs. He is simultaneously senior advisor to the Overseas Development Council and chairman of its Program Advisory Committee. From 1979 to 1981, Mr. Lewis was chairman of the OECD's Development Assistance Committee. He has served as a member of the U.N. Committee for Development Planning. For many years, he has alternated between academia and government posts, with collateral periods of association with The Brookings Institution and The Ford Foundation.

ISBN: 0-88738-044-1 (cloth)
ISBN: 0-87855-991-4 (paper)
1986

$19.95
$12.95
208 pp.

GROWTH, EXPORTS, AND JOBS IN A CHANGING WORLD ECONOMY: AGENDA 1988

John W. Sewell, Stuart K. Tucker, and contributors

Agenda 1988, the eleventh of ODC's well-known assessments of U.S. policy toward the developing countries, contributes uniquely to the ongoing debate on U.S. jobs and trade competition with other nations.

The administration that takes office in 1989 faces a situation without precedent in the post-1945 period. Like many developing countries, the United States has to balance its trade accounts, service its foreign debts, and rebuild its industrial base. The challenge is twofold.

The immediate task is to restore the international economic position of the United States by taking the lead in devising measures to support renewed *global* growth, especially rapid growth in the developing countries.

Meanwhile, however, the world is on the threshold of a Third Industrial Revolution. Rapid technological advances are radically changing the familiar economic relationships between developed and developing countries. The kinds of policies needed to adjust to these technology-driven changes—policies on education, training, research and development—generally have longer lead times than the immediate measures needed to stimulate global growth. In the next four years, the United States must therefore proceed on *both* fronts at the same time.

Contents:

John W. Sewell has been president of the Overseas Development Council since January, 1980. From 1977 to 1979, as the Council's executive vice president, he directed ODC's programs of research and public education. Prior to joining the Council in 1971, Mr. Sewell directed the communications program of the Brookings Institution. He also served in the Foreign Service of the United States. A contributor to past *Agenda* assessments, he is co-author of *Rich Country Interests and Third World Development* and *The Ties That Bind: U.S. Interests in Third World Development.* He is a frequent author and lecturer on U.S. relations with the developing countries.

Stuart K. Tucker is a fellow at the Overseas Development Council. Prior to joining ODC in 1984, he was a research consultant for the Inter-American Development Bank. He has written on U.S. international trade policy, including the linkage between the debt crisis and U.S. exports and jobs. He also prepared the Statistical Annexes in ODC's *Agenda 1985-86.*

U.S.-Third World Policy Perspectives No. 9
ISBN: 088738-196-0 (cloth) $19.95
ISBN: 0-88738-718-7 (paper) $12.95
February 1988   286 pp.

Forthcoming 1989
ENVIRONMENTAL AND ANTI-POVERTY STRATEGIES FOR THE 1990s*
H. Jeffrey Leonard and contributors

Few aspects of development are as complex and urgent as the need to reconcile anti-poverty and pro-environmental goals. Do both of these important goals—poverty alleviation and environmental sustainability—come in the same package? Or are there necessary trade-offs and must painful choices be made?

A basic premise of this volume is that environmental degradation and intractable poverty are often especially pronounced in particular ecological and social settings across the developing world. These twin crises of development and the environment can and must be addressed jointly. But they require differentiated strategies for the kinds of physical environments in which poor people live. This study explores these concerns in relation to irrigated areas, arid zones, moist tropical forests, hillside areas, urban centers, and unique ecological settings.

The overview chapter highlights recent efforts to advance land and natural resource management, and some of the real and perceived conflicts between alleviating poverty and protecting the environment in the design and implementation of development policy. The chapters that follow offer economic investment and natural resource management options for reducing poverty and maintaining ecological balance for six different areas of the developing world.

Contents:

H. Jeffrey Leonard—Overview

Montague Yudelman—Maintaining Production on Irrigated Lands

Dirk Strycker—Technology, Human Pressure, and Ecology in Arid Regions

John O. Browder—Agricultural Alternatives for Humid Tropical Forests

John de Boer—Sustainable Approaches to Hillside Agriculture

Tim E. S. Campbell—Resource Dilemmas in the Urban Environment

Alison Jolly—Meeting Human Needs in Unique Ecological Settings

---

H. Jeffrey Leonard, guest editor of this volume, is the vice president of the World Wildlife Fund and The Conservation Foundation and Director of the Fairfield Osborn Center for Economic Development. Dr. Leonard has been at The Foundation since 1976. He is the author of several recent books, including *Pollution and the Struggle for the World Product, Natural Resources and Economic Development in Central America,* and *Are Environmental Regulations Driving U.S. Industries Overseas?* He is also editor of *Divesting Nature's Capital: The Political Economy of Environmental Abuse in the Third World* and *Business and Environment: Toward a Common Ground.*

*Tentative title.

Forthcoming 1989

THE POLITICS OF ECONOMIC ADJUSTMENT: FRAGILE COALITIONS*

Joan M. Nelson and contributors

The global economic crisis of the 1980s forced most developing nations into a simultaneous quest for short-run economic stabilization and longer-run structural reforms. Effective adjustment is at least as much a political as an economic challenge. But political dimensions of adjustment have been much less carefully analyzed than have the economic issues.

Governments in developing countries must balance pressures from external agencies seeking more rapid adjustment in return for financial support, and the demands of domestic political groups often opposing such reforms. How do internal pressures shape external bargaining? and conversely, how does external influence shape domestic political maneuvering? Growing emphasis on "adjustment with a human face" poses additional questions: Do increased equity and political acceptability go hand in hand? or do more pro-poor measures add to the political difficulties of adjustment? The capacity of the state itself to implement adjustment measures varies widely among nations. How can external agencies take such differences more fully into account? The hopeful trend toward democratic openings in many countries raises further, crucial issues: What special political risks and opportunities confront governments struggling simultaneously with adjustment and democratization?

The contributors to this volume explore these issues and their policy implications for the United States and for the international organizations that seek to promote adjustment efforts.

Contents:

Joan M. Nelson has been a Visiting Fellow at the Overseas Development Council since 1982; since mid-1986, she has directed a collegial research program on the politics of economic adjustment. She has been a consultant for the World Bank, the Agency for International Development, and for the International Monetary Fund, as well as a staff member of USAID. In the 1970s and early 1980s, she taught at the Massachusetts Institute of Technology, the Johns Hopkins University School of Advanced International Studies, and Princeton University's Woodrow Wilson School. She has published books and articles on development assistance and policy dialogue, political participation, migration and urban politics in developing nations, and the politics of economic stabilization and reform.

*Tentative title.

Forthcoming 1989

THE FUTURE OF THE IMF*

Catherine Gwin, Richard E. Feinberg, and contributors

The global economic environment in which we now live is radically different from the one foreseen when the International Monetary Fund was created in the wake of World War II. The important changes have to do not only with the end of U.S. economic hegemony and the demise of the fixed exchange rate system, but also with the internationalization of financial markets, shifting patterns of global production and trade, and a prolonged slowdown in global economic growth.

The Fund has not kept pace with the changes and has not been fulfilling its needed role. This volume poses the fundamental questions regarding the responsiveness of Fund policies and practices to change, and the member countries' willingness to let the Fund play a more constructive role in coping with the new realities of international monetary and financial matters. It also addresses the overarching question of the Fund's dual role—its systemic role and its role as a financial institution for countries that do not have market access, or whose access is temporarily interrupted. The study sets out a plan for revisions that must be made in light of the major changes in the global economy.

Contents:

Catherine Gwin and Richard E. Feinberg —Overview

Jacques J. Polak—The IMF's Future in the Management of International Monetary and Financial Affairs

Jeffrey Sachs—The Reorganization of IMF Program Strategies

Louis Goreux—IMF Repayment and the Role of Concessional Funds

Peter B. Kenen—The IMF's Use of its Resources

Guillermo Ortiz—The Future Strategy for the IMF in the International Debt Crisis

---

Catherine Gwin is Special Program Adviser at The Rockefeller Foundation. She served as a consultant for the Group of Twenty-Four's 1987 report on the future of the International Monetary Fund. In 1981-83, she was a Senior Associate at the Carnegie Endowment for International Peace, where she directed a Study Group on international financial cooperation and the management of developing-country debt. In 1980-81, she was North-South Issues Coordinator at the U.S. International Development Cooperation Agency (IDCA). Prior to that assignment, she was a staff member, and subsequently Staff Director, of the Council on Foreign Relations' 1980s Project. Dr. Gwin has taught, consulted, and written widely on international financial and development issues.

Richard E. Feinberg is Vice President of the Overseas Development Council. He served as the Latin American specialist on the Policy Planning Staff of the Department of State from 1977 to 1979. He has worked as an international economist in the Treasury Department and with the House Banking Committee, and has been an adjunct professor of international finance at the Georgetown University School of Foreign Service. Dr. Feinberg has written numerous articles and books on U.S. foreign policy, Latin American politics, and international economics, including *The Intemperate Zone: The Third World Challenge to U.S. Foreign Policy;* (as editor) *Central America: International Dimensions of the Crisis;* and *Subsidizing Success: The Export-Import Bank in the U.S. Economy.*

*Tentative title

THE UNITED STATES AND MEXICO: FACE TO FACE WITH NEW TECHNOLOGY

Cathryn L. Thorup and contributors

Rapid technological advance is fast changing economic and political relations between industrial and advanced developing countries. The new technologies encompass innovations in automation and robotization, the substitution of synthetic for natural materials, advances in communications and information technology, and changes in social organization. These advances are transforming production, trade, and investment in manufactures, commodities, and services—with major repercussions on jobs, wages, and politics in many countries.

This study explores what adjustment to this worldwide transformation means close to home—for people and policies in Mexico and the United States, and for relations between the two nations.

The authors come from both sides of the border—bringing together varied experience and expertise from government, business, and academic institutions. They highlight the interplay of economic, political, social, and cultural forces in the process of technological change. Among the themes they explore are the relationships between technological advance and employment, immigration, foreign debt, and protectionism. From their analysis of the objectives and policies of both countries emerge insights into the politics of technology change—the policy constraints faced in each country, the limits of political will, and the changing horizons of domestic interest groups.

The study draws together specific recommendations on improving the efficiency of bilateral economic interaction, reducing the adjustment costs of technological change, and avoiding diplomatic tensions between the two nations.

Contents:

Cathryn L. Thorup is the director of the U.S.-Mexico Project of the Overseas Development Council. Prior to joining ODC in 1980, she spent six years in Mexico, studying and working as a journalist for the Mexican news magazine *Razones*. She has written extensively on U.S. policymaking toward Mexico, conflict management in U.S.-Mexican relations, regional security, and Mexican economic and political reform. Ms. Thorup is a member of the Board of Directors of the Consortium for U.S. Research Programs for Mexico (PROFMEX).

ISBN:0-88738-663-6 (paper) **$12.95**
October 1987 **No. 8, 238 pp.**

BETWEEN TWO WORLDS:
THE WORLD BANK'S NEXT DECADE
Richard E. Feinberg and contributors

In the midst of the global debt and adjustment crises, the World Bank has been challenged to become the leading agency in North-South finance and development. The many dimensions of this challenge—which must be comprehensively addressed by the Bank's new president assuming office in mid-1986—are the subject of this important volume.

As mediator between international capital markets and developing countries, the World Bank will be searching for ways to renew the flow of private credit and investment to Latin America and Africa. And as the world's premier development agency, the Bank can help formulate growth strategies appropriate to the 1990s.

The Bank's ability to design and implement a comprehensive response to these global needs is threatened by competing objectives and uncertain priorities. Can the Bank design programs attractive to private investors that also serve the very poor? Can it emphasize efficiency while transferring technologies that maximize labor absorption? Can it more aggressively condition loans on policy reforms without attracting the criticism that has accompanied IMF programs?

The contributors to this volume assess the role that the World Bank can play in the period ahead. They argue for new financial and policy initiatives and for new conceptual approaches to development, as well as for a restructuring of the Bank, as it takes on new, systemic responsibilities in the next decade.

Contents:

Richard E. Feinberg is vice president of the Overseas Development Council and co-editor of the U.S.-Third World Policy Perspectives series. From 1977 to 1979, Feinberg was Latin American specialist on the policy planning staff of the U.S. Department of State. He has also served as an international economist in the U.S. Treasury Department and with the House Banking Committee. He is currently also adjunct professor of international finance at the Georgetown University School of Foreign Service. Feinberg is the author of numerous books as well as journal and newspaper articles on U.S. foreign policy, Latin American politics, and international economics. His most recent book is *The Intemperate Zone: The Third World Challenge to U.S. Foreign Policy* (1983).

ISBN: 0-88738-123-5 (cloth)   **$19.95**
ISBN: 0-88738-665-2 (paper)   **$12.95**
June 1986   208 pp.

HARD BARGAINING AHEAD: U.S. TRADE POLICY AND DEVELOPING COUNTRIES

Ernest H. Preeg and contributors

U.S.-Third World trade relations are at a critical juncture. Trade conflicts are exploding as subsidies, import quotas, and "voluntary" export restraints have become commonplace. The United States is struggling with record trade and budget deficits. Developing countries, faced with unprecedented debt problems, continue to restrain imports and stimulate exports.

For both national policies and future multilateral negotiations, the current state of the North-South trade relationship presents a profound dilemma. Existing problems of debt and unemployment cannot be solved without growth in world trade. While many developing countries would prefer an export-oriented development strategy, access to industrialized-country markets will be in serious doubt if adjustment policies are not implemented. Consequently, there is an urgent need for more clearly defined mutual objectives and a strengthened policy framework for trade between the industrialized and the developing countries.

In this volume, distinguished practitioners and academics identify specific policy objectives for the United States on issues that will be prominent in the new round of GATT negotiations.

Contents:

Ernest H. Preeg—Overview: An Agenda for U.S. Trade Policy Toward
    Developing Countries
William E. Brock—Statement: U.S. Trade Policy Toward Developing Countries
Anne O. Krueger and Constantine Michalopoulos—Developing-Country
    Trade Policies and the International Economic System
Henry R. Nau—The NICs in a New Trade Round
C. Michael Aho—U.S. Labor-Market Adjustment and Import Restrictions
John D. A. Cuddy—Commodity Trade
Adebayo Adedeji—Special Measures for the Least Developed and Other
    Low-Income Countries
Sidney Weintraub—Selective Trade Liberalization and Restriction
Stuart K. Tucker—Statistical Annexes

Ernest H. Preeg, a career foreign service officer and recent visiting fellow at the Overseas Development Council, has had long experience in trade policy and North-South economic relations. He was a member of the U.S. delegation to the GATT Kennedy Round of negotiations and later wrote a history and analysis of those negotiations, *Traders and Diplomats* (The Brookings Institution, 1969). Prior to serving as American ambassador to Haiti (1981-82), he was deputy chief of mission in Lima, Peru (1977-80), and deputy secretary of state for international finance and development (1976-77).

ISBN: 0-88738-043-3 (cloth)   **$19.95**
ISBN: 0-87855-987-6 (paper)   **$12.95**
1985   **220 pp.**

INVESTING IN DEVELOPMENT: NEW ROLES FOR PRIVATE CAPITAL?

Theodore H. Moran and contributors

The tone of the debate about foreign direct investment in Third World development has changed dramatically since the 1970s. There are expectations in both North and South that multinational corporations can play a key role in restoring growth, replacing aid, providing capital to relieve the burden on commercial bank lending, and (together with the private sectors in the local economies) lead to an era of healthier and more balanced growth.

To what extent are these expectations justified? This volume provides a reassessment of the impact of multinational corporate operations on Third World development. It covers not only direct equity investment in natural resources and manufacturing, but non-equity arrangements extending to agriculture and other sectors as well. It examines whether the efforts of less developed countries to attract and control multinational corporations have constituted a serious "distortion" of trade that threatens jobs in the home nations. It analyzes the link between international companies and the "umbrella" of World Bank co-financing as a mechanism to reduce risk. Finally, it attempts to estimate how much of the "gap" in commercial bank lending might plausibly be filled by direct corporate investment over the next decade.

In each case, it draws policy conclusions for host governments, for home governments (focused particularly on the United States), for multilateral institutions such as the World Bank and the agencies of the United Nations, and for the multinational firms themselves.

Contents

Theodore H. Moran is director of Georgetown University's Landegger Program in International Business Diplomacy as well as professor and member of the Executive Council of the Georgetown University School of Business Administration. A former member of the Policy Planning Staff of the Department of State with responsibilities including investment issues, Dr. Moran has since 1971 been a consultant to corporations, governments, and multilateral agencies on investment strategy, international negotiations, and political risk assessment. His publications include many articles and five major books on the issues explored in this new volume. He is a member of the ODC Program Advisory Committee.

ISBN: 0-88738-044-3 (cloth) **$19.95**
ISBN: 0-88738-644-X (paper) **$12.95**

UNCERTAIN FUTURE: COMMERCIAL BANKS AND THE THIRD WORLD

Richard E. Feinberg and Valeriana Kallab, editors

> "useful short papers by people of differing backgrounds who make quite different kinds of suggestions about how banks, governments and international bodies ought to behave in the face of the continuing debt difficulties"
> —*Foreign Affairs*

> "the very best available to academia and the general public . . . on the criteria of reader interest, clarity of writing, quality of the research, and on that extra something special that sets a work apart from others of similar content"
> —James A. Cox, Editor
> *The Midwest Book Review*

The future of international commercial lending to the Third World has become highly uncertain just when the stakes seem greatest for the banks themselves, the developing countries, and the international financial system. Having become the main channel for the transfer of capital from the North to the South in the 1970s, how will the banks respond in the period ahead, when financing will be urgently needed?

The debt crisis that burst onto the world stage in 1982 is a long-term problem. New bank lending to many developing countries has slowed to a trickle. The combination of high interest rates and the retrenchment in bank lending is draining many developing countries of badly needed development finance. While major outright defaults now seem improbable, heightened conflict between creditors and debtors is possible unless bold actions are taken soon.

New approaches must take into account the interests of both the banks and developing-country borrowers. No single solution can by itself resolve the crisis. A battery of measures is needed—reforms in macroeconomic management, in the policies of the multilateral financial institutions, in bank lending practices as well as information gathering and analysis, and in regulation.

Contents:

Richard E. Feinberg—Overview: Restoring Confidence in International Credit Markets
Lawrence J. Brainard—More Lending to the Third World? A Banker's View
Karin Lissakers—Bank Regulation and International Debt
Christine A. Bogdanowicz-Bindert and Paul M. Sacks—The Role of Information: Closing the Barn Door?
George J. Clark—Foreign Banks in the Domestic Markets of Developing Countries
Catherine Gwin—The IMF and the World Bank: Measures to Improve the System
Benjamin J. Cohen—High Finance, High Politics

ISBN: 0-88738-041-7 (cloth) **$19.95**
ISBN: 0-87855-989-2 (paper) **$12.95**
1984 **144 pp.**

ADJUSTMENT CRISIS IN THE THIRD WORLD

Richard E. Feinberg and Valeriana Kallab, editors

"major contribution to the literature on the adjustment crisis"
—B. T. G. Chidzero
Minister of Finance, Economic Planning
and Development Government of Zimbabwe

"The adjustment crisis book has really stirred up some excitement here"
—Peter P. Waller
German Development Institute (Berlin)

"good collection of papers"
—*Foreign Affairs*

Just how the debt and adjustment crisis of Third World countries is handled, by them and by international agencies and banks, can make a big difference in the pace and quality of *global* recovery.

Stagnating international trade, sharp swings in the prices of key commodities, worsened terms of trade, high interest rates, and reduced access to commercial bank credits have slowed and even reversed growth in many Third World countries. Together, these trends make "adjustment" of both demand and supply a central problem confronting policy makers in most countries in the mid-1980s. Countries must bring expenditures into line with shrinking resources in the short run, but they also need to alter prices and take other longer-range steps to expand the resource base in the future—to stimulate investment, production, and employment. Already low living standards make this an especially formidable agenda in most Third World nations.

What can be done to forestall the more conflictive phase of the debt crisis that now looms ahead? How can developing countries achieve adjustment *with growth?* The contributors to this volume share the belief that more constructive change is possible and necessary.

Contents:

ISBN: 0-88738-040-9 (cloth)   **$19.95**
ISBN: 0-87855-988-4 (paper)   **$12.95**
1984   **220 pp.**